ALEXANDER McKEE

From Merciless Invaders

The Defeat of the Spanish Armada

GRAFTON BOOKS

A Division of the Collins Publishing Group

LONDON GLASGOW
TORONTO SYDNEY AUCKLAND

Grafton Books
A Division of the Collins Publishing Group
8 Grafton Street, London W1X 3LA

Published by Grafton Books 1988

First published in Great Britain by
Souvenir Press Ltd 1963
Second edition, revised with additional material 1987

Copyright © Alexander McKee 1963, 1987

ISBN 0-586-20090-8

Printed and bound in Great Britain by
Collins, Glasgow

Set in Times

Contents

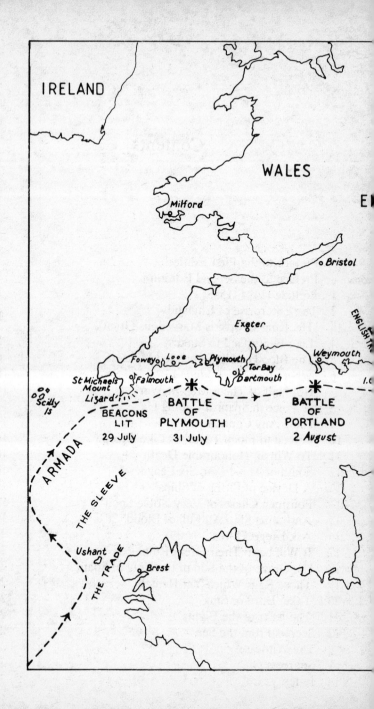

The dates are the "New Style" used by the armada and everyone today.

Preface to the First Edition

There cannot be fewer than 150 ships of all Sorts; and several of them called Galleons and Galleasses, are of a size never seene before in our seas, and appear on the surface of the water like floating Castles. But at Sun-set we had the Pleasure of seeing this invincible Armada fill all their sails to get away from us.

Report in the *English Mercurie*, 23 July 1588

The London journalist who thus wrote up the story of the first sighting of the Armada was working for a newspaper 'published by Authoritie for the prevention of false reportes'; but the slight sensationalism with which his tale was tinged started many hares in the pages of later writers. The first historian to approach the subject, Petruccio Ubaldino, had the inestimable advantage of being able to interview some of the chief witnesses on both sides, including Lord Howard, Drake, and Don Pedro de Valdes; but the necessity for tact, and possibly security considerations also, prevented his work from being as informative as it might have been. It was not until the 1890s that the existing mass of documentary evidence, both English and Spanish, was collected, edited, and published; affording a field day to naval historians whose interests were largely technical and critical.

When I came to study the documents, in 1954, as the basis of a feature programme for the BBC, what impressed above all was the quality of the eye-witness narratives. Never, in the long history of England's wars, can a set of combat reports have been written to equal these. The red-hot phrases shower from the battle like sparks from a grinder. One ceases to marvel so much at Shakespeare.

Therefore, I have chosen to present this story of the Armada Campaign strictly as a narrative of adventure told by more than a hundred eye-witnesses, drawn impartially from both sides. In them, the atmosphere of the age is almost perfectly preserved; and such errors, exaggerations, or evasions as there may be, are genuinely Elizabethan.

But as essays in interpretation cannot quite be avoided, I would claim for the method of close reconstruction from contemporary narratives that it forces the author to consult at every step the statements of participants; hinders the too easy formulation of delusive theories; and arms the reader against any errors into which the author, nevertheless, may fall.

Some areas of dispute will most probably always remain. Although arguments on technicalities, such as that concerning Armada guns, might even now be resolved by undersea exploration, a field of research much neglected by students of maritime affairs, only Sir Francis Drake in person could settle authoritatively those discussions which concern tactics; Ubaldino had the chance, but neglected to take it, losing us the opportunity forever. I must, however, acknowledge my personal debt to him; for when I came a few years ago to write the history of the Battle of Britain, which is a real parallel to the story of the Armada, I took a leaf out of his book, disdained the documents, and sought out the witnesses instead.

ALEXANDER McKEE
Hayling Island, Hampshire
March, 1963

Preface to the Second Edition

The Preface I wrote for the original edition of this book, published more than twenty years ago, requires a further introduction. Potential readership has changed radically, from people with vivid personal memories of the bloodiest and possibly the cruellest conflict in the story of man, to a younger audience who may not yet realize that war as seen on TV is not war at all. There is nothing I can do about this but crave their indulgence.

In one respect this book, based on research for my BBC script of 1954 and the full-length work published in 1963, is nearer to reality than I could manage now. In 1954, I had been out of the British Army for only two years (after spending ten years in uniform); and was that much closer to two of the three striking parallels with the Spanish Armada.

From a variety of vantage points on the south coast in 1940, I had watched Hermann Göring's Luftwaffe roar over as the powerhead of the German invasion that never came; the English sky a stage for events which would decide the fate of the world.

In 1944, only four years later, I had seen the wave of history go the other way in a conflict equally critical, when I went to Normandy as a minor cog among millions in the greatest seaborne invasion in history. Once more, the decision seemed to hang in the balance.

These two campaigns together highlighted clearly the essential ingredients for success in an amphibious operation. Admittedly, Elizabeth did not have to guard against paratroops and the Armada did not have to bother about air cover, U-boat torpedoes and mines; but the use of wind-driven ships held special difficulties and hazards, as did the food and water supply in an age before refrigeration or the tin can. Movement on land was limited to the power of the horse, the ox, the mule, and mere human muscle. The railway and the motor vehicle, which revolutionized war, were centuries in the future.

A third but this time almost contemporary parallel to the story of the Spanish Armada of 1588, was the invasion from ships of the great French Armada of 1545, the French threat being launched from nearer home, with rather larger forces, and with more success. Even so, there were limitations. I began to study this campaign, waged by Francis I of France against Henry VIII of England, soon after 1962, the year I started serious research into the loss of Henry's flagship *Mary Rose* in that hot invasion summer of 1545. The result of my work, after twenty years or so, was significantly to improve on the existing meagre evidence for the technical side of Renaissance fleets – the ships and the guns.

In the final paragraph of my Preface to the 1963 edition of this book, I mentioned the vast, untapped field of research represented by undersea exploration, which was then occupying a good deal of my spare time. Between 1968 and 1985, no less than nine Armada wrecks were to be found by divers, mostly by deliberate design, which provided at last a modicum of solid evidence to replace controversy. In this respect, an updating was clearly necessary.

However, I would rate the excavation of the *Mary Rose* as providing far more evidence about ships and life at sea in the time of the Spanish Armada than any actual Armada shipwreck.

Firstly, unlike the Armada ships so far discovered, a large part of the hull and much of its contents lay invisible and undisturbed deep under mud and clay. King Henry VIII's great carrack had not been smashed up in the shallows in any common stranding. Secondly, although built in 1509–10, rebuilt in 1536 and sunk in action in 1545 (with every man still at battle stations), there were many ships of her type in the Spanish Armada and not a few even in the English fleet. The carrack was obsolescent but not yet obsolete in 1588. In 1963 only a few meagre facts were known about them, whereas now, in the recovered *Mary Rose*, we have an encyclopaedia of Tudor maritime and martial history.

Nevertheless, the fundamental format of this book is unchanged. It is a narrative of the Armada campaign as experienced – and described in their own words – by more than a hundred witnesses drawn impartially from both fleets. This is the story of the clash as it really was, carried out in what to our minds must appear to be slow motion – for the ships mostly moved at barely walking pace in an age when almost everyone was a pedestrian. Basically, however, it was not unlike modern war: much preparation, much waiting, much boredom, many partings, great griefs, the tales told by governments and propagandists usually false, but very often believed even into our own time.

It is more than thirty years now since I first sat down to immerse myself in the contemporary documents, but I can still recall my reaction: astonishment, that everything I had believed about the Armada campaign seemed to be untrue; often the very opposite was the case.

ALEXANDER MCKEE
Hayling Island, Hampshire
September, 1986

1
Prelude (1494–1583)

From merciless invaders,
From wicked men's device,
O God! arise and help us
To quell our enemies!

Strike deep their potent navies,
Their strength and courage break,
O God! arise and arm us,
For Jesus Christ his sake.

Though cruel Spain and Parma
With heathen legions come,
O God! arise and arm us,
We'll die for our home!
John Still (1542–1607)

The summer of 1588 was miserable with rain and sudden, gusty storms. The sound of the sea breaking on the shores of the island was more often a roar than a murmur. In this year of decision the very elements themselves seemed to favour England, presenting to the invader an impassable barrier of sullen, gale-white water. The bonfires ready on hill and headland were soaked by the driving rain or torn by the winds that howled about them. Somewhere beyond those grey leagues of tossing sea was the mighty, long-awaited Armada of Spain, storm-bound and seasick. Surely it would not come now?

In the western entrance to the Channel, the watchful English pinnaces pitched and rolled, too few to guard that massive stretch of water; but the English western fleet, under Howard and Drake, had put back to Plymouth, victuals exhausted, after their abortive strike against the invasion fleet in its own harbours. With this south-westerly wind blowing straight into their Plymouth anchorage, they would find it hard to get out in a hurry. They might even be trapped there, if the enemy could use a brief advantage. But even if they could get out, they would starve, for the supply system was as dire as it had been early in King Harry's reign.

Out at sea, a few sails moved upon the waters, those of merchant ships. To their owners, captains and crews time was money. Among them was a nameless bark from Mousehole in Cornwall. All we know of her master is that he was a resolute man, determined to pass across the Channel to France, collect a cargo of salt, and return. On his way, he was hailed by a French flyboat, also on patrol, in this uneasy time which was neither peace nor war. The Frenchman closed him and, finding that this was an English ship, shouted across the heaving water: 'In any wise, as you love your life, do not proceed, for the Spanish fleet is on the coast!'

But the Cornish ship stood on for France, on the day that by English reckoning was the 19th of June (by the New Style calendar in use on the continent it was the 29th, as it would be in our own time). A few hours after encountering the Frenchman, the Cornish master saw, rising slowly up over the horizon, a forest of masts. He could have turned away, but he did not. He altered course to intercept, steering into history with empty holds, but prudently aiming for the windward position. If this was the great Armada, French salt would keep.

By the time the Cornishman was able to start counting the numbers of the distant ships, it was clear that they had sighted his small craft. Two flags fluttered out briefly at the mastheads of the leading vessels, a sighting report for their flagship, no doubt of that. It was strange to know that if these were Spaniards then at this moment, a few miles away, the guns were being readied, the matches prepared, the soldiers buckling on their armour. An enemy would want information; he would want a capture. Well, information was what England needed, too.

As the miles closed, the mass of masts and sails grew in size and definition, became a squadron of great ships, some very large indeed, towing boats or pinnaces behind them. The oddest thing was the markings on their sails. Each vessel had a great red cross, not unlike the English Cross of Saint George, worn by the Queen's ships, emblazoned on her foresails. Rapidly, the silhouettes of some of the strange vessels began to alter. They were turning out of line towards the bark from Mousehole. But her master survived to report to Sir Francis Godolphin, MP for Cornwall, who would pass the news to Drake and Howard's fleet at Plymouth.

Being bound for France to lade salt, I encountered with nine sail of great ships between Scilly and Ushant, bearing in North-East with the coast of England. Coming near unto them, and doubting not they were Spaniards, I kept the wind of them. They, perceiving it, began to give me chase. So in the end, three of them followed me so near that I doubted hardly to escape them. They were all great ships, and, as I might judge, the least of them from 200 tons to five and 800 tons. Their sails were all crossed over with a red cross.

This was the first sighting report – a Spanish squadron of nine great ships. The western entrance to the English Channel is wide, more than a hundred miles across. Yet another Cornish trading vessel, voyaging in another area of it, soon brought news of two more Spanish formations approaching England. One squadron consisted of six sail, the other of fifteen. Hot with the excitement of battle, this master also poured out his news to Godolphin. He had closed them to the edge of risk; when they opened fire, his frail vessel had been hit. All these ships, too, noted Godolphin, had been marked on their sails with a great red cross.

Nine, six and fifteen. Thirty ships in all, all bearing what appeared to be a special marking for the invasion fleet, almost a copy of the flag of England . . . That was just the insulting arrogance one might expect from Spaniards! Doubtless there were a hundred or more ships crowding on behind these first-comers, and certainly they must outnumber the Plymouth fleet, but did they think they had conquered England already?

The opening moves of the Armada campaign identified the weaknesses and limitations of the opponents. The English fleet was divided and the western part penned in Plymouth by lack of victuals and a south-westerly wind. The English seamen knew – and had told London more than once – that a wind which kept them in port brought the Spaniards out; and equally, a wind which was fair for a descent on the coast of Spain would have the Spaniards in harbour. A glance at a globe could tell you that. They knew it, London knew it, but here they were. The raid on Armada ports had been abortive; unfavourable winds and a shortage of food and drink had forced them back. Always, they were hobbled by the Queen, who could not make up her mind or, if she could, soon changed it. Oh, to have Harry VIII back again!

Spain, too, lacked the right man now, for their great admiral, victor of many actions – the Marquis of Santa Cruz – was lately dead and the new man, appointed by a slow and cautious king, although decent, honourable and earnest, had no grip on the situation at all; and that was not his fault but King Philip's. The situation as it really was – not as the English thought it was – tended to farce and fiasco unbecoming to a nation of warriors.

What the masters of two Cornish merchant ships had taken for the battle fleet of continental Europe was no such thing. The real warships, the ships built and armed for fighting, were with their new commander-in-chief, huddled in home ports, sheltering from the gales outside, still more than five hundred miles from England. The only ships which had braved the mountainous seas and bitter winds as far as the enemy's coast were the rag-tag and bob-tail – the hurriedly conscripted, under-gunned, ill-armed vessels of the storeship squadron carrying the nails, spare boots and medicines of the great Armada. Drake and Howard's western fleet, if it could have got out of Plymouth, and if it had had victuals for just a few days at sea, could have destroyed the enemy's Fleet Train at the outset – with decisive results.

As it was, the thirty storeships, after hanging around waiting for their commander-in-chief – who had threatened severe pen- alties for any malingerers who held back from England – grew tired of waiting for him and sailed wearily homeward again.

Elizabeth has had her defenders – and it is true that it was genuinely difficult to supply fully mobilized forces with the meagre organization she had. And true, England might be considered a poor country, provided you only counted heads, the population being half that of Spain. But the Queen's indecision was a by-word, and not least to her enemy, Philip, who was very well informed of what went on at Court.

Nevertheless, even the King of Spain, ruling the largest, most powerful and by far the richest empire in the world, had to work within strict constraints. The extraordinary valour of a handful of Spanish adventurers had won him and his country gold mines almost beyond count and, quite literally, a mountain of silver. And these, to the sixteenth century, like oil to the twentieth, were the sinews of war. But even this monarch was not without troubles peculiarly his own.

The two great exploring nations of Europe were Portugal and Spain. The Portuguese sailed southwards down Africa and eventually discovered the Cape and a route to the East. The Spaniards employed an Italian-born Portuguese reject named Columbus to find them a way to the East by sailing west across the Atlantic. His debatable discoveries (which Columbus claimed to be China) sparked a commonsense decision by these two nations to agree spheres of influence. In 1494 the Treaty of Tordesillas was agreed, between, on the one hand, Isabella of Spain and, on the other, Joao II of Portugal. They divided the world in two. Everything west of a line 370 leagues out in the Atlantic from the Cape Verde islands was Spain's. Everything to the east was Portugal's.

By 1503 Spain's trade with her colonies in the 'Indies' was important enough to merit the setting up of the Casa de Contratación at Seville to regulate the trading fleets. By 1555 mining technology had produced a method of separating precious metals from common ores by using mercury; the result was a bonanza of silver and gold never seen in the world before. The ships of the 'Silver Fleets' came home in great convoys, escorted by the galleons of the 'Indian Guard'. And the end result was a roaring inflation. A French economist, Jean Bodin, wrote in 1568:

It is incredible, and yet true, that there have come from Peru since the year 1533, when it was conquered by the Spaniards, more than a hundred millions of gold, and twice as much silver . . . But the fact is that the Spaniard, being compelled by unavoidable necessity to come here (to France) for wheat, cloths, stuffs, dyestuffs, paper, books, even joinery and all handicraft products, goes to the ends of the earth to seek gold and silver and spices to pay us with.

Spain itself was not rich in natural resources for either agriculture or manufacture. The people themselves bitterly referred to the treasures brought from the Indies as 'raindrops', because they vanished into the ground almost as soon as they arrived – to pay for the upkeep of empire, the holding down of rebellious subjects, the wages of soldiers and sailors. It was not long before the Spanish Crown was forced to mortgage the revenues of the treasure fleets in advance of their arrival. All other nations were forbidden by Spain to trade with her colonies; but the prospects were too tempting. The French, the Dutch, the English swarmed in. And many of them were heretics already, or would soon be so.

To simple greed was added deep iniquity (which varied according to the viewpoint), for the Protestant Reformation had been met by the Catholic Counter-Reformation. People could be burnt alive or disembowelled for their beliefs (the method varying according to the viewpoint, and all acting in the name of Christ).

1555 was a significant year. Not only was it the year of the new treasure-mining technology, but the year which saw Cardinal Caraffa, head of the Inquisition in Italy, elected as Pope Paul IV. And in this year also, the German Emperor, Charles, handed over to his son, Philip of Spain, both the land and the people of the Netherlands.

1559 was a year of change also. Until then, England was officially Roman Catholic and a satellite of Spain; while Scotland was officially Roman Catholic and a satellite of France. And as the two great powers, Spain and France, were rivals, so the English and the Scots were enemies. Now that enmity ceased and the two smaller states could not easily be controlled from abroad, either by Kings or by Popes.

The famous fight of San Juan de Ulua took place in 1568. John Hawkyns, the West Country merchant shipmaster, led a slaving fleet to Africa and then across the Atlantic to sell the captives and other goods to the Spanish colonists in the New World. It was forbidden, of course, but the colonists were keen to trade. The venture was demi-official, for Hawkyns was using a Queen's ship as his flag vessel, the great carrack *Jesus of Lübeck*, bought by Henry VIII in 1545 as a major warship but almost instantly pressed into service with the salvage fleet unsuccessfully trying to refloat the sunken *Mary Rose* at Spithead. The two ships were very similar.

But the *Jesus* suffered storm damage off Cuba and the only useful port available was San Juan de Ulua, designed by the Spaniards as a base for the loading of the Silver Fleets; and a thirteen-strong convoy was about to sail in and pick up the treasure. It was thus an inauspicious time for a fleet of Lutheran heretics, led by an English battleship, to arrive and seek harbour facilities. Within two days the Plate Fleet arrived, carrying also the new Viceroy of Mexico. The result was an international incident of grave proportions. One can sympathize with the Spaniards in their resentment and suspicion of the interlopers, which led them to double-cross Hawkyns and bring on a battle in which the English were routed. Hawkyns lost the *Jesus* but escaped in another ship – although many of his men died of starvation – and was apparently deserted by the young Francis Drake, recently appointed to his first command. Drake, however, brought most of his men safely home, although his fortunes were nearly ruined. He determined to retrieve them, in due course, from Philip's empire.

At almost exactly the same time, sinister events were taking place in the Netherlands. In 1559 Philip had appointed as his regent there the Duchess of Parma, who knew the place and the people; but in 1567 the King replaced her with the ferocious Duke of Alva. He ruled by an informal body known as the Council of Blood, which rapidly gained an infamous and never-to-be-forgotten reputation. When I first saw it in 1944, Alva's sinister fortress by the Scheldt in Antwerp, with its Spanish torture chambers, could still produce a shudder, although the more recent Gestapo had only been gone from the city a few weeks. Revolt was easier in the 1570s than it was in the 1940s, and Alva provoked it.

Events began to move rapidly. In 1570 Pope Pious V declared Queen Elizabeth of England to be excommunicated. This meant that anyone who assassinated her would be doing no wrong; indeed, would be openly encouraged. If Elizabeth died, another Tudor – Mary, Queen of Scots – was likely to succeed to the throne; and she was a Catholic and a client of France. Not all Englishmen would accept her; probably there would be civil war.

In 1571 Don John of Austria, an illegitimate relative of the King of Spain, won the great naval victory of Lepanto over the Turks at the head of a largely Italian and Spanish force. But no sooner was the Mediterranean quiet than trouble erupted elsewhere. In 1572 the Dutch 'Sea Beggars' seized the town of Brill in the Spanish Netherlands, so giving the rebellious element a base and a rallying point. In that year and the following one, Drake was carrying out commando-style raids in the Spanish colonies. The year 1572 also saw the public ruin of the Ridolfi Plot to murder Elizabeth and put the Queen of Scots (for many years a prisoner in England) on the throne; and also the summer of the St Bartholomew massacre in France, when some 30,000 Protestants – men, women and children – were slaughtered.

Intentions, for good or ill, depended on the possession of gold and silver, but even King Philip, the richest ruler in the world, taking for the state a fifth of the treasures brought to Spain from the Indies, was sometimes unable to pay his own soldiers. In 1576, the Spanish army in the Netherlands mutinied at Alost, marched on the great trading city of Antwerp and, in a murderous military riot, famous as the 'Spanish Fury', slaughtered 8,000 of the inhabitants.

The following year Elizabeth loosed Drake with a handful of small ships to strike a virgin target – the Spanish treasure fleets operating on the Pacific side of South America. The junction of the fleets, the 'Piccadilly Circus' of the whole convoy system in the Caribbean and Gulf of Mexico, had been raided often and was defended; but Spanish ships off the coast of Peru were operating in almost peacetime conditions. Their security lay in the fact that the only way into the Pacific was through the Straits named after Magellan, the first and so far the only seaman to get through. Drake made his fame and his fortune by doing the same, returning home in 1580 with a treasure perhaps greater than the Queen's whole budget for a year; as she had been a principal investor in the voyage, Drake – a former cabin boy – received a knighthood.

1580 was a fateful year nearer home, too. In 1579 a Papal force which included Spanish troops had landed in Ireland to support a revolt against the English; 1580 saw them defeated and massacred. The back door to England was now closed to Philip. But this was also the year when he annexed Spain's neighbour, Portugal – the other power with whom the world had been divided. Now, legally – in theory at least – the whole oceanic world belonged to the King of Spain as a vast commercial empire in which no other nation was allowed to trade.

Advantage and disadvantage tended to cancel out. In 1581 the Netherlands formally renounced allegiance to Philip of Spain, on the grounds that he was a tyrant – a revolutionary stance at the time. But the following year, when a French fleet under the Florentine Filippo Strozzi sought to capture the Azores for the Portuguese claimant – and as a base to attack the Silver Fleets – they were bloodily defeated in a hand-to-hand boarding battle by the Spaniards under the Marquis of Santa Cruz. In 1583 he defeated a further French expedition, and then, from the crest of victory at sea, sat down to write a letter to Philip.

Your Majesty is now master of the Portuguese empire. I am prepared, if you will allow it, to add England to your Dominions. Everything is favourable. The troops are ready, the fleet in high condition. The cost may be great, but the cost of the English raids is greater. If one looks at difficulties, nothing will be done. I beg Your Majesty to take courage and undertake this campaign, and I hope in God to come successfully out of it, as I have out of everything else.

2
The Enterprise of England

My promise was, and I record it so,
To write in verse (God wot though little worth)
That war seems sweet to such as little know
What comes thereby, what fruits it bringeth forth:
Who knows none evil his mind no bad abhors,
But such as once have felt the scorching fire,
Will seldom efte to play with flame desire.

I set aside to tell the restless toil,
The mangled corpse, the laméd limbs at last,
The shortened years by fret of fevers foul,
The smoothest skin with scabs and scars disgraced,
The frolic favour frounst and foul defaced,
The broken sleeps, the dreadful dreams, the woe,
Which one with war and cannot from him go.

I list not write (for it becomes me not)
The secret wrath which God doth kindle oft,
To see the sucklings put unto the pot.
To hear their guiltless blood send cries aloft,
And call for vengeance unto him, but soft
The soldiers they commit those heinous acts,
Yet Kings and Captains answer for such facts.
George Gascoigne (1525?–1577)
Veteran of the Netherlands campaign

The King of Spain attempted to control his empire from a
purpose-built headquarters on the slopes of the Guadarrama
mountain range thirty miles from his capital of Madrid. The
construction was a 'palace' in name only; rather, it resembled a
cross between a fortress and a monastery, designed to ensure
privacy for Philip while he processed his paperwork. 'Chief
clerk' of the Spanish empire he has been called, aptly.

He lived frugally, and worried constantly. He would have

been appalled to learn that anyone thought of him as a tyrant. His decisions, slow in coming, were always carefully weighed. He wanted to be quite sure that God would approve of what he at length decreed. And yet this headquarters, this complex of buildings called after the nearest village, the Escorial, was almost the most imposing construction of its kind in Europe, second only to the Vatican, although very different in character. One might compare the mountain eyrie Hitler made, the Berghof, in the spacious days before he launched his armies across Europe, with, in contrast, the gloomy Eastern Front headquarters in the woods at Rastenburg, the 'Wolf's Lair', from which he attempted to control his forces on every front in the years when they were being forced back on Germany.

That earlier ruler of expanding empire had no telephones, no radio, no ciphering machines, no great road and rail networks; and no typewriters – not even carbon paper. It was all done by hand, the incoming documents piled up on tables for Philip to read and annotate.

The King was conscientious – far too much so – but was possessed also of that blindness common to kings and princes. When poison was poured into his ear, he had his own secretary assassinated; not tried and executed, but murdered. In 1584 William of Orange, the principal leader of the revolt in the Netherlands, was shot down by a single assassin. Protestants thought they knew who gave the order.

The same fate could strike Elizabeth any day. And then, almost certainly, her successor would be the Catholic Mary, Queen of Scots. Protestants could remember the public burnings, not so long ago, under Elizabeth's Catholic sister, Mary Tudor, who had married Philip while he was still a Prince and not yet King of Spain. In quiet rage, a number of leading gentlemen formed themselves into the 'Bond of Association', by which they swore, if Elizabeth was murdered, to murder likewise anyone who benefited by it.

1585 was the year of undeclared war. Some English ships, trading peacefully in a Spanish port, were seized. Elizabeth retaliated by sending an army of 6,000 men to the Netherlands to help the Dutch; and despatched Drake with twenty-five ships to raid the Spanish Main. In one of those fallen Spanish colonial towns, the prisoners were herded into their ornate Government House, with jeers and insults. One of Drake's captains reported:

By some of our company it was told them that if the Queen of England would resolutely prosecute the wars against the King of Spain, he should be forced to lay aside that proud and unreasonable reaching vein of his; for he should find more than enough to do to keep that which he had already, as by the example of their lost town they might for a beginning perceive well enough.

Philip's reaction was to take up the matter of the invasion of England which the Marquis of Santa Cruz had authoritatively suggested in 1583. People, particularly the exiled Jesuits in Rome, had been advocating such a step for twenty years, but Santa Cruz was a veteran and victorious man-of-war. He replied to the King's request for estimates of the force required and its cost:

It will be necessary to mobilize, and to concentrate in the English Channel, the whole naval power of Your Majesty's dominions; together with large land forces.

The great admiral itemized them: 596 ships, manned by 17,000 seamen; carrying an invasion army of 55,000 soldiers, equipped with 130 pieces of artillery for the field, 1,600 horses, 1,400 mules, a siege train, quartermaster stores, and a field hospital. To take the assault troops ashore, 200 special landing craft would have to be constructed, and carried on deck by the storeships. This was much more than a mere battle fleet – it was an enormous amphibious task force, completely self-contained.

It did not yet exist, but would have to be created – by construction, by conversion, by conscription. Santa Cruz worked out how it could be done – by the dockyards, by the requisitioning of Spanish and foreign merchant ships, by the withdrawal of forty galleys from the Spanish Mediterranean Fleet. The loss of 10,000 men, by the wastage of battle, sickness and desertion, would have to be allowed for. The stores of food, drink, powder, shot, etc, would have to be calculated on the basis of a campaign likely to last eight months. He went on to consider how many sandals must be held in the storerooms, and how many pikes, and how much medicine, and how much it would all cost. And perhaps he was employing the standard method of military demand in all countries throughout the ages, by which everyone indents for twice what is actually required in the certain knowledge that half of it will be disallowed anyway. Philip replied, after due thought: 'The plan I think extremely good, but very costly. I must consider it.'

Early in 1586 yet another proposal for the invasion of England was put forward. This came from the Duke of Parma, the most brilliant general of the age, who was now commanding the Spanish forces in the Netherlands with gratifying success. It was a simple plan. It required only the existing Spanish army in the Netherlands, plus a fleet of flat-bottomed boats, guarded by a fleet of twenty-five warships. The first waves of the 30,000 strong force could be put ashore in the south-eastern tip of England – Kent or Essex – in eight or ten hours. (Such an improbable nightmare also worried illustrious minds in England in 1940.) Philip put his finger on one weak point – the fact that the necessary surprise could not be achieved because of the size of the force. The German army, struggling in the continental Channel surf on landing exercises in 1940, could have mentioned a great many other relevant factors which were not apparent until you actually tried to do it. And they had internal combustion engines to propel their craft, and air superiority above them.

Nevertheless, from these conflicting plans, and others, Philip produced an alternative which to him appeared workable. It was to combine the suggestions of Santa Cruz and Parma, by effectively splitting the force. Parma would provide the bulk of the soldiers and the assault boats from his Army of the Netherlands, while an armada would issue from Iberian ports to join him off the coast of the Low Countries. At a stroke, Philip had reduced by two-thirds the number of soldiers who would sail from home ports, thereby making an immense saving in trained manpower, in warlike and other stores, in draught animals, and in the staggering amount of water and fodder which the latter consume. At the same time, the tonnage of merchant shipping required to transport the army could be brought down to something like manageable proportions, without much affecting the power of the fleet in battle. Indeed, by reducing the number of slow and semi-armed transports and store ships, the fighting part of the fleet would be more efficient in action.

Philip also set a date for this 'Enterprise of England': 1587.

The part to be played by the English Catholics in supporting the invaders was important, even vital. An English exile, the Jesuit Father Parsons, assured the King and the Pope:

Sixteen times England has been invaded. Twice only the native race have repelled the attacking force. They have been defeated on every other occasion, and with a cause so holy and just as ours we need not fear to fail. Two-thirds at least are Catholic at heart, though many conceal their convictions in fear of the Queen. The puritans have none of them ever seen a camp. They have not a man who can command in the field. In the whole realm there are but two fortresses which could stand a three days' siege. The people are enervated by a long peace, and, except for a few who have served with the heretics in Flanders, cannot bear their arms.

Of course, Father Parsons, Cardinal Allen and all the other Catholic exiles longed to return home. A rosy view of the prospects for a Catholic reconquest of England was natural; but conditions had changed since they had gone into exile and were now altering rapidly. In the summer of 1586 yet another plot to assassinate Elizabeth and put Mary, Queen of Scots on the throne was exposed. The men who had formed the Bond of Association decided to put an end to the menace; and pressured the Queen to order her execution. Elizabeth agonized over this because, it seems, she thought that such a theatrical state killing set a dangerous precedent for royalty generally. She was, of course, quite right, as Charles I subsequently discovered. Elizabeth wanted the Queen of Scots quietly eliminated, killed off anonymously, slaughtered on the side, as it were. But she could find no one prepared to do that.

So she had to sign a death warrant, and when it was executed, went into a rage with her secretary, blaming him for her own reluctant decision. There were precedents, for her own sister, the Catholic Mary, had executed Lady Jane Grey and her husband because the lady was a rival for the throne. However, about the repercussions there could be no argument: when the severed head of the Queen of Scots (the candidate of France) struck the boards of the scaffold, war with Spain was inevitable, the way being now clear for Philip himself as a claimant to the throne, descended as he was from Edward III through the marriage of John of Gaunt and Constance of Castile.

Both the cautious monarchs concerned – Philip and Elizabeth – had been a long time making up their minds. Henceforth the power would tend to drain away from them to the commanders in the field and at sea – Parma and Santa Cruz; Howard and Drake.

Even before the execution, plans had been made for a pre-emptive strike against the Armada, slowly assembling in Portuguese and Spanish ports. Drake was to be given the command of twenty-three ships (including the four formidable Royal warships *Elizabeth Bonaventure*, *Golden Lion*, *Dreadnought* and *Rainbow*), manned by 2,200 men, and to sail in the spring of 1587 with provisions for three months. On 20 April that year a Spanish agent in London was able to report (with no more than minor errors of fact) that:

Drake left Plymouth on Saturday, 11 April with 34 ships of the fleet, four of them being Queen's ships, the best she has, of 700 and 800 tons, and two of her pinnaces, all armed with bronze pieces. The rest are merchantmen, but comprise some of the best ships in the country. They are well armed, victualled for eight months, and carry 2,000 men, all seamen and no soldiers. The intention is to intercept the silver fleets from Peru, which they are confident of capturing if they meet them. Some people say that if the weather serves they will run into Cadiz, and do what damage they can to the shipping and the city . . . André de Loo arrived here last week from Brussels with the reply of his Highness respecting peace. The Queen instantly sent couriers to Plymouth to stop Drake from sailing until further orders, but they were too late and he was gone.

What the Spanish spy did not know was that a fast pinnace, sent out carrying the amended orders allowing no offensive action, had inexplicably found the weather too rough and reported being unable to deliver them. The messenger was a relative of John Hawkyns, which may explain a good deal. Further, Drake had got away very quickly indeed, penning a brief note for London that 'the wind commands me away'.

On 16 April English Style (26th April Spanish Style) the English fleet was off the main assembly point for the Armada – Lisbon in Portugal. Drake was an expert in attacking Spanish naval bases and he judged that this one was too strong and too difficult navigationally; he therefore carried on to Cadiz in Spain, not far from Cape Trafalgar and the Straits of Gibraltar. When the Spanish agent's message reached Spain, it would be of historic interest only; Drake had achieved complete surprise. Indeed, the stoutest defender of the Spanish port was an English naval officer, William Borough, sent along to hold Drake's hand and ensure that he did not misbehave (according to the divided command system practised at the time). Borough found Drake rash and wilful. He argued against any attack at all, but cautioned at least to hold back and send in a proper challenge to the enemy (so that he would be able to arm himself in readiness). Nelson, in a similar situation later off Tenerife, neglected surprise and achieved only total failure and the loss of an arm. Drake just went straight in without lingering.

Two harbour guard galleys were disposed of at once. There were about sixty Armada vessels in the outer harbour, in various stages of preparation for invading England; some were able to move to an inner harbour. The rest were sunk, burnt or taken. Next day Drake led a flotilla of pinnaces into the inner harbour. Among the vessels he gutted was Santa Cruz's own flagship, as unready as the rest. In all, he destroyed thirty ships and captured six supply ships full of provisions. But when it was time to leave, the wind dropped dead calm; and a number of war galleys came out to pound the helpless English vessels.

At least, that is what should have happened. And no doubt this was a contingency Borough had worried about. During the exceptionally hot and calm summer of 1545, the big ships on both sides had often been powerless to move; and the formidable war galleys of the French Mediterranean Fleet (brought into the Channel for the purpose) had been able to annoy the English carracks without suffering much themselves. But Drake's ships were far handier and his men more experienced; by laying out anchors they could turn their vessels so as always to present their broadside batteries to the galleys, which were frail and had only a few sizeable guns firing only forward; moreover, their motive and manoeuvring power, the hundreds of oarsmen, were frighteningly vulnerable to cannon shot or, indeed, small arms fire. Firing solid shot into heavy wooden hulls, on the other hand, was an unproductive business.

Drake wrote to his brother captain, Thomas Fenner, with the decisive news:

I assure your honour there is no account to be made of his galleys. Twelve of her Majesty's ships will make account of all his galleys in Spain, Portugal and all his dominions within the Straits (of Gibraltar), although they are 150 in number. If it be to their advantage in a calm, we have made such trial of their fights that we perfectly see into the depth thereof.

A Spanish naval officer, Captain Luis Cabreta, had already warned Philip:

It is all very well to say that Your Majesty has a hundred galleys. They may be of some little use in the Mediterranean but they are of small importance elsewhere, especially on the high seas.

Santa Cruz had earmarked a large force of forty Mediterranean galleys for the Armada. It is usually assumed that, because of his experiences at Lepanto – fought between rival galley fleets – he intended them to be part of the battle fleet. But the French experience of 1545 had shown that the key role for galleys in an invasion was as assault landing craft for the infantry. They could be beached precisely together, like ranks of soldiers, and the real soldiers could leap on to the beach from the projecting beakheads; disembarkation could be rapid and exact. Because of their shallow draft the galleys could also be vital in guarding Parma's invasion barges out of port to deep water, through the shallows which the Dutch 'Sea Beggars' at present ruled with their small armed craft. The chief disadvantage of galleys was their reliance on fresh water – they carried huge crews of oarsmen and had very little hull space for water and provision stowage.

The results of Cadiz were technological bad news for the Armada, and the forty galleys were in the event reduced to four. If Parma was unwise enough to let his invasion barges go out, then his splendid army was due for a bloodbath in the surf.

Drake's next battle was with William Borough, his vice-admiral. Having got out of Cadiz with few losses, Drake intended to capture Sagres on the Algarve coast of Portugal and hold it as a base from which to pounce on the shipping routes leading to Lisbon. Borough was even more pessimistic about this operation than he had been about Cadiz, and Drake put him under arrest. But Sagres, an important watering point, fell to the English; and perhaps as many as half-a-hundred small Spanish supply ships were plundered and destroyed; they included a number carrying the staves to make water casks for the Armada. In a sailing or rowing navy, water is the limiting factor. The lack of proper containers for the water supply was to be grimly felt in the Armada before too long.

Drake wrote home for reinforcements – with six of the Queen's second-class ships, he felt that he could hamstring the Armada for good, pointing out that 'There must be a beginning of any great matter, but the continuing unto the end until it be thoroughly finished yields the true glory.'

But then he heard of a giant Portuguese carrack which was due in the Azores from a voyage to the East Indies. His feeling for rich prizes was uncanny. After sixteen days, some of them spent battling a gale, he intercepted the *San Felipe*, 'the greatest ship in all Portugal, and richly laden'. She was a strong ship, being built to bring safely home the treasures of the East, but Drake captured her and put a prize crew aboard. Her contents were to be valued at £114,000, of which the Queen's share was £40,000 and Drake's £17,000. These were enormous sums in the sixteenth century, when an admiral's pay might be 10s. (50p.) a day, a soldier's 10s. (50p.) a month.

The only Spanish success in the summer of 1587 was the capture by the Duke of Parma of Sluys, a port in the Low Countries facing the short crossing to England. With the cover-story of an attack on Ostend, Parma proposed to assemble his invasion force in this area, together with the boats in which it would cross. Surprise might be obtained. If it was not, then the English fleet presented a deadly danger because, Philip observed in a letter to Parma, of 'the strength and character of their ships'.

Philip turned down the idea of using the Armada to create a diversion; the English, he felt, would not be deceived. He ordered the Armada to rendezvous with Parma:

We calculate that by the time you have invested Ostend you will have over 30,000 men ready for the main business, whilst 16,000 Spanish infantry, a part of them veterans, will go in the Armada from here, the whole force of soldiers and sailors in the fleet reaching 22,000 men . . . The Marquis of Santa Cruz will go direct to Lisbon, take charge of the fleet which will be awaiting him and with God's blessing sail straight to the English Channel. He will anchor off Margate Point; having first sent notice to you at Dunkirk, Newport or the Sluys, of his approach. You in the meanwhile will be quite ready, and when you see the passage assured by the arrival of the Armada at Margate, or at the mouth of the Thames, you will, if the weather permits, immediately cross with the whole army in the boats which you will have ready. You and the Marquis will then co-operate, the one on land and the other afloat . . .

The date of this letter is 4 September by New Style reckoning (which is what it would be today). That is, a month or so before the time of the equinoctial tides and gales. Sometimes in October there is a 'Saint Martin's Summer' in the English Channel, lasting perhaps a week or ten days, but severe gales of Force 10 are more likely. With the knowledge of the facts, Philip was ordering a winter campaign, warning Parma:

The most important of all things is that you should be so completely ready that the moment the Marquis arrives at Margate, you may be able to do your share without delay. You will see the danger of any such delay, the Armada being there and you behind-hand; as until your passage is effected he will have no harbour for shelter, whereas when you have crossed over he will have the safe and spacious River Thames. Otherwise he will be at the mercy of the weather, and if, which God forbid! any misfortune should happen to him, you will understand what a state it would put us into . . . You must not forget that the forces collected, and the vast money responsibility incurred, make it extremely difficult for such an expedition again to be got together if they escape us this time, whilst the obstacles and divisions which may arise (and certainly will do so) next summer, force us to undertake the enterprise this year, or else fail altogether . . .

Philip also wrote to the Marquis of Santa Cruz, Parma's co-commander:

It is clear that great risks are involved in the moving of a mighty Armada in winter, particularly in the Channel with no port secured; but the other reasons which have induced His Majesty to take this resolution are even weightier . . . Our forces, if skilfully united, would assure us of victory, if we do not delay to use them, in view of the enemy's present unpreparedness, and the fact that the expedients he is devising for next year cannot serve him in this, and would utterly collapse if we should win the first move. The roadstead of Margate is excellent, but without defences; the river of London is also undefended.

But October passed, and most of November, and still no Armada was sighted. On 27 November the Queen of England held a Council of War. Among those present were Drake and Raleigh. They concluded that the most likely areas for a landing numbered eight: Milford in South Wales; Helford and Falmouth in Cornwall; Plymouth and Torbay in Devon; Portland in Dorset; Portsmouth in Hampshire; and, south of Portsmouth, the Isle of Wight, where French soldiers had landed from a French fleet safely anchored offshore in 1545, little more than forty years before.

Clearly, the English fleet would have to engage the enemy off all these main objectives, and so harass them that they could not put soldiers ashore from the boats and galleys. There was no chance whatever of boarding and capturing any of the large Spanish ships, which was the normal way to victory; because the English had only a handful of soldiers in their ships. They would have to succeed by gunfire alone. And normally, guns did not sink ships.

So, if the fleet failed and the Spanish army did get ashore at any of these places, the English army had to consider its strategy. There are only two options in such cases, as the Second World War once more demonstrated: either fight them on the beaches with what few troops you have there, or concentrate much larger forces inland and then strike. The British army in 1940 and the German army in 1944, had very similar debates. In 1587 the decision was: 'That at his landing he may be impeached, if conveniently it may be done'. In short, the forward strategy on the beaches instead of 'drawing them to a head' and then fighting the decisive battle inland.

But there was no disagreement about what was to be done if
the enemy established his beachhead and broke out. Scorched
earth and guerilla warfare. Or, as they put it in 1587:

If he march forward, we advise that the country be driven so as no
victuals remain to them but such as they shall carry on their backs,
which will be small . . . And that he may be kept waking with
perpetual alarms. But in no case should any battle be adventured until
such time as divers lieutenants be assembled to make a gross army,
except upon a special advantage.

Sir Walter Raleigh summed up the problem of the defenders:

Great difference I know there is, between such a country as France is,
strengthened with many fortified places; and this of ours, where our
ramparts are but the bodies of men. I say this, that an army transported
over the sea, and the landing place left to the choice of the invader,
cannot be resisted on the coast of England, without a fleet to impeach
it; except that every creek, port, or sandy bay, had a powerful army in
each of them, to make opposition. I hope that this question shall never
come to trial; Her Majesty's many movable forts will forbid the
experience. I take it to be the wisest way, to employ good ships on the
sea, and not trust to any intrenchment upon the shore.

Sir Francis Drake similarly put his views on paper; but he
went much further, advocating a bold counter-offensive. He
was sure that the Armada could be best fought on its own
coasts, while still assembling. He wrote to the Secretary of
State, Walsyngham:

I assure your honour the like preparation was never heard of or
known, as the King of Spain hath and daily maketh to invade England.
Prepare in England strongly and most by sea. Stop him now and stop
him ever.

Drake was not alone in holding these views. Another English
seaman had already advised a raid on the Spanish fishing fleets
working the Newfoundland banks:

Give me five vessels, and I will go out and sink them all, and the
galleons shall rot in Cadiz harbour for want of hands to sail them. But
decide, Madam, and decide quickly. Time flies, and will not return.
The wings of Man's life are plumed with the feathers of death.

Likewise, Drake was shortly to urge in vain: 'The advantage of time and place in all martial actions is half a victory; which being lost is irrecoverable.'

On 21 December, 1587, four weeks after the Council of War had met to decide invasion policy, Elizabeth made her choice of the chief command at sea. It went to Lord Charles Howard, the ninth member of his family to be appointed Lord Admiral of England. Drake was to be second-in-command; no more. For a former cabin boy, this was meteoric promotion. On the other hand, in Spain no one had ever heard of Lord High Admiral Howard, whereas when the Spaniards spoke of 'Drake', they really meant the whole English fleet, so awe-inspiring was his reputation. There were many other successful leaders at sea, to be sure, Hawkyns and Frobisher, to mention only two of those best known in England, but Drake was a world figure. He also had actual experience of handling fleets of ships at sea; although no one in England had ever controlled a fleet as large as the one now being prepared.

A contemporary wrote of Drake that he never failed in any action wherein he had the sole command. But it has to be admitted that he did not work well in harness. During the voyage of circumnavigation, he had executed his partner Doughty as a threat to his authority; and off Cadiz he had arrested Borough and asked the Queen to execute him, because of a disagreement on policy. Now he would have to work with Howard, to whom he was subordinate; but under him, he would have his kinsman John Hawkyns who had previously been Drake's superior, and the ferocious Sir Martin Frobisher, who despised and hated Drake.

There were similar command problems on the Spanish side. In January of the New Year, 1588 – with the Armada still far from ready to sail – these suddenly became critical, for the Marquis of Santa Cruz took to his bed and died. The commander-in-chief of the fleet – who was also the chief architect of the 'Enterprise of England' – was removed from the scene. As in England, there were plenty of experienced seamen of reputation, any one of whom could succeed him. But, as in England, it was not as easy as that.

3
'The King's Force is Marvellous Great'

> Farewell, adieu, that court-like life!
>   To war we 'tend to go;
> It is good sport to see the strife
>   Of soldiers on a row:
>   How merrily they forward march
>   Their enemies to slay!
>   With hey trim and trixy too
>   Their banners they display.
>
> The drum and flute play lustily,
>   The trumpet blows amain,
> And vent'rous knights courageously
>   Do march before their train,
>   With spear in rest so lively dressed
>   In armour bright and gay,
>   With hey trim and trixy too
>   Their banners they display.
>   *John Pickering* (1567)

The King had made his choice, carefully weighed in advance of the death of Santa Cruz, of his successor; when it became clear that the great admiral was dying, he wrote to the premier nobleman of Spain, the Duke of Medina Sidonia:

Dear Duke and Cousin, I have decided to confer on you the office of my Captain General of the Ocean. Your first action will be to take charge of the Armada which I have ordered to assemble in Lisbon. And as speed is particularly important, if within eight or ten days you find you are able to set out with the galleons provided with their full complement of sailors and soldiers, I charge you to embark and proceed straight to the mouth of the river of Lisbon without loss of time.

The Duke was Captain General of Andalusia, responsible for the overall management and defence of that province; when

Drake had raided Cadiz, he had hurried there with the militia and may have prevented further damage. Mild and modest, he replied to the King's secretary, Juan de Idiaquez:

I first humbly thank His Majesty for having thought of me for so great a task, and I wish I possessed the talents and strength necessary. But, sir, I have not health for the sea, for I know by the small experience I have had afloat that I soon become sea-sick, and have many humours. Besides this, as I have often told you verbally and in writing, that I am in great need, so much so that when I have had to go to Madrid I have been obliged to borrow money for the journey. My house owes 900,000 ducats, and I am therefore quite unable to accept that command. I have not a single real I can spend on the expedition.

Besides, the force is so great, and the undertaking so important, that it would not be right for a person like myself, possessing no experience of seafaring or of war, to take charge of it. I possess neither aptitude, ability, health, nor fortune, for the expedition. I would simply be groping in the dark, since I should suddenly, without preparation, enter a new career. In his Majesty's own interests, I cannot attempt a task for which I have no doubt I should give a bad account.

These are merely the most striking phrases from a long and convincing letter, but they did not convince Philip. On 18 February (8 February by the English calendar) the King gave the Duke a direct order to go to Lisbon and take command of the leaderless Armada. It was to cost Medina Sidonia personally a ruinous sum – 7,827,358 maravedis. Of course, more ambitious men would have cared little about their lack of qualifications. Seeing a bandwagon, they would have jumped on it eagerly.

Probably the King did not want a bold war leader, which the original scheme put up by Santa Cruz required. Philip's own revised plan called, he may have thought, merely for a manager who, acting on the advice of experienced subordinates, would complete the preparations at Lisbon and then sail direct to the Straits of Dover to join the Duke of Parma – who would naturally assume command of the whole enterprise. Medina Sidonia would not object to that, whereas Santa Cruz certainly would have done. There were a number of experienced admirals who could have commanded the Armada, but they were proud men and jealous of each other. None, however, could object to serving under a grandee of Spain. The King's reasons for choosing Medina Sidonia were basically the same as the Queen's for nominating Howard to the chief English command. He therefore rejected the Duke's protest that he would give only a 'bad account' of the task, and issued his detailed instructions. As Medina Sidonia knew so little, he had to be told everything – or almost everything. There were three separate instructions, including directives that would have riven diplomacy generally and this enterprise in particular, if the details had become known at the time. One of these documents was sealed, not even to be opened by Medina Sidonia, but only by Parma.

First, there was a General Instruction covering propaganda, tactics for fighting the English fleet, co-operation with the Duke of Parma's invasion force, discipline in the fleet and the quality of the food.

The second document contained the Secret Instructions. These told the King's Captain General of the Ocean what to do in the event of the Armada being, not invincible, but a failure. With the Secret Instructions was a third, a Sealed Document addressed to the Duke of Parma (nowadays it would be classified TOP SECRET). But it was to be given to Parma in two circumstances only: (a) if Medina Sidonia had landed in England, or (b) if Medina Sidonia had decided that a landing was impossible. In any other event, it was to be returned unread to the King of Spain. This Sealed Document spelled out the King's peace terms to Queen Elizabeth of England, which would vary according to the success, or otherwise, of the Armada. But the terms are the key to the entire enterprise because they make clear what Philip really hoped to gain.

If the result be not so prosperous that our arms shall be able to settle matters, nor, on the other hand, so contrary that the enemy shall be relieved of anxiety on our account, and affairs so counter-balanced that peace may not be altogether undesirable, you will endeavour to avail yourself as much as possible of the prestige of the Armada, bearing in mind that there are three principal points upon which you must fix your attention:

1 That in England the free use and exercise of our holy Catholic faith shall be permitted to all Catholics, native and foreign, and that the exiles shall return.

2 That all places in my Netherlands which the English hold shall be restored to me.

3 That the English shall recompense me for the injury they have done to me, my dominions, and my subjects; which will amount to an exceedingly great sum. (This third point may be dropped; you may use it as a lever to obtain the other two.)

There was no suggestion here of a complete conquest of England; like Adolf Hitler's abortive Operation Sealion of 1940, the Enterprise of England was a threatening gesture – a bluff backed by invasion boats. But if the English had been so mauled in the fighting as to accept points one and two of the Spanish peace offer, their capacity to resist in a further clash would have been severely weakened. The chances of a successful Catholic coup in England would have been much improved, while the capacity of the Dutch to hold down the threatening Spanish army in the Netherlands would have been considerably reduced. As usual, the clever, cautious Philip was thinking in the long term. But all this was not for the eyes of Medina Sidonia. It was a secret kept for three centuries.

Medina Sidonia journeyed from his estates in Andalusia to Lisbon on Portugal's Atlantic coast, where the Armada was being stored and gunned from the warehouses on the quayside. Some of the ships were anchored off in the dirty green waters of the Tagus; others were in the hands of shipwrights busy cutting gunports in what were mostly merchant ships, building up castles at bow and stern for the infantry and fitting tall wooden blinds in the waists of the vessels so as to screen the gunners and soldiers there from enemy view.

At first sight, all was chaos; and a babel of tongues. This Armada was not Spanish, it was international. Captive Portugal was to supply a squadron of modern galleons and four galleys. Italy had sent a squadron of armed merchantmen and four Neapolitan galleasses (hybrid warships, half sail, half oar-propelled). A great many Dutch mariners were serving in the fleet, as well as German artillerymen and Frenchmen. There were Scotsmen, whose country was neutral; Irishmen, whose country was captive to England; and many English renegades who would help to govern such English territory as might be captured. Almost any nationality might be found among the

slaves labouring at the great sweeps of the galleys and galleasses; there were Spanish convicts, Frenchmen, and at least
one Welshman amongst them. All told, the Duke was now
responsible for the fitness, discipline, training and moral wel-
fare of some 30,000 men; and for the readiness of some 130
ships – warships, armed merchantmen, and a crowd of fast,
light craft for scouting and despatch-carrying: zabras (Biscay
smacks) and pataches or pinnaces. Even the galleons of the
Indian Guard were there, for Philip had stripped his treasure
fleets of their best vessels. There were carracks from the
Mediterranean and hulks from the Baltic. It seemed as though
the whole of continental Europe was mobilizing against
England.

And this was only part of the story. Half the Spanish army in
the Netherlands was earmarked for England. On 19 April,
1588, Parma reported the latest muster as: 8,718 Spanish
infantry; 5,339 Italian infantry; 3,278 Burgundian, Irish and
Scots infantry; 17,825 Walloon infantry; 8,616 Low German
infantry; 3,650 Italian and Spanish light horsemen.

A unifying factor among King Philip's forces was the Catholic
religion. He had instructed Medina Sidonia to emphasize the
holy image.

In the first place, victories are God's to give, and His to take away, as
He sees fit. But the cause you are defending is so peculiarly His as to
give us hope of His help and favour if it is not made unworthy by our
sinfulness. For this reason you must take particular care in the Armada
against sin of any kind, but especially the sin of blasphemy, by
providing heavy penalties, to be rigorously carried out . . .

The Duke arranged for a unifying ceremony in the centre of
Lisbon, with the standard of the Armada being blessed in the
cathedral on the great square and then at the Dominican
convent. On the banner was a Latin inscription which said:

Arise, O Lord, and vindicate thy cause.

It is hard to guess at the exact effect of this on individuals; it
cannot always have been what was intended. Undoubtedly, the
Duke's Lisbon ceremony would have been taken in England as
proof – if proof were needed! – that the Armada was a Roman

plot by the Pope to scourge the English back to Catholicism. But then the people of England were not privy to the despatches of diplomats; and it was just as well for Philip of Spain that these remained secret for centuries. True, the Vatican was in favour of recovering England to the faith, by force if necessary; and Medina Sidonia in Lisbon was saying the same thing in his sailing orders:

From the highest to the lowest, you are to understand the object of our expedition, which is to recover countries to the Church now oppressed by the enemies of the true faith. All personal quarrels are to be suspended, and I charge you, one and all, to abstain from profane oaths.

But the diplomatic quarrel between Pope Sixtus V and Count de Olivares, Spanish ambassador to the Vatican, continued, unknown to the general populace. Sixtus had said that he would give Philip a million gold ducats when a Spanish force landed in England; but not before. Olivares was trying to get at least some of the money in advance even of the Armada's sailing. In his secret despatches to the King he wrote of the Pope:

The answer he gives *me* is that the terms of the agreement have not yet been fulfilled. His excuse to *others* for not paying the money is that the Armada business is nothing but a trick, and that Your Majesty has not raised the fleet for the English enterprise at all, but for brag, and to frighten the Queen of England into making peace. He shows reports he has received to this effect. However unlikely a report may be, it matters not to His Holiness if it serves his purpose.

But of course the Pope had read the signs correctly – he might almost have read the very Sealed Instruction that the Duke of Medina Sidonia was to give to Parma, unread. And it was true also that the Pope made no secret of his doubts to the ambassadors of other powers. Giovanni Gritti, the Venetian ambassador, reported to the Doge and Senate that the Pope had told him:

The King goes trifling with this Armada of his, but the Queen acts in earnest. We are sorry to say, but we have a poor opinion of this Spanish Armada, and fear some disaster.

That was the coldly informed view. But a great military enterprise can seem unstoppable; the mustered forces give an intoxicating impression of power, so that the participant seems to be swept along as part of a whirlwind. The Armada was never officially proclaimed as 'Invincible', merely 'Fortunate', but some in Lisbon felt it was. Antonio de Taso Aquereis, captain of infantry, wrote home to Andalusia:

Do you pray to God that in England he doth give me a house of some very rich merchant where I may place my ensigne. But I do fear that they will instantly yield and agree unto all that the King will demand of them, for that the King's force is marvellous great as well by sea as by land. It is impossible to signify unto you the people that are therein as well soldiers, gentlemen, as of noblemen; only I can say that every day is given twenty-two thousand rations of meat, and this only to Spaniards, besides strangers. All things are now embarked even to the mules that must draw the artillery; and commanded here, upon pain of death, no man to go ashore; only do we tarry for a fair wind to go to sea.

This sanguine letter may have been one result of a morale-building speech made by Medina Sidonia:

By God's help, the war in Flanders will be ended, and we shall be saved the drain of blood and substance which it draws from Spain; it will be profitable also because of the plunder and endless riches we shall gather in England, and with which, by the favour of God, we shall return, gloriously and victoriously, to our homes.

The Pope was now positively unhappy, reported the Count de Olivares in the second week of March:

The grief he exhibits now that the time has nearly arrived for him to pay the million, fills me with anxiety that I shall have small chance of success in obtaining the second million. Since the 28 ultimo, when he learnt that the affair was really in earnest and that the moment was approaching when he would have to disburse, his extreme and extraordinary perturbation is evident to everybody. He does not sleep at night; his manners to all are more than ordinarily abrupt; he talks to himself, and generally conducts himself most shamefully.

The first million was due on the day Spanish soldiers landed on English soil. Perhaps that was why Philip's Secret Instruction to Medina Sidonia contained an alternative which should ensure the payment of the money:

If the Duke of Parma should not be able to cross to England, nor you for that reason to meet him, then you will see whether you are able to capture the Isle of Wight, which is not so strongly defended as to be able to resist you. Once captured, however, it can be defended, and you will have a secure port in which the Armada may take shelter and which, being a place of importance, would open the way for further action by you.

In the light of the French experience in July, 1545, this was wishful thinking. The French drove the English back and anchored inside the protection of the Isle of Wight; but their fleet had numbered 235 ships and over 30,000 men, which were opposed initially by only sixty English ships (later increased to 105). Henry VIII had been forced to fight a strictly defensive battle at sea. On land, however, the odds were different. The French managed to put about 5,000 men ashore, but Henry by that time managed to have his garrison in Wight reinforced to some 7,000 men. The French considered holding on to the Bembridge peninsula (in 1545 almost an island) and after careful thought concluded that it was logistically impossible (although their own coastline was only 100 miles away).

In 1588 the English had more ships than Spain could field in the Armada and they were mostly better ships, better armed. The King had warned Medina Sidonia about that:

You should take special note that the enemy's aim will be to fight from a distance, since he has the advantage of superior artillery and of the large number of fireworks with which he will come provided.

Our aim must be to attack, and to come to grips with the enemy at close quarters; and to succeed in doing this you will need to exert every effort. That you might be forewarned, you will receive a detailed report of the way in which the enemy arranges his artillery so as to be able to aim his broadsides low in the hull and so sink his opponents' ships.

This was not a licence for Medina Sidonia to go bald-headed for the English fleet, in all circumstances. In particular, he was not to turn back in order to parry another English raid; but he was authorized to engage if he was himself pursued by an

English force, and should definitely engage if he found a divided English fleet guarding the entrance to the Channel, because it is always sound strategy to fight a portion of the enemy's force with the whole of yours, if he is foolish enough to give you the chance. But the King summed up with a contradictory instruction:

It is understood that you will fight only if you cannot otherwise make secure the passage across to England of the Duke of Parma . . . It will be well to keep our forces intact.

Given that God granted Medina Sidonia a victory, he was warned by the King:

As a prudent commander you should see that your squadrons do not break their battle formation and that their commanders, moved by greed, do not give pursuit to the enemy and take prizes.

The Queen did not see fit to issue a similar instruction for the English fleet, but if she had, it would have been justified; as events were to prove.

The Great Armada took weeks to come down from the Lisbon quaysides to the mouth of the Tagus. This was to be expected. In peacetime, to cross from England to Normandy as a paying passenger takes less than half a day. In July, 1944, when I made the same journey, from central London to Juno Beach off Courseulles, the British Army, employing motor vehicles and steam-driven ships, took six days to get me there. This is what 'meticulous military precision' really means in the twentieth century; almost all military, naval and air forces are like that. The sixteenth century was no different, except in the means of propulsion of their vehicles.

On one occasion, some years ago, in order to carry out a diving operation I had to rely on a modern cruising yacht as a means of transport. It took three hours to get there and about 20 minutes to get back, whereas a motor boat would have taken about half an hour each way. The difference is explained by the fact that the wind was dead against us on the way out, and directly behind us on the way back. Consequently, the owner of the yacht had to tack across the wind in long zig-zags on our tedious way to the dive site, but simply ran back with the wind astern. The yacht was an efficient fun craft; the Armada's ships were not. The majority were cargo carriers accustomed to working in trades where time is of no great consequence; the warships were only marginally faster. The really speedy craft were the small patches and zabras, fast fishing boats, which the English called pinnaces; used by the Spaniards for scouting and communications.

There was no secret whatever about the composition of the invasion force. On 29 April, Medina Sidonia had sent a full list to the King of the ships, guns and men actually assembled for the Enterprise of England. An almost identical list, not quite so detailed and with some confusion over the foreign names, was in the hands of the English government by 1 May. Reports from other spies and also escaped prisoners, often greatly exaggerated, also reached England, adding to the aura of invincible power which now shone on Spanish arms.

The Great Armada was divided into squadrons, also called armadas, mostly on a territorial basis. The Duke of Medina Sidonia himself was to sail in the strongest ship of a strong squadron, which consisted of ten galleons: *San Martin, San Juan, San Marcos, San Felipe, San Luis, San Mateo, Santiago, Florencia, San Cristobal, San Bernado*, accompanied by two zabras, fast and light, for communications duties. Most were Portuguese warships; an exception was the *Florencia*, a galleon belonging to the Duke of Florence. Medina Sidonia's flagship was the *San Martin* of 1,000 tons by Spanish reckoning (less by the English method of measurement). The two smallest galleons were of only 352 tons. Standardization of ships (and guns) was still more than three centuries into the future.

Next listed was the Armada of Biscay, under the veteran Admiral Juan Martinez de Recalde, whom the English recognized as 'a man of service'. He also had ten sizeable vessels not, however, classified as galleons: *Santa Ana* (the flagship), *Gran Grin, Santiago, La Concepcion de Zubelzu, La Concepcion de Juanes de Cano, Magdalena, San Juan, Maria Juan, Santa Maria de Montemayor*, and four patches for scouting and communications.

After this came the Armada of Castile under Admiral Diego Flores de Valdes. Ten of his ships were Spanish galleons: *San Cristobal, San Juan Bautista, San Pedro, San Juan, Santiago el Mayor, San Felipe y Santiago, Ascencion, Nuestra Senora del Barrio, San Medel y Celedon, Santa Ana*. In addition there were four large vessels described simply as 'ships': *Nuestra Senora de Begona, Trinidad, Santa Catalina, San Juan Bautista*. Two pataches accompanied this squadron. Two vessels bore the same name, it will be noted – one a galleon, the other a merchant ship.

The Armada of Andalusia, under Don Pedro de Valdes, consisted of ten large vessels of various types: the ships *Nuestra Senora del Rosario* and *San Francisco*, the galleon *San Juan* (yet another of that name!), the ships *San Juan de Gargarin* and *La Concepcion*, the hulk (a Baltic type) *Duquesa Santa Ana*, the ships *Santa Catalina, La Trinidad, Santa Maria del Juncal, San Bartolome*, and one patache.

Another ten large vessels formed the Armada of Guipuzcoa under Miguel de Oquendo. Nine of them were listed as 'ships': *Santa Ana, Santa Maria de la Rosa* (also referred to as *Nuestra Senora de la Rosa*), *San Salvador, San Esteban, Santa Marta, Santa Barbara, San Buenaventura, La Maria San Juan, Santa Cruz*; the tenth, the *Doncella*, being described as a 'hulk'. Two pataches were attached to this squadron.

The Armada of the Levant, under Martin de Bertondona, similarly consisted of ten large vessels, one of them, the flagship *La Reganzona*, being the largest in the whole Armada, at 1,249 tons. The others were *La Lavia, La Rata Encoronada, San Juan de Sicilia, La Trinidad Valencera, La Anunciada, San Nicholas Prodaneli, La Juliana, Santa Maria de Vision, La Trinidad de Scala*.

The first two ships on each list were of course the flagship and vice-flagship. This was true also of the storeships listed as the 'Fleet of Hulks' under Juan Gomez de Medina. Ranging from 750 to 160 tons, they were: *Gran Grifon, San Salvador, Perro Marino, Falcon Blanco Mayor, Castillo Negro, Barca de Amburg* (Hamburg), *Casa de Paz Grande, San Pedro Mayor, El Sanson, San Pedro Menor, Barca de Anzique* (Danzig), *Falcon Blanco Mediano, San Andres, Casa de Paz Chica,*

Ciervo Volante, Paloma Blanca, La Ventura, Santa Barbara, Santiago, David, El Gato, Essayas, San Gabriel. Twenty-three ships in all, vulnerable and under-gunned, to be stationed in the middle of the fleet.

Apart from the small craft specially assigned to particular squadrons of the Armada, there were twenty-two pataches and zabras held centrally under the command of Don Antonio Hurtado de Mendoza. As they did not take part in the battles or suffer shipwreck, it does not seem worthwhile listing them here, whereas the names of many of the fighting ships and store vessels will occur and recur in the unfolding story – some of them to continue into our own times, when their remains were found. It will be apparent, from the similarity of many of the names (the innumerable *San Juans*, for example), that some confusions will occur.

In quite a different category from all the above were two special, oared squadrons forming part of the Great Armada. There were the four Galleys of Portugal under Don Diego de Medrano: the *Capitana* (flag galley), *Princessa, Diana, Bazana*. Aboard these four were 888 galley slaves, one of whom was a Welshman who would subsequently tell his story to the English. This type of vessel had performed well for the French during their invasions of 1545; but during 1588 there were to be few calms suitable for galleys.

The admitted deficiencies of the galley had resulted in the invention of a hybrid, the galleass, which combined auxiliary oar propulsion with a broadside fire from guns mounted above the heads of the rowers. Stronger than galleys, nevertheless their hulls had to be kept light, otherwise the oars would not have moved them much. At Lepanto in 1571 they had been very effective against the Turkish galleys, and four Neapolitan galleasses were to accompany the Armada under Don Hugo de Moncada: *San Lorenzo, Zuniga, Girona, Napolitana*. Both galleasses and galleys carried masts and sails, using their oars only in battle or other emergency, where extra speed and manoeuvrability were required.

When it sailed from Lisbon, the Great Armada numbered 130 ships carrying 29,453 men, of whom some 19,000 were soldiers (17,000 Spanish, 2,000 Portuguese) commanded by six

Maestres de Campo, or Regimental Commanders: Don Diego de Pimental, Don Francisco de Toledo, Don Alonso de Luzon, Nicholas de Isla, Don Agustin Mexia and Gaspar de Sosa. These officers, and the men they commanded, formed the basic fighting strength of the invasion force, both at sea and on land. We shall meet some of them again, in triumph and disaster. In overall charge, as land forces commander, was Don Alonso de Leyva, general of Milanese cavalry, whose headquarters ship was the 820-ton *Rata Encoronada* of Martin de Bertondona's Levant squadron. If Medina Sidonia was killed, he was to take over.

Among those embarked were 180 monks and friars, 167 artillerymen, and a hospital staff of eighty-five (which included five physicians, five surgeons and four priests, a pessimistic proportion). In comparison, the staff of the Commander-in-chief, Medina Sidonia, consisted of twenty-two gentlemen and fifty servants, an astonishing number compared to those usual in English fleets of the Tudor period, where ten or a dozen might be appropriate to an admiral.

All the ships must have been desperately overcrowded, so that a race for the best places aboard ensued, with particularly haughty individuals putting up artificial partitions to give themselves privacy, while others installed unofficial beds. One sympathizes, although the conditions were probably not so bad as on a troopship going to Normandy in 1944, because what can be endured by soldiers for a few days becomes dangerous from disease when the time is counted in months. We, however, would never have got out if the ship had been hit by a fifteen-inch shell or struck a mine (in the latter case, she would sink in four minutes, the crew told us, gleefully).

While at low level thousands of men were settling into unfamiliar quarters, trying to make themselves at home, at command level there had been a hasty reshuffling of jobs, ships and responsibilities, as a result of the death of the project's originator and organizer, the Marquis of Santa Cruz. Medina Sidonia was nominally in charge; but as he himself said, he knew little of war or the sea, let alone that most difficult aspect, an amphibious operation involving all arms. His flagship, the galleon *San Martin*, was nominally the Armada *capitana*, or fleet flagship. But firstly he needed a seaman adviser. Diego Flores de Valdes, admiral of the Armada of Castile, had to leave his own *capitana* and go on board the *San Martin*, leaving Gregorio de las Alas to command in his place. Secondly, he needed someone to advise him on military tactics at sea. The Duke asked for the Marquis de Penafiel who was commanding the Portuguese galleon *San Marcos*, but Penafiel preferred to go to war in good company, with his old comrades, and refused the honour of holding Medina Sidonia's hand. So the job of military adviser went to Don Francisco de Bobadilla, an experienced regimental commander. In effect the Great Armada was to be commanded by a committee of three.

This far from ideal solution was made more confused by two other, virtually rival, appointments. Diego Flores de Valdes was nobody in particular. The senior sailor, the admiral of greatest reputation, was Juan Martinez de Recalde, commander of the Armada of Biscay. He could hardly be left out, and under the reorganization shifted his flag from the *Santa Ana* to the great *San Juan* of Oporto, which thereby became the vice-flagship, or *almiranta*, of the entire force. Nevertheless, he was not appointed successor to the Duke, for that place was given to the Milanese general of cavalry, Don Alonso de Leyva, an equally redoubtable officer, commanding in the *Rata Encoronada* of the Levant squadron.

Out of this apparent confusion came good advice and contentment for the Duke. Two months' hard toil had turned a motley collection of ships and men, drawn from all over the Latin world, into a united, disciplined force. From 1 to 18 May (11–28 by the Spanish calendar), the ships were passing down the river in groups, as the wind and their degree of readiness allowed. The war galleys were proving useful – as tugs and hufflers. They could push the clumsy sailing ships round with their bows, point them in the right direction or, if the wind shifted, get them out of trouble. On the 18th, the Duke wrote:

The weather is not good, and a NNW wind is blowing, but I have sent some ships down the river, and some more went down today with a great deal of trouble. They are at anchor on the bar. If a land wind blows tomorrow morning I will go down with the rest of the fleet. Not an hour has been, or shall be, lost.

He was feeling easier in his mind about the fighting, too. His experienced advisers had been feeding him with facts and ideas and, in place of an unwelcome blank, the Duke thought he now knew what to expect, and exactly how to deal with it.

A stream of reports from Spanish spies in England showed that the enemy fleet was in three separate sections: Drake's formidable force at Plymouth, a smaller force in the Straits of Dover, and a mass of ships fitting out in the Thames as reinforcements. Men were being pressed into them from the streets, those to become soldiers being given red coats, those to be sailors blue coats.

Drake would be badly outnumbered when he first sighted the Armada and would hardly dare to attack; it would be much more sensible merely to follow the Spanish force until the other English fleet lying off Dover came in sight; and then both English fleets would fall on the Armada from front and rear simultaneously.

But this, the Duke's advisers had explained, could be countered by adopting a fleet formation based on that used by galleys. In his turn, Medina Sidonia explained to the King:

I have taken every precaution. Either of the two horns of our formation, with their supports, and two of the galleasses which accompany the first four ships, would be able to cope with one of the enemy's fleets; whilst I with the rest of our vessels leading, could deal with the fleet in front of us, my centre being supported by the vessels I have appointed for the purpose, and the other two galleasses which are attached to my flagship.

The Duke was now filled with a spirit of aggression. His advisers obviously did not agree with King Philip's pious hope that the enemy might be ignored; they advocated fighting a decisive battle at sea before attempting invasion:

The opinion of those whom I have consulted here is that the best course would be to break up the enemy's sea force first. When this is done, as I hope it will be, if the enemy will meet me, the rest will be safe and easy. I will redouble my care, that if the enemy will face us he will meet the fate he always has done when he has encountered Your Majesty's forces.

The Great Armada, united, sailed on 29 May, the Duke noting: 'All the men are in good health and spirits, ready for the fight if the enemy will face us.'

There was a flash and a cloud of smoke from the Duke's flagship, followed seconds later by the sound of the explosion rolling across the sea. In all the ships, crisp orders were barked; men ran to be ready at anchor cables and at the rigging. Soldiers came up from below, to watch. The newly mounted guns emphasized the purpose of their journey. It was a moving moment for everyone, this final departure into the unknown. How many would come back? How rich would be the plunder? How great the fame?

A bugle shrilled out from the flagship, sad and lonely across the tossing wastes of water, echoing one part of their mood.

The capstans ground, hauling in the dripping anchor cables, wet and slimy from the sea. The flagship shook out her sails. The rest followed suit and began to form up, each ship striving for its allotted space. The white wakes tumbled astern as the vessels heeled under the wind, came alive and began to move forward – to England.

4

'Like Bears Tied to Stakes'

Vulcan begat me, Minerva me taught,
   Nature my mother, craft nourish'd me year by year;
Three bodies are my food, my strength is nought;
   Anger, wrath, waste, and noise are my children dear;
Guess, friend, what I am, and how I am wrought,
   Monster of sea, or of land, or of elsewhere;
Know me and use me, and I may thee defend,
And if I be thine enemy, I may thy life end.
                                   Sir Thomas Wyatt (1503–1542):
                                         'Description of a Gun'

Lord Charles Howard of Effingham was appointed Lord High Admiral of England just before Christmas, 1587, a few weeks earlier than the Duke of Medina Sidonia's appointment as Spain's Captain General of the Ocean. The Englishman had this much advantage, that the position was his by right of birth; he was the ninth member of his family to hold the post. He was also of the correct religion – he was a firm Protestant, unlike most of the Howards. As he had grown up with the right background, he could understand the technical issues, and was not incapable of making swift and sound decisions. But, like Medina Sidonia, he began the campaign on a mundane level, issuing a fleet order concerning lighted candles. Reporting a small fire in the galleon *Elizabeth Bonaventure*, he wrote:

There were two poor knaves that came from Chester, that strived for a place to hang up their netting for to lie in, and the one of them had a piece of candle in his hand, and in striving, the candle fell down where there lay some oakum. It might have bred some mischief, but it was quickly put out.

The next mishap was more serious: one man killed and another wounded by the bursting of a gun in one of Drake's ships at Portsmouth while carrying out practice firing. Howard thought better of giving a direct reprimand to his famous subordinate and instead asked Walsyngham, the Secretary of State, to do it: 'If you would write a word or two unto him to spare his powder, it would do well.'

Still new to his command, Howard had touched on one of the two serious weaknesses in the otherwise strong English fleet: shortage of ammunition and shortage of food. He was soon to realize that telling Drake to cut down on practice powder was no answer at all. This was to be a very special campaign at sea. There had been nothing like it before and there was to be nothing like it again.

For centuries sea battles had been decided, not by sinking the enemy's ships, but by boarding and capturing them; and for centuries after the time of the Armada, sea battles were still to be decided by boarding. At Trafalgar in 1805, the dying Nelson did not ask how many enemy ships had been sunk, but how many had been taken. That is to say, battles were finally decided by putting a sufficient force of armed men on to the enemy's decks.

Of course, the battle was always begun by a rain of missiles designed to kill, confuse or intimidate the enemy's crews. Anything, from catapults to crossbows, was used. Then, in 1313, the monk Berthold Schwarz of Freiburg in Germany made the first gun, and a new factor appeared – noise and terror. At first, as at Agincourt, it was only the enemy's horses which were frightened. But soon there was a distinct shock effect to be obtained, not merely from the actual discharge of the weapon but from the whistling scream of the missiles hurtling towards you. The actual effect on the nerves cannot be appreciated by a TV-trained audience, for the simple reason that no recording machine, and no transmitter for that matter, can reproduce the sound at full volume.

Very early on, there are mentions of guns at sea. In 1356 a French fleet had a few guns, in 1359 a Spanish ship used a big gun in action, in 1379–80 guns were used in the Genoese-Venetian war, in 1410–12 guns appeared in the lists of English carracks (although not more than three guns per ship). These early guns were made of wrought-iron and constructed in the same way as a wooden cask – which is why the tube of a gun is still called the barrel. Almost all were breech-loaders and, because so much of the expanding gases escaped, were not very powerful.

A great step forward in power was obtained when muzzle-loading guns were cast in bronze and then combined with a stronger propellant. In the late fifteenth century this produced a revolution in land warfare, as far as sieges were concerned. Such guns could send the projectile faster than ever before and obtain a closer grouping of shots on a castle or city wall, causing a breach to appear in a relatively short time. Strongholds which had withstood sieges of many years now fell to the new methods in weeks or even days.

It was not long before complete batteries of such guns were mounted in strong-built warships. A French shipwright is credited with producing the first watertight gunport in 1501, which enabled the heavy guns to be mounted low down in the hull instead of high up in the waist or castles; and in 1509 the teenage Henry VIII ordered the first English ship to be constructed to take the new armament – the *Mary Rose*. She carried an array of heavy bronze muzzle-loaders as well as heavy wrought-iron breech-loaders, plus a large number of light swivel guns. In design, she was an Italian carrack, retaining the high fighting castle at the bow which was the dominating feature of the type. Both this and the slightly lower stern castle were placements for infantry, pikemen and bowmen, which previously had formed the main striking power of ships at sea.

In the *Mary Rose*, they were still there; but in reduced numbers. The guns were not expected to win the battle alone. Her ammunition lists show that on average only about 15 rounds per gun were carried; although the lighter pieces were better supplied. Clearly, a prolonged gun battle was never intended. A reading of the narratives and the fighting instructions of the time show that the aim was first to beat down the enemy crew's opposition by gunshot and bowshot, and then, in the smoke and confusion – and in the shocked state of the enemy – carry first his fighting tops which dominated his upper deck and then the deck itself. This was all more easily advised than done, for as I know from experience, to leap from one ship to another, when both are pitching and rolling in the waves – encumbered by light armour or leather jerkins and while carrying weapons – is a difficult and dangerous feat, even if no one is shooting at you at the same time. Imagine doing it with arrows and bullets whistling up at you, and the sharp steel points of pikes waiting below to impale you if you survive the hail of fire.

I have no doubt whatever that it was not a practical proposition unless the enemy's infantry had been stunned and shocked into immobility – or actually cut down – by the nerve-tearing thunder of gunfire, heavy and light.

This was what the artillery was supposed to do: assist the infantry in the assault. This was exactly what the artillery in the Armada was supposed to do when it met Drake in the Channel. Many of the Spanish ships were similar to the *Mary Rose* and many of the guns, particularly the bronze muzzle-loaders, were of the same types; some of the ships still carried wrought-iron breech-loaders like hers.

The problem faced by the English admirals, however, was unique. They had no infantry; or hardly any. Perhaps 1,500 men could be considered soldiers as compared to the 19,000 men – mostly the formidable Spanish veterans – embarked in the Armada. The guns would have to do all the work, instead of just the preparatory part. And no English ship dare close with a Spanish ship, or even risk damage to sails and rigging, for fear of being instantly overwhelmed by a rush of boarders which could not be stemmed. They would have to stand off and bang away at a distance. And that meant powder and shot, and plenty of it. But the allowances in Elizabeth's time were based on the wars of Henry VIII, when English ships had their full complement of excellent infantry and, ship to ship, could take on any opponent on equal terms at least.

No one at the Queen's court appreciated this. Even Howard, when he first took up his command, did not understand it. It was left to Drake to rock the boat, make a damned nuisance of himself, and tell the blunt truth:

The proportion in powder and shot for our great ordnance in her Majesty's ships is but for one day and half's service, if it be begun and

Fighting Ships: The Vikings to the *Victory.*

Viking longship, 850–900 AD. A large, light open boat with auxiliary oar propulsion. Many examples known.

Mid-13th-century English cog. A ship rather than a boat, with temporary castles built on in time of war. No plans exist.

Late-14th-century 'nef' with permanent built-in castles. No plans exist.

Grace Dieu, a huge early-15th-century carrack built by Henry V after Agincourt. Remains of lower hull can still be seen in Hamble River.

Mid-16th-century carrack. A four-master with heavy guns as main armament. No plans exist.

English galleon of about 1586. Still a four-master, but the towering castles have been reduced. Result: improved sailing qualities. A few plans exist.

Swedish galleon *Wasa* of 1628. Deliberately discovered by Anders Franzén in 1956 and salvaged intact in 1961.

First rate line-of-battle ship HMS *Victory* as she appeared in 1805. A giant headquarters ship for an Admiral.

continued as the service may require; the powder for 24 of the merchant ships will be scant sufficient for one day's service.

This was a crisis indeed. The English fleet had no teeth. But in addition, it had no food; and Howard took his complaints right to the top, to Walsyngham, the Secretary of State:

I do warrant you our state is well enough known to them in Flanders, and as we were a terror to them at our first coming out, so do they now make but little reckoning of us; for they know we are like bears tied to stakes . . . I have a good company here with me, so that if the Queen's Majesty will not spare her purse, they will not spare their lives.

The ships were being rationed for so limited a period that they could hardly put to sea, let alone sail down to the enemy coasts and smash the Armada at source, as Drake and Hawkyns wanted to do, and as they soon convinced Howard he must do. Elizabeth was necessarily a frugal ruler, but food and ammunition are not items for cheeseparing at the start of a decisive campaign. Perhaps she had some faint hope of the peace negotiations still dragging on across the Channel, or divined Philip's real purpose. But it was all very risky, as Howard pointed out to Walsyngham on 10 March:

Sir, I pray you to let me hear from you how the peace is like to go on; for if I may hear in any time that it is not like to come to pass, I will make some provision for the choking of Dunkirk haven . . . Yester-night there came one to me of purpose from Dunkirk, who doth assure me that the Spanish forces by sea are for certain to part from Lisbon the 20th of this month with the light moon. I pray to God her Majesty do not repent this slack dealings. All that cometh out of Spain must concur to lie, or else we shall be stirred very shortly with heave and ho. As for her Majesty's four great ships, I am out of hope to see them abroad; they shall be to keep Chatham Church when they should serve the turn abroad.

Sir William Wynter, commanding the English fleet blockading Parma in the Narrows, had no time for peace negotiations or Government excuses of poverty. He was to write in June:

If we did make a sharp war out of hand (entertaining Scotland as our friend) and to spare the pride of our backs and some of our glutton's fare I do not doubt (by God's grace) we should then make Her Majesty's enemies come to reason shortly.

By 30 March (9 April New Style) Drake, who thoroughly agreed with this aggressive philosophy, was urging: 'With fifty sail of shipping we shall do more good upon their own coast, than a great many more will do here at home.'

But still the English ships were 'like bears tied to stakes'. Drake was forced to write with restraint, but Howard was able to use terms to Burghley, the Lord High Treasurer of England, that few have since dared to employ to the Treasury. He wrote on 8 April:

We shall now be victualled, beginning the 20th of this April, unto the 18th of May, at which time the last month's victual doth end; and by the advertisements that giveth the largest time for the coming out of the Spanish forces, is the midst of May, being the 15th. Then we have three days victual. If it be fit to be so, it passeth my reason. I think ever since there were ships in this realm it was never heard of but a month's victual was prepared. King Harry, her Majesty's father, never made a lesser proportion of supply than 6 weeks.

Here was the point of giving Howard the chief command; no mariner, no matter how brilliant, could talk to the Government like that. Howard could, because he was one of them. The young Henry VIII did in fact have supply problems in his 1513 campaign, because the victualling fleet was kept penned in West Country ports by unfavourable winds. To be fair to his daughter, that must be said.

News of the imminent sailing of the Armada came in almost daily. An exceptionally well-informed witness arrived at Portsmouth on 28 May (7 June New Style). His extraordinary story would make a firm foundation for a tale of romantic adventure (but in reality must have been highly unpleasant). His name was Giles Napper and he had been captured from a ship of Sir Thomas Leighton's some four years earlier, served as a galley slave under the Turks for two-and-a-half years; and then as a galley slave with the Spaniards for one-and-a-half years; and had escaped from Spain in a French ship as late as 26 April (6 May).

The Great Armada had then been on the point of sailing. He

could not speak for the Dons themselves, but as for the common people in the ships, they had told him:

That if they set foot on land, they hope to find some friends, and look for help from the Scots: but that they think the Englishmen will be hard for them at sea.

But on the very day that Giles Napper got home to England again, Howard was continuing his endless battle with Burghley, the Treasurer, fighting for adequate rations with which to fight, and beginning to sneer:

Your Lordship shall understand that we have scarcely three weeks victuals left. My good Lord, there is here the gallantest company of captains, soldiers and mariners that I think ever was seen in England. It were a pity that they should lack meat, when they are so desirous to spend their lives in her Majesty's service. God send us the happiness to meet with the Spaniards before our men on the land discover them, for I fear me a little sight of the enemy will fear the land men much.

The letter was dated from Plymouth, 28 May by the English calendar. The Armada had already been nine days at sea.

The strength of the English fleet was that it was entirely English: the land forces also were composed only of Englishmen. The force was all of one nationality, one language, and one purpose. The Queen had not, as the King of Spain had feared, reinforced the native troops with Germans or other foreigners; nor were the English at sea relying on the Dutch rebel warships to keep Parma locked up in Nieuport, although these were perfectly capable of doing so; they were relying entirely on themselves. Indeed, in this crisis, there was a dislike of all foreigners, friendly or otherwise, openly and contemptuously expressed; so much so that the authorities tried to suppress it on the grounds that it might lead to public disorder. A foreign historian resident among them, the Florentine Petruccio Ubaldino, noted with care the precautions taken against the mass of aliens, many of them refugees from religious oppression, who had flocked to England in recent years.

Because of the common danger, watch had to be kept on the great crowd of foreigners from the Low Countries, France, and other places, who lived in London on their earnings as craftsmen. No more was known of some of them except that they had come on account of their religion; but the city was full of such as might be faithful or not under the cloak of the same religion. And not being so very sure of them as could be wished, amid such cares and dangers, they needed watching. Every day these foreigners received insulting words from the prentices and the lower classes, people who are naturally the enemies of foreigners, which fact disturbed the careful magistrates. For that reason all the principal cross roads were guarded day and night for the keeping of the peace.

Some 350 years later, in a similar situation, a British Prime Minister was to order: 'Collar the lot'. Elizabeth was not so sweeping, but the precautions she did take were not baseless. There were indeed Spanish spies in London; their reports, unsigned, are in the Spanish archives today. They operated under code names, such as 'David'. One at least was a native Englishman, who on 16 July (26 July New Style) reported:

People here do not fear the Spaniard any more, as they are convinced that he has returned to Spain. All the principal Catholics have been sent to the Isle of Ely in the custody of Lord North.

The latter was perfectly true. A limited number of the leading English Catholics had been interned in Wisbech Castle, but not as suspected traitors. Elizabeth was far too wise, far-seeing, and politic for that. It is hard to read a man's soul. It was merely suspected that some might be tempted to turn traitor, if the Spaniards landed in force. That, in the absence of any proof, was not justification enough to brand them all publicly as traitors to Queen and country. Therefore, she did not do so. She publicly proclaimed that their internment was not for the safety of her realm, but for their own safety, because, in case of a Spanish landing, the more riotous elements of the popula-tion, already insulting all foreigners, might well attack them. Considering that there had already been a number of Catholic plots to assassinate her, this showed iron nerve on Elizabeth's part, more impressive by far than Winston Churchill's grand gesture of 1940.

In the view of Ubaldino the Florentine, she was absolutely right. Catholics could hardly avoid wishing to see the return of the old religion – but at the price of Spanish conquest and control?

The change of religion threatened by the Spaniards did not so much encourage their rebellion as anger them, when they heard that the Spaniards had determined to conquer the kingdom. It being easier to find flocks of white crows than one Englishman (and let him believe what he will about religion) who loves a foreigner, either as a master or companion in his own home, even if a benefactor.

To gather in the waverers, and buttress the determination of the loyal, a distinctly modern policy was used, as Ubaldino noted:

In those days news was spread (and perhaps not by chance in London, for preachers in several churches discussed the matter extensively), which served to incite even further the feelings of the English people. These preachers, in public sermons, stated that the Spaniards were carrying in their fleet a large number of women of every kind, and together with this report was spread the rumour that in the Spanish ships were many instruments of torture with which to afflict the English people. These things being easily believed, the whole of the lowest and most credulous part of the people were moved to a mortal and dangerous hatred of all foreigners living there.

A report from a Genoese living in England and serving Spain contains further details of this propaganda:

Being in great alarm, they made the people believe that the Spaniards were bringing a shipload of halters in the Armada to hang all the Englishmen, and another shipload of scourges to whip women, with 3,000 or 4,000 wet nurses to suckle the infants. It was said that all children between the ages of 7 and 12 would be branded in the face, so that they might always be known. These and other things of the same sort greatly irritated the people. During the time the Armada was in the Channel all foreigners in London were forbidden to leave their homes, and the shops were to remain closed.

The English precautions were undeniably efficient. The flow of letters from agents died to a trickle and then stopped, while the actual fighting was taking place in the Channel. In effect, the English sealed off their coasts; and little got through, even from privileged diplomatic sources. The precautions were not technically so complete as those enforced in 1940, when the entire south coast of England was declared a prohibited area and road blocks set up to prevent all unauthorized entry; nor so complete as in 1944, when the awaited invasion was in the other direction. But the sparsity of population and slowness of communications in the time of Elizabeth rendered them just as effective. The Spanish spy network was hamstrung and, if indeed there was a fifth column, it had been rendered harmless with the minimum of cost and fuss. There was no Chief of the Imperial General Staff charging round, spreading baseless stories of traitors in high places. That was to be left to an imaginative, escaped galley slave called David Gywnn. There was no fifth column scare; Elizabeth did not allow it.

In the fleet papers there is one reference to a single case of suspected treason; and that was in February, in the *White Bear*, commanded by Lord Sheffield, a nephew of Howard's. The Secretary of State, Sir Francis Walsyngham, set this particular hare in motion by briefing Howard personally. Howard, on going abroad, found his nephew in a hurry to get off to London:

And yet my Lord himself, as great haste as he had, made the barber, and three or four more which he suspected, to be sworn. And so they were; and they utterly renounced the Pope's authority. After my Lord's departure, Mr Ha. Sheffield, his lieutenant, took great pains and did examine the barber, and found that two or three years agone, he was something inclined to papistry, but being matched by his wife with an honest race, as it seems, they converted him. I have talked with the man myself. He offers to receive, and to do anything that a good Protestant should do. This was the cause I think that bred the doubt in him. He had a book that was done by an English papist beyond the seas; a bad book; but he brought it the preacher, with dislike of the book; and the preacher is counted to be a most zealous man and very honest.

There are 'bad books' today, which will get you into a lot of trouble in some places. In the case of this barber-surgeon, the ship's doctor of the *White Bear*, the 'bad book' may have been a pamphlet by either Father Parsons or Cardinal Allen, the Rome-supported renegades, who argued that as the Queen had been excommunicated by the Pope, no English Catholic could owe allegiance to her, or be guilty of treason against her. But

Elizabeth certainly would regard it as treason, and the penalty for that was hanging, drawing and quartering – a terrible, disgraceful butchery of the offender's living body carried out in public. One can almost smell the fear behind Howard's plea to Walsyngham:

> The barber had many good books, as the New Testament, the Book of Common Prayer, the book of the Psalms which he daily sang with the company. The man was prest by the Company of Surgeons, and not by my Lord; and he hath sailed often in her Majesty's ships, and accounted a very honest man. I think my Lord Sheffield will send you the party, and I believe you will not mislike him.

Anyone supporting a suspect could himself come under suspicion, so as well as pointing out that the doctor had been conscripted by the man's own guild, the Company of Surgeons, and not by Lord Sheffield, Howard added that Sheffield himself was 'very earnest and zealous in religion' and had been heard to be:

> most vehement against Papists, so be-traitoring them, saying that he that was in his ship that would not be sworn against the Pope, he would take him for a traitor, and so use him.

Howard was probably wise to ignore Walsyngham's suspicions and let the doctor have the benefit of the doubt, for when it came to David Gywnn's turn to spread stories of treason, the most important man he named was Sir Francis Walsyngham. Once denunciations began, there was no knowing where they would stop – nor how flimsy might be their basis.

For the moment, however, Gywnn was still slaving at the oar of a Portuguese galley bound for England with the Armada. Another seaman with experience of Spanish galleys, Captain Thomas Cely, was making a nuisance of himself by writing to the Lord Treasurer, Lord Burghley, for redress, interspersing his painful reminiscences with advice to the Government: 'My good Lord, a sharp war and a short. The Queen's subjects doth desire it.'

Cely had a pet scheme of his own, which he had been trying to push, without success:

When I have begun to enter into any matter of importance, one of them (the Council) told me and said this unto me: 'Cely, it is told me that you meddle with Councillors matters.' A rebuke I had, and so went my way. Another told me that if I could do her Majesty any service, so that it cost money, never speak of it, for she will not consent unto it. So I went my way with a flea in mine ear. My good Lord, I am a poor man, and one that hath a patched carcass; for I had thirty-two sundry torments in the Inquisition; and eight years in prison lacking but two months; and in the King of Spain's most filthy galleys, and seven other prisons.

Cely was not the sort of 'armchair expert' who flourishes in wartime because of the censorship. Downwind, a galley stank for miles, and it was just as well to remind Burghley of it. Nor was his letter wasted. Soon, Cely was to get suitable employment against his old enemies.

In other respects also, the time of waiting for the Armada, from the end of May to the end of July, 1588, seems to parallel the experience of 1940, from the last week of May to the middle of August – at least, on the threatened south coast which had seen the Armada pass and was now facing the Luftwaffe. I was at Portsmouth, and can remember clearly the first enemy aircraft I saw – at night, a mine-laying Heinkel 111 held in a searchlight beam at 2,000 feet in front of our house and being fired on by guns mounted on Southsea Castle, the artillery fort built by Henry VIII in 1544 against French invasion and still a viable strongpoint.

Like the Armada, the Luftwaffe had been built up by propaganda (British as well as German) as a mighty force; but all we got in those early months were a few tentative probes at our defences. Consequently I was taken totally by surprise when the first really big attack by dive-bombers took place on Portsmouth, Gosport, and the Isle of Wight. Our defences were poor, but no one thought we would be defeated; the tradition of the unbeaten island was too strong.

This is not to imply that we were all heroes, but in the beginning, there is usually a mixture of fear and rashness which with experience tempers into professionalism. I recall, on 13 August, 1940, short-range AA guns blazing away at all sorts of hopeless ranges at Junkers 88s ducking in and out of cloud over

Portsmouth dockyard, as they returned from a raid on Southampton. There were gunners just like that in Tudor times, too. Sir Arthur Gorgas (1557–1625), who served as a volunteer against the Armada in 1588, put down on paper some of the observations he made then:

Moreover, whereas in seafights you shall have some men, many times out of fear, some out of vain shows, that will discharge the broadsides upon an enemy ship when he is out of all reach and beyond culverin shot which fetched furtherest. That is a very indiscreet wasting of shot and powder and but a bravado that discovers fear or folly to a wise and valiant enemy which we must not do. For having the weather of them, we should come as near as our ordnance will do good safely, which is like a true man-of-war, and so bestowing our broadsides we may fall again at our pleasure and shall be able to avoid boarding, which they will by all means come to as their best advantage and shortest trial. Whereas otherwise in loose fights we shall still gall them and tire them out.

The best weapon of the Armada was its infantry, for they were battle-experienced veterans, long past the fearful or vainglorious stages so vividly condemned by Gorgas. The English had no match for them, but must harass any landing attempt with their more speedy and manoeuvrable ships and far superior gunnery. But as the weeks went by and the Armada did not appear, many began to doubt that it would ever come.

5

'The Blood of His Beheaded Mother'

> They now to fight are gone;
> Armour on armour shone;
> Drum now to drum did groan;
>   To hear, was wonder.
> That, with the cries they make,
> The very earth did shake;
> Trumpet, to trumpet spake;
>   Thunder, to thunder.
> *Michael Drayton* (1563–1631)

On 30 May by Spanish reckoning the Duke of Medina Sidonia wrote to King Philip, announcing that the Armada had sailed and giving his position as three leagues out to sea off Portugal. In common with the humblest men in that force, not all of his thoughts were with the Enterprise; he asked the King to show favour to his children 'whom he has left so poor'.

In strong contrast was the outward show of deference to the Duke's official position, given in the General Orders he issued to the fleet:

The ships will come to the flagship every evening to learn the watchword and receive orders . . . The flagship must be saluted by bugles if there are any on board, or by fifes, and two cheers from the crews. When the response has been given the salute must be repeated. If the hour be late, the watchword must be requested, and when it has been obtained another salute must be given, and the ship will then make way for others. In case the weather should make it impossible to obtain the watchword on any days, the following words must be employed: on Sunday, Jesus; on Monday, Holy Ghost; on Tuesday, Most Holy Trinity; on Wednesday, Santiago; on Thursday, The Angels; on Friday, All Saints; on Saturday, Our Lady.

With such a miscellaneous force, much of it vulnerable, stress was very properly laid on formation-keeping.

It is of great importance that the Armada should be kept well together
. . . Great care and vigilance must be exercised to keep the squadron
of hulks always in the midst of the fleet. The order about not preceding
the flagship must be strictly obeyed, especially at night.

There was a crisp disciplinary decision about the following
paragraphs:

No ship belonging to, or accompanying the Armada, shall separate
from it without my permission. If any should be forced out of the
course by tempest, before arriving off Cape Finisterre, they will make
direct for that point, where they will find orders from me; but if no
such orders be awaiting them, they will then make for Corunna, where
they will receive orders. Any infraction of this order shall be punished
by death or forfeiture.
   On leaving Cape Finisterre the course will be to the Scilly Isles, and
ships must try to sight the islands from the south, taking great care to
look to their surroundings. If on the voyage any ships should get
separated, they are not to return to Spain on any account, the
punishment for disobedience being forfeiture and death with disgrace . . .

Those orders had been drafted when the ships were in the
Tagus, comfortably moored. The quiet lapping of the waves
against the hulls was almost soothing, even when the wind blew
strongly, as it had in the first week of May:

God ordains all things and He has not seen fit to send us weather for
the sailing of the Armada; it is as boisterous and bad as if it were
December.

Now that the Armada was at sea, such a wind was a different
matter. The bows rolled and plunged, lifting bursts of white
spray back across the deck; the masts swept back and forth
across the horizon in the gusts, the wind roaring through the
loose, flying rigging; nothing in the high-perched, tottering
stern cabins stayed still for a moment, unless it was lashed
down, and to walk, a man had to sway with the ship and with
at least one hand hold on to something firm. In the low troop
decks amidships, the situation was indescribable. The soldiers,
seeing to their own comfort, had brought masses of kit aboard;
many of them had embarked truckle beds instead of hammocks;
and all this gear was loose, slithering backwards and forwards
on the heaving, vomit-slimy planks, colliding with the guns run

in behind closed ports, smashing into the piles of ready-to-use ammunition and powder bags, bringing down rows of stacked pikes and other weapons.

To the sailors, whose quarters were now confined to the fore and after castles, it was of course nothing much; indeed a sailing vessel is steadier and has a more comfortable motion than a modern, powered ship, which can be butted head-on into wind-driven rollers, or pointed directly across them. But to the land men – one of whom was the Captain-General of the entire enterprise – it was hell without end. It would not cease, could not cease, until the whole expedition was over and the Armada safe at anchor in the land-locked Thames. The men longed for England in a way they had not done before. If Drake came and drowned them all, it would not matter. Nothing mattered, if only the world would be still for once.

Those people who intended to keep diaries, or 'relations', made few entries. An Army officer, Pedro Estrade, sailing in the Portuguese galleon *San Marcos*, noted: 'We were with foul weather until 14 June, that we saw Cape Finisterre, whereas we were turning up and down till Sunday the nineteenth of the same.'

Facing strong headwinds, the Armada was beating up and down, gaining very little distance towards the first rendezvous, the Scilly Isles. The barren coasts of Portugal slowly gave place to the barren coasts of north-west Spain, between the headland of Finisterre and the port of Corunna; but the fleet was still not in sight of the Bay of Biscay. Nevertheless, the Duke kept busy reporting progress to the King. The dates on his letters are naturally according to the new, Spanish calendar, ten days ahead of the old style still in use by the English. On 1 June he complains of the slowness of the hulks, the ill-armed storeships. On 10 June he reports that one of them, the hulk *David Chico*, has been dismasted and sent in to Galicia for repairs; and that he is sending Captain Moresin ahead in a past vessel to the Duke of Parma, to tell him that the Armada is on its way but will not rendezvous with him, but will wait off the English coast until such time as Parma has sent news that his invasion barges are ready. To the King, he writes that provisions are bad, the hulks slow, the weather contrary – a long voyage may be anticipated. The victuals are so rotten and stinking that many have been thrown overboard to prevent pestilence; please will the King send fresh supplies after the Armada. On 14 June he reports that he has begged the governor of Galicia to requisition as much food as possible from the countryside and send it on after the Armada. On 18 June, headwinds are still holding him up; the pilots advise him to enter Corunna or Ferrol, but he has refused for fear that the soldiers and sailors will desert, 'as usual'.

His progress report next day is dated 19 June, from Corunna. The flagship is safe in harbour with some of the ships; most are still at sea but expected to make port the next morning. But on 20 June his news is that a great storm has scattered the ships, damaging many, and driving them into various ports on the coast of Biscay, Asturias and Galicia.

On 24 June the Duke wrote two letters to the King. On that date thirty-three ships and two of the galleasses were missing still, with 6,567 soldiers and 1,882 sailors in them, nearly one-third of the Armada's strength. Some might merely be storm-bound on the Spanish coast, but . . . a chill suspicion oppressed Medina Sidonia.

I have sent pataches and caravels in all directions to order the ships to rendezvous at Corunna. I hope that eventually all, or nearly all, will come in, notwithstanding the violence of the storm. It has also occurred to me that some of our ships may have run as far as the Scillies, in accordance with the General Orders given to the fleet. I have consequently sent two very swift oared pataches, well armed, with an experienced ensign in each, to order any ships that may be there to return. If they find none of our vessels, they will be useful in reconnoitring the enemy's fleet.

The Duke's second letter of the day started by lamenting the weather and ended by advising the King to seek peace terms with England.

The weather, though it is June, is as wild as in December. No one remembers such a season . . . We have now arrived at this port scattered and maltreated in such a way that we are much inferior to the enemy, according to the opinion of all those who are competent to judge. Many of our largest ships are still missing, as well as two of the galleasses; whilst on the ships that are here there are many sick, whose number will increase in consequence of the bad provisions. These are not only very bad, as I have constantly reported, but they are so scanty that there cannot be more than sufficient to last two months . . . To undertake so great a task with equal forces to those of the enemy would be inadvisable, but to do so with inferior force, as ours is now, with our men lacking in experience, would be still more unwise . . . Your Majesty may believe me when I assure you that we are very weak . . . Well, Sire, how do you think we can attack so great a country as England with such a force as ours is now? . . . The difficulties might be avoided, by making some honourable terms with the enemy.

One of the two pataches ordered to go quickly to the Scillies was commanded by Ensign Esquival, but he did not get away until 27 June; probably the weather was too rough. His task was to check around the Scilly Isles for Spanish ships, because this had been the first rendezvous listed in the Duke's General Order to the fleet, issued at Lisbon, which strictly enjoined that if:

any ships should get separated, they are not to return to Spain on any account, the punishment for disobedience being forfeiture and death with disgrace.

It might not have occurred to all ship captains that the first ship to give up and put into a Spanish port would be the flagship of the whole Armada, the powerful galleon San Martin serving as headquarters for the Duke of Medina Sidonia. Some might have pressed on in spite of the gales. When Esquival put out to sea, twenty-eight ships were still missing, with nearly 6,000 men, and the Duke was holding a council of ten of his senior officers, for advice as to what to do.

When Esquival's patache reached the Scillies they found nine Spanish supply ships parading up and down, waiting for the Duke of Medina Sidonia. When Esquival told them where the Duke was, he did not record their replies; only that he told them to retire to Corunna, which they did, arriving on 5 July.

Esquival had now entered a potential battle zone which rapidly became a real one; every sail which came up over the horizon was a portent of possible annihilation for the weaker vessel. Until the distance had been closed appreciably, it would not be clear which was which. To complicate matters, there was a screen of English ships on patrol, some of them disguised as English or foreign merchantmen, and there were many genuine merchantmen, as well as fishing craft close inshore; plus French warships.

The nameless bark from Mousehole on course for France, which was warned by a French flyboat that the Spanish fleet was on the coast, seems to have been genuinely on passage to fetch a cargo of salt. The 'nine sail of great ships' which he counted were almost certainly some of the hulks of the Armada's supply squadron. The date of that sighting was 19 June by English reckoning, which was the 29th by the new continental calendar, three days after Esquival had left Corunna. The following day, 30 June New Style, two groups of Spanish ships, of six and fifteen sail, were reported by what was most probably an English spy ship. According to Lord Howard:

One Simons of Exeter gave advertisement that he was chased with a fleet of great ships, having some of his men hurt with shot from them; escaping their hands, landing in Cornwall, and came post to Plymouth unto the Lord Admiral. Seven of the ships they met withal were of 800 and 900 tons. The others were Biscayans of 300. It is very likely that this stormy weather hath parted their fleet.

But, he added, there was nothing he could do about picking off these stragglers. The fresh rations had only just arrived, and although 'no man shall sleep nor eat' until they had been loaded, the English fleet would be unable to sail until the following day.

Medina Sidonia, prudent and careful as always, had appointed a second rendezvous beyond the Scillies, which was actually on the coast of Cornwall near Mousehole – Mount's Bay and the Lizard – so Esquival took his patache there. To make himself less visible in the failing light on 1 July, he had the sails taken down. The pinnace was then rowed in towards the English coast for some four leagues; until land was only a few miles away.

We then stood by for night to come on, and a sail passed to leeward at two leagues distance. I wished to chase her, but the pilots opposed it, as it was late, and we were uncertain of catching her. The general opinion was that, being so near the land, we should hardly fail to catch a fisher-boat during the night.

The changeable Channel weather undid their plans. The wind got up from the usual south-westerly direction, blew a full gale, and then raged round the compass. The greatest danger to ships is not the sea, but the land. The Spaniards had to tack constantly to keep from being driven on to the rocks of Cornwall by the veering winds. By dawn, the wind had settled to a northerly and, although Esquival tried to keep heading in the general direction of Ireland, the patache shipped so much water over the side that he was forced to turn stern-on to it and, carrying the foresail low, run before it to the southward, the wind meanwhile steadily increasing again.

At four o'clock in the afternoon, after we had already received several heavy seas, a wave passed clean over us, and nearly swamped the pinnace. We were flush with the water, and almost lost, but by great effort of all hands the water was baled out, and everything thrown overboard. We had previously thrown overboard a pipe of wine and two butts of water. We lowered the mainmast to the deck, and so lived through the night under a closely reefed foresail.

At nine o'clock on the morning of Sunday, 3 July (it was still the month of June by English dating), the Spaniards sighted six sails – three to the north of the patache and three to the south-east – which suggested that this was an English search squadron divided so as to cover a great expanse of sea. Esquival took the bold decision to carry on and break through their search line.

We ran between them with our foresail set, and two of those to the south-east gave chase. We then hoisted our mainmast and clapped on sail, and after they had followed us until two o'clock, they took in sail and resumed their course. At nine o'clock we sighted another ship lying to and repairing, with only her lower sails set. On Monday, 4 July, we sighted land off Rivadeo.

Two days later thirteen supply ships, out of the fifteen sighted by Simons of Exeter on 30 June, got safely into Corunna, led by the vice-flagship of the hulks, the 650-ton *San Salvador*, twenty-four guns. The two missing were soon reported as safe in the port of Muxia. These were the *Paloma Blanca*, 250 tons, 12 guns, 20 sailors, 56 soldiers, and the *Casa de Paz Chica*, 350 tons, 15 guns, 24 sailors, 162 soldiers. They had had an exciting time, obeying their Duke's order to the letter, to carry on to the rendezvous point off the Scillies.

But nothing of interest had occurred (except for the gales which had sent the Duke's flagship into Corunna) until 28 June – ten days after they had lost sight of the Armada. Then sails were sighted towards Ushant. The *San Salvador* gave chase but was unable to catch up before the coastline had grown uncomfortably close. When night fell, signal lights were seen on land and six ships came out to reconnoitre the Spaniards. Three of them opened with gunfire on the rearmost hulk, the *San Pedro el Menor*, 500 tons, 18 guns, 23 sailors, 157 soldiers. Then they hoisted a lantern and turned away. France was in a ferment of civil strife, and no one could know on whose side a French ship might be.

On 1 July the Spanish squadron was fifteen leagues south of the Scilly Isles. In the cold, grey, dawn light, the heaving wavetops torn by violent wind from the north, two ships were seen emerging from St George's Channel between Cornwall and Ireland. The Spaniards did not hesitate. They attacked first and asked questions later.

The 400-ton *El Gato*, 9 guns, with 22 sailors and 400 soldiers aboard, drove alongside one of the strange ships with a grinding, splintering squeal of timbers against timbers, and the Spanish boarders poured down into her. For a moment there was a desperate mêlée on deck, before the crew surrendered, with two of their number dead and another mortally wounded. But the merchant ship had been so shattered from the shock of collision with the heavier vessel, that she heeled over and began to sink, disappearing under the wild grey seas with the wounded man still aboard. Meanwhile, reported the *San Salvador*:

The *Paloma Blanca* attacked the other vessel, capturing four men; but she drifted away from her, having broken her main yard-arm. The Admiral went on board the prize to make her fit for sailing, but the sea was terribly rough, and the Admiral was only saved by a miracle, for he broke two of his ribs whilst leaving the prize. We took him on board again, also one of the soldiers from the hulk *Paloma Blanca*, who had got on board during the attack.

Now the Spaniards had prisoners for interrogation. But they turned out not to be English. One ship was Irish, bound for Biscay in Spain with a cargo of wheat and tanned hides. The other was Scots, bound for France with a cargo of coal and two refugee friars, a Bernardin and a Franciscan, who were fleeing from the English troops in Northern Ireland.

Two important monasteries had been burnt in the last six weeks, the friars being burnt as well. These two had fled to the woods. The friars said they were escaping from terrible cruelties.

The *San Salvador*'s log reported immense seas driven by a north-easterly wind.

At night fall the *Paloma Blanca*, seeing that the ship that had been captured was going down, was ordered by the Admiral to cast her off, which she did. We then ran towards Corunna, as we could do no more, and we were sure that no ships of the Armada were off Cape Longnose, Mount's Bay, or Scilly.

The *Paloma Blanca*'s captain, when he reached Muxia, had a stirring tale to tell, which the Duke of Medina Sidonia himself passed on to the King, perhaps because it smacked of a victory.

The *Paloma Blanca* was chased by an English ship, which took her for a merchantman. She followed her over two leagues, the hulk allowing the Englishman to come up with her and then discharged a volley of artillery and musketry which made the enemy retire. The hulk would have chased her but for an accident which happened. One of the soldiers' powder-flasks caught fire and fell on some cartridges, which might have resulted in the burning of the whole ship. It was thought best to set all hands to avert this danger rather than follow up the Englishman . . .

These dutiful storeships were very lucky. Realizing that the Armada had been dispersed by storm and that there were good pickings to be had off Scilly, Howard had not waited to load all the rations which had been delivered, but got out of harbour with the bare minimum. He himself went to Scilly, while Drake made for the French coast. With ten fighting ships screened by three or four pinnaces, the great corsair came close upon the trail of the hulk *Paloma Blanca*. Off Ushant he came up with one of the English spy ships, posing as innocent traders, which had been on that station for the past ten days. Her master told Drake that, although he himself had not seen the Armada, he had hailed:

. . . an Irish bark which had been with the great ships of the Spanish fleet west of Scilly. The Spaniards had taken out of the said bark five of her most principal men, and left in her but three men and a boy. One of the greatest Spanish ships towed her at the stern by a cable, which in the night time, the wind blowing somewhat stiff, brake, and so she escaped in the storm.

According to the log of the *San Salvador*, however, she was a ghost ship, cast off because she was going down. Just another example of the fact that official documents cannot entirely be relied on. On the other hand, the story of the pursuing English ship being lured into gun range of the *Paloma Blanca* might have been correct, for Howard reported: 'My own pinnace hath been well beaten and hath had 18 great shot, which hath torn her hull and sails.'

At the other end of the Channel, off Dunkirk, there had been a similar flurry of mistaken identities and small actions on 2 July. Admiral Lord Henry Seymour who, with Sir William Wynter, was conducting the blockade of Parma's army from his flagship the *Rainbow*, saw two small vessels slip out of Dunkirk and crowd on all sail for Gravelines. The big *Rainbow*, manned by 250 men, could not close that shallow coast, with its treacherous banks; but the light vessels could.

Two of our pinnaces chased them, with the discharging of some saker shot, and yet they would not strike, till at last one of our shot struck down the mainmast of one of their vessels, being a French bottom belonging to Calais, and had Monsieur Gourdan's hand for his pass. I demanded to know what he meant, not to strike his sails and come to the Queen's ships, knowing us so well. He answered that he took us for the King of Navarre's fleet, making himself ignorant of what to do. I replied that if the Duke of Parma, or the Duke of Guise, should do the like, I would sink them, or they should distress me; adding further that my Sovereign Lady was able to defend her country against the

Holy League, besides able to master any civil discord; and so dismissed them, with some little choler.

Another case of mistaken identity, or shoot first and ask questions later! The second ship, whatever she was, was no luckier than the first, which had a pass from the French Governor of Calais, Gourdan.

He ran himself hard aground right over against Gravelines, and they voided themselves out of their vessel, wading through the water, and cut their sails from the masts, taking them also away. My boat, which I manned with some shot (musketeers or caliver-men), came upon their skirts, but a little too late; yet came there very near a hundred men, horse and foot, and durst not approach us. By which time our men had some little leisure to cut down their masts, and would have fired her, but that suddenly the wind arose at North and by East, enforcing us to weigh for Blackness, where we anchored, with marvellous foul weather, some thirty hours.

Admiral Seymour added a postscript, to explain that he had dictated the letter because 'I have strained my hand with hauling on a rope'; yet another casualty of flag rank. The two sea skirmishes, the Spanish battle by boarding off the Scillies, and the English gun action off Dunkirk, were, as it happened, exactly representative of the different tactics which the two main opposed fleets were to employ in the great Channel conflict to come. They explain it better than any learned treatise could. The rapid and violent fate of the two ships which tried to get out of Parma's invasion port of Dunkirk makes very clear the reason for his reluctance to emerge with hundreds of clumsy troop barges before the Armada was firmly in control of the crossing.

Parma had just written to King Philip (on 22 June) not only to ask for reinforcements from the Armada of 6,000 men, but adding:

He (Medina Sidonia) also seems to have persuaded himself that I may be able to go out and meet him with these boats. These things cannot be, and in the interest of your Majesty's service I should be very anxious if I thought the Duke were depending upon them . . . With these little, low, flat boats, built for these rivers and not for the sea, I cannot diverge from the short direct passage across which has been

agreed . . . If I were to attempt going out to meet the Duke, and we
came across any of the armed English or rebel ships, they could
destroy us with the greatest of ease. Neither the valour of our men nor
any other human effort could save us.

Admiral Seymour absolutely agreed; he was hoping Parma
would come out.

His own private strength doth not exceed 40 sails of flyboats and 220
bylanders. All I fear is that they will never offer themselves. We have
twice showed ourselves at Gravelines, desiring nothing more than to
suffer them to come out, rather than to stop them in by sinking vessels
with stone or timber.

On 27 June the Duke of Medina Sidonia had held his council
on board the Armada flagship *San Martin* at Corunna. Some of
the squadron commanders and regimental camp masters were
in the missing ships, so the full leadership was not present. The
first question the Duke asked was whether they should wait in
harbour for the missing ships to arrive, or should the Armada
go out and look for them. The decision was unanimous that it
would be best to wait for them to rejoin.

The Duke then asked the council to decide whether the
Armada should sail for England at once, with the ships which
they had now in the ports of Corunna, Vivero and Rivadeo,
without waiting for the missing ships to rejoin.

At this point the Inspector-General, Don Jorge Manrique,
stated that the missing vessels numbered twenty-eight, some of
them the best in the fleet, with 6,000 men on board – that is,
one-third of the Armada's strength. He arrived at this estimate
because, although it was asserted that 27,884 men had been
shipped in the Armada, after deducting general and field
officers, staff, cabin and ships' boys, gentlemen adventurers,
officers of justice, hospital staff, artillery officers and ministers
of religion, as well as the oarsmen in the galleys and galleases,
he found the total number of effectives to be only 22,500. Now,
deduct from that figure the 6,000 men in the missing ships, he
said, and recollect that there are some hundreds of dead and
sick – and you are left with a total of 16,000 effectives, here at
this moment. Personally, he felt that the Armada ought not to

sail without the missing vessels. All those present, bar one, agreed. Don Francisco Bobadilla, a regimental commander who was the Duke's military adviser, was particularly adamant:

If the Armada goes at full strength, its task will be safe and easy; and this general feeling in the fleet will enable us to overcome any difficulties, the men being confident and in good spirits, with the assurance of victory. But if we go short-handed, the risk will be great, especially in face of the forces we know the enemy now has. In case of misfortune to the Armada the Indies would be lost, and Portugal and Flanders in dire peril of being lost as well.

Everyone present agreed, with the single exception of Don Pedro de Valdes, who made a tactless speech which certainly enraged the Duke of Medina Sidonia, mild man though he was, as it reflected on the leadership, the close group of three sailing in the *San Martin* – the Duke, his military adviser, Don Francisco de Bobadilla, and his naval adviser, Diego Flores de Valdes, cousin to Don Pedro.

My experience of English affairs, and the fact that no intelligence has been received that the enemy will receive any foreign aid, lead me to the conclusion that the portion of the Armada now here, ought to proceed on the expedition. It is perfectly evident that the enemy's forces must be divided between two or three places, for the purpose of impeding the passage of the Duke of Parma, and to oppose the entrance of this Armada into the Channel. I am also of opinion that most of our missing ships will very shortly be heard of – because the storm that overtook them was not very violent, unless, for reasons of their own, any of the vessels wished to make bad weather of it.

That sally was received with a venomous glance or two, because it was the *San Martin* which had abandoned the voyage first, leaving less formidable ships to obey the Duke's inflexible orders, and brave both the storm and the English.

Nevertheless, went on Don Pedro, the food stores in his own squadron gave cause for concern; the only fresh food on board was the meat and fish which had been loaded in this port of Corunna; of the stores shipped at Lisbon, the bacon, cheese, fish, sardines and vegetables were all rotten; and some of the biscuit was in bad condition. On this point everyone agreed.

Most of the victuals were of no use whatever, for the men would not eat them.

Everything that Don Pedro had said was true; but, he complained to the King, because his opinion had been so different from those expressed by the other commanders, he had offended the Duke, who was 'looking upon him with an unfriendly eye, and had used expressions towards him which had greatly grieved him.'

The King was now bombarding Medina Sidonia with exhortations, mingled with detailed criticisms.

But you must take great care that the stores are really preserved, and not allow yourself to be deceived, as you were before . . . The information you sent me produced an impression very different from what has turned out to be the truth. The same remark applies also to the question of water. I gathered that you were informed that you had sufficient water on the fleet for two months; and now I find that on the very day of your arrival at Corunna, you discovered that some of the ships had no water left.

Probably this was because some of the water casks were made of unseasoned wood, as a result of Drake's raid on the Armada supply lines the previous year. In another letter of an urgent series designed to bolster the Duke's morale, Philip wrote: 'His Majesty continues firm in the resolution to carry forward the task.'

He repeated the public line he was taking, that the enterprise was 'least of all influenced by motives of personal interest', the 'chief consideration being God's cause'. The Duke had suggested making an honourable peace with England, but if the affair was abandoned now, what capital the Protestants would make out of it!

The enemies of the Catholic religion would interpret the damage inflicted by the storm as authority for their heresies, twisting in their favour God's tolerance.

To the Duke's protests that his 'weak force' was now inferior to the enemy, the King replied with scathing comments on the English fleet and, above all, its lack of allies.

Of the enemy's ships, some are old; others small, and inferior to ours in strength and general excellence; do not forget the numerical superiority of our crews, and the long experience enjoyed by many of them. The enemy's crews, on the other hand, consist of novices, drawn from the common people – a tumultuous crowd, lacking military discipline . . . Had aid come from France, it might have been formidable; but they are in no condition there to send help owing to their internal feuds. The rebels in Holland and Zealand care more for their own interests. The German Protestants are at most able to create some slight diversion which cannot avert the blows which the Armada will deliver. The Danish king, the enemy's most powerful supporter, who could have reinforced the English fleet, is dead, and that news has caused hope to fade in England of receiving help from that quarter. As for the King of Scotland, no help can be looked for from him, for the blood of his beheaded mother is not yet congealed. One might rather expect that the Scottish forces would themselves move to attack the English from their side. Thus there appears to be no possibility of considerable reinforcements or help reaching the enemy from any source whatever . . . From its present anchorage, the Armada can, with six days of fair weather, reach the appointed place. If it were now to remain in Corunna, this would be construed as a proof of our weakness, and far from enhancing our prestige at the treaty negotiations (if, indeed, we were working to conclude a treaty) would provide the enemy with an opportunity to rise to greater heights of insolence.

But the Duke was already in more hopeful mood. The dread he must have felt, that the twenty-eight ships and their 6,000 men might never return, because they had perhaps obeyed his own order for them to go to the Scilly Isles, on the doorstep of England, that bleak fear was banished as, one by one and squadron by squadron, the lost ships came safely into Spanish ports, 'smelling of England', as Recalde put it. How close they had been to disaster, he could not know. He replied to the King's letters, apologizing for the delays and adding that 'those that go down to the sea in ships are exposed to these vicissitudes.'

On 15 July he could report:

With God's help, I hope to have everything ready for sailing tomorrow, or the day after, weather permitting. I have already had the squadrons of Diego Flores, Valdes, Oquendo, and Ojeda towed out of the harbour, and the rest will go outside tomorrow. We can then take advantage of the first fair wind to get clear away.

On 19th July the Armada was entirely ready but still waiting for the south-westerly wind. The Duke had received 400 infantry reinforcements from Galicia and Monterey, but they:

. . . are so useless that they are no good, even for pioneers. Besides this they are nearly all married and have large families; and are, indeed, absolutely unserviceable old men. Their wives have been coming in with their troubles and lamentations to such an extent that it goes against my conscience to ship the men. The captains themselves have refused to have anything to do with them, as it is evident that all the use they would be is to die on board the ships and take up space. Not a soul of them knows what a harquebus is, or any other weapon, and already they are more dead than alive; some of them have not eaten anything for two days. I have thought it best to send them all away and they have gone to their homes.

Some of the infantry officers, too, were not all that could be desired. Admiral Juan Martinez de Recalde had written to the King on 11 July:

I hear great complaints about the command of those companies which are conferred on quite young fellows because they are gentlemen. Very few of them, therefore, are soldiers, or know what to do, and their officers the same. It would be much better to re-form them with not less than 120 men in each company, for we are going to a place where they cannot be recruited.

On 20 July Medina Sidonia held a consultation with his senior officers regarding the sailing of the Armada. The discussion was technical, some of it beyond our understanding because no such ships exist today and we would not know how to handle them if we had any. From Corunna, to get clear of the land round Cape Priorio to the north, and then set course for England, required a trouble-free run of nine or ten leagues; but if a cross-wind sprang up or a calm fell, many of the ships would be in great danger. Don Pedro de Valdes stated:

The Spanish ships of the Armada might weather the point, as they were swift and could go well to windward, but neither the hulks nor the Levanters could do so without danger.

On the 20th there had been heavy seas, but on 22 July these had flattened, with only a light south-west wind blowing; and the Armada got out. At two o'clock in the afternoon the light wind died away to a flat calm, the Armada having covered only three leagues, with Cape Priorio still a potential danger to the north. The ships could not be moved except by using the tidal streams into or out of Corunna, but at three o'clock in the morning of 23 July, the wind began to blow off the land, growing to a brisk south-easterly. Soon after 6 P.M. that day, the Armada had doubled not merely Cape Priorio, but Cape Ortegal on the northern coast of Spain; with a strong southerly wind behind them, England was less than a week's sail away, even for the slowest ships. Medina Sidonia was told that the best ships, if they spread all sail, could be on the enemy's coast by 25 July.

6

'Whereupon They Made Fires and Smokes'

'Stand to it, noble pikemen,
　And look you round about;
And shoot you right, you bow-men,
　And we will keep them out:
You musket and calliver men,
　Do you prove true to me,
I'll be the foremost man in fight,'
　Says brave Lord Willoughbèy.
The sharp steel-pointed arrows,
　And bullets thick did fly;
Then did our valiant soldiers
　Charge on most furiously;
Which made the Spaniards waver,
　They thought it best to flee,
They feared the stout behaviour
　Of brave Lord Willoughbèy.
　　Anonymous (late sixteenth century)

22 July, the day on which the Armada sailed again, was 12 July by the English calendar, and on that day the ships of Drake and Howard came into Plymouth with fury aboard. This was their second abortive sortie in a row. The first time they had come within a day of catching the Spanish storeships parading off the Scillies, but had been forced back by shortage of victuals. Now they had got to within two days' sail of Corunna, where the Armada was temptingly dispersed, only to be forced by an adverse wind to return at once because they were too short of victuals to persevere. Captain Thomas Cely, ex-Spanish galley slave and now master of the *Elizabeth Drake*, had been with them:

My Lord (Howard) was in a good way, if God had not sent a contrary wind. If the wind had holden two days and two nights longer, we had them in the Groyne, and within three leagues of the Groyne, all their whole fleet in three sundry harbours.

Now it was the English fleet which was likely to be caught penned up in harbour, the men starving and dying of disease. Some 500 Spaniards were in hospital at Corunna, but what they were suffering from was mainly food-poisoning. The English sick lists were much more serious, corpses being thrown overboard daily and ships being decommissioned for lack of men. In the Eastern fleet, under Admiral Seymour, six ships had been discharged because there was no food to feed their crews; while four had been sent away on convoy duty, escorting the cloth fleet to Stade on the Elbe, near Hamburg. Depression after depression was coming out of the Atlantic and sweeping over Europe, making Seymour's blockade of the invasion ports difficult or even impossible.

Such summer season saw I never the like; for what with storms and variable unsettled winds, the same unsettleth and altereth our determination for lying on the other coast . . .

That letter was dated 12 July, from the Downs, the bad weather refuge off the Kentish coast. Inland places such as London do not, of course, have weather; the wind may scream unrestrained on the coasts, but hedges, trees, houses and hills inland serve as a series of screens. The wind may blow a wild fury at sea, but in London there can be calm. At this moment, all the ten-second experts and sidewalk superintendents of the capital were anxious for news of the Armada and blaming the Lord Admiral for not getting it. Chief among them was the Queen. She passed on her views and suggestions through Walsyngham, the Secretary of State. It took ten days to reach Howard because he had himself been on the Spanish coast, and he had to waste time with his reply, dated 13 July (being 23 July by the Spanish calendar and the Armada already clear of Corunna and on course for England):

Sir, we are here to small purpose for this great service, if that hath not been thought of. Both before my coming, by Sir Francis Drake, and since my coming, there hath been no day but there hath been pinnaces, Spanish caravels, flyboats, and of all sorts, sent out to discover there.

The winds hath been so southerly, and such foul weather as that they could not recover the coast of Spain so near as to take any of their fisher boats; and to send some of our fisher boats to discover there, they would do as much good as to send oysterboat of Billingsgate . . . I know not what weather you have had, but there was never any such summer seen here on the sea . . . I would her Majesty did know of the care and pains that is taken here of all men for her service. We must now man ourselves again, for we have cast many overboard, and a number in great extremity which we discharged, I have sent with all expedition a prest for more men.

Afraid that perhaps neither Walsyngham nor the Queen would believe that he knew what he was talking about, Lord Howard enclosed a brief supporting note from Sir Francis Drake regarding the various reconnaissance craft, including spy ships (one of which was a Spanish-built caravel) being used to get news of the Armada.

It hath pleased my Lord Admiral to command me to write my knowledge touching our espials. I assure your Honour there could not have been more care taken than his Lordship hath from time to time given order for; and it is now certainly known that they are all returned back, much distressed; and as for fisher boats, they are neither meet and cannot endure the seas.

On 17 July, by English reckoning, the English were frantically busy, writing. The Lord Treasurer, Burghley, was complaining to Mr Marmaduke Darell that the ration returns for the fleet had been incorrectly rendered.

There was some fault in you, in that you made not your last certificate so perfect as had been requisite; for that you neither particularly mentioned the numbers of men, nor the vessels wherein they serve; which I pray you by your next certificate to reform.

Poor Mr Darell, who had been given the task of victualling more than a hundred vessels virtually single-handed, with no proper organization at all, probably wished Lord Burghley to the devil for nit-picking, but could not very well say so. Howard could. On the same day that Burghley was writing to Darell, he was writing to Burghley.

I have caused Sir Francis Drake and Mr Hawkyns to consider of your charges, for that our company grow into great need, and many occasions in such an army doth breed sundry great and extraordinary charges. I have sent herein enclosed an estimate thereof, praying your Lordship that there may be some care had that we may be furnished with money, without the which we are not able to continue our forces together.

Also on the English 17th, Howard wrote in more friendly fashion to Walsyngham:

But there shall be neither sickness nor death which shall make us yield until this service is ended. I never saw nobler minds than be here in our forces.

Two days later, Burghley was writing to Walsyngham in exasperation:

I have received letters from my Lord Admiral and Mr Hawkyns, with a schedule declaring that they have great lack of money for wages, besides victuals; for Mr Quarles hath 6,000*l.* this last week, and now Mr Hawkyns' declaration that, to make a full pay to the 28th of this month, there must be paid 19,070*l.*; and of that 6,000*l.* which he had, there remaineth with him but 500*l.* I marvel that where so many are dead on the seas the pay is not dead with them . . . A man would wish, if peace cannot be had, that the enemy would not longer delay, but prove, as I trust, his evil fortune: for these expeditions do consume us . . . I have had conference with Palavicino (a banker) and Salton-stall (Governor of the Merchant Venturers) how 40,000 or 30,000 might be had for 10 per cent; but I find no probability how to get money here in specie, which is our lack . . . yet there is some likelihood that our merchants of Stade might practise for 20,000 or 30,000, for which there shall be some profit very secretly. I shall but fill my letter with more melancholy matter if I should remember what money must be had to pay 5,000 footmen and 1,000 horsemen for defence of the enemy landing in Essex.

That day, 19 July by the English calendar, was the 29th by Spanish reckoning; and time had finally run out.

Already, on 25 July, Medina Sidonia had sent on a pinnace to warn the Duke of Parma and his invasion army of the imminent arrival of the Armada in the Channel, after three days of favourable winds.

No better weather could have been desired. Really, if three or four of our ships had cared to clap on sail, even though they were not very swift, they might have arrived at the mouth of the Channel by now. But I, in this galleon, could only sail as fast as the scurviest ship in the fleet, as I have to wait for the slowest of them – verily some of them are dreadfully slow – so I was obliged, anxious as I was to get forward, thus to tarry on the way.

But the next day, 26 July, the Armada had been becalmed, the ships drifting, scattered in a dense fog that lay on the quiet sea. That afternoon the fog had been blown away by a rising wind from the north; violent squalls splattering the waves with sudden rain, and the wind continuing to increase, veering west. Soon, foaming white horses had flecked the wave crests and the ships had begun to roll and plunge violently.

The four galleys were soon in trouble. Apart from the flag galley, the *Capitana*, there were the *Princessa, Diana* and *Bazana*. Each carried five guns, their crews consisting of respectively 109 men, 81, 79 and 72 (sailors and soldiers combined), plus nearly 900 slaves chained to the rowing benches, among them the Welshman, David Gywnn, who was in the *Diana*.

Their long, low hulls were almost hidden from sight by the Biscay rollers; occasionally the beakhead (or boarding platform) of one of them would rear skyward on a wave, the white water pouring back from her sides, and seeming to engulf her amidships. Then she would rise under the lift of the wave and stagger forward again, heeling a little under her lateen sail.

Admiral Medrano, commander of the oared squadron, sent a pinnace to the flagship with the news that Pantoja, the *Diana*'s captain, had decided to turn back for Spain; and to ask for the flagship's permission for the three remaining galleys to run for the shelter of the French coast.

I begged him to make every effort to continue with the fleet. I sent two pataches to stand by the galleys in case they should require assistance, and all that day the three galleys were in sight. But after nightfall, when the weather became thick, with very heavy rain, they were lost sight of and we have seen them no more.

But the King had news of his galleys long before Medina Sidonia did, and informed his ambassador to the French:

Of the four galleys that sailed from Corunna, one arrived two days afterwards at Vivero on the coast of Galicia and two of the others, after having reached Ushant, were so clumsy, that instead of entering one of the Breton ports they came to the ancient channel near Bayonne, where one was wrecked and the other ran ashore, the crews escaping and deserting from both of them.

The wretched, escaped galley slaves, Gywnn among them, begged their way across France to Rochelle; and there Gywnn, ragged, destitute and starving, approached some English merchants with tales of how much he knew about the Spanish fleet, and the English traitors in high places who, he said, were only waiting for the right moment to make a prisoner of the Queen.

Even the great ships of the Armada had suffered damage, reported Medino Sidonia to the King:

Not only did the waves mount to the skies, but some seas broke clean over the ships, and the whole of the stern gallery of Diego Flores' flagship was carried away. It was the most cruel night ever seen. The next day (28 July) was clear and bright, with less sea, although it was still very rough. On counting the ships of the Armada, forty were found to be missing, namely Don Pedro de Valdes' ships, the hulks, and some of the pataches.

Once again, however, it was the flagship which had lagged behind. Don Pedro had sailed on for England and was waiting for his Captain General to catch up, being duly reported by the English pinnaces to Howard:

Upon Friday, being the 19th of this present month [29th by Spanish reckoning], part of the Spanish navy, to the number of 50 sail, was discovered about the Isles of Scilly, hovering in the wind as it seemed to attend the rest of the fleet . . .

This performance was almost a repetition of the Armada's first fiasco when, after leaving the Tagus, the storeships had sailed on to the Scillies while the fighting ships had fled into Corunna, led by the flagship. Now, however, some vessels really were missing. Apart from the four galleys, last seen labouring in the gale, the 768-ton great ship *Santa Ana*, of the Biscay squadron, was not in sight. She had been Juan Martinez de Recalde's flagship, but he had transferred out of her into the

San Juan of Oporto. Her captain was Juan Perez de Mucio and she was commanded by one of the Camp Masters, Nicholas Isla, with 284 soldiers and ninety-eight sailors; and also, according to the Armada's chief accountant, Pedro Coco Calderon, 50,000 ducats in gold from the Royal treasury. Unknown to the Duke, she had put into a Breton port for shelter and then, keeping to the French side of the Channel, sailed on alone towards Le Havre.

At four o'clock in the afternoon of Friday, 29 July, the coast of England rose out of the sea beyond the bows of the Armada's flagship. The thunder of a three-gun salute poured out from the sides of the galleon, and a standard was hoisted to her maintop; hoisted also were a crucifix and a representation of the Virgin. Prayers were said, and the Duke penned a letter to the King, which would go back to Spain in a fast pinnace.

God Almighty grant that the rest of our voyage may be performed as we and all Christendom hope it will be. Written in sight of Cape Lizard, on board the galleon *San Martin*.

As the great fleet surged slowly on past Cornwall, smoke began to rise from a headland, and then from the next, and the next. 'Many fires were made on the land as a signal that they had seen us', noted Bernado de Gongora, a friar serving in the *Nuestra Senora del Rosario*, flagship of Don Pedro de Valdes. Now they were in enemy waters and at any moment might have to fight for their lives. The Duke, too, noted the menacing beacons.

The 30th at dawn, the Armada was near with the land, so as we were seen therefrom, whereupon they made fires and smokes.

There was nothing new about a smoke-signalling system, not merely as a simple alert – like the sinister wailing of an air-raid siren – but as a method of sending messages. Henry VIII had used a hilltop beacon system in the Isle of Wight, when his militia were battling the French driving inland from the beaches during July, 1545, forty-three years before, almost to the very day. The only difference was that this time the invaders were Spaniards, previously the allies of England against France.

Although short of four galleys and one great ship, the Armada was still a formidable force, and these were proud hours for the Duke. The cliffs of England in plain sight, and not a sign of an English ship, let alone the great Drake. They were daring the English fleet in its own waters, defying the common prediction that 'the English would be hard for them at sea'. As recently as April, the Venetian ambassador in Madrid had reported on public opinion in the Spanish capital in pessimistic terms.

It is generally held that the King of Spain will not undertake so vast an enterprise, although His Majesty is justly provoked, it is thought he will not, for the sake of revenge, hazard upon a doubtful and uncertain battle the peace and liberty of his many states and kingdoms. For he knows well how high he must rate a fleet like the enemy's, seeing the number of its vessels, and that the Englishmen are of a different quality from the Spaniards, bearing a name above all the West for being expert and enterprising in all maritime affairs, and the finest fighters upon the sea. A battle will in any case be very bloody; for the English never yield; and although they be put to flight and broken, they ever return, athirst for revenge, to renew the attack, as long as they have breath of life.

The Armada reached England with about 124 ships (it is difficult to calculate exactly because Medina Sidonia frequently detached pinnaces for message-carrying). During the campaign the English employed 197 ships, not all of them at the same time and not all of them against the Armada (e.g. the escort which accompanied the wool ships to Stade). But, just as the Armada was a mixture of purpose-built warships and ordinary merchant ships, so too was the English fleet.

Militarily, the Armada was organized in precise squadrons of about ten large galleons, carracks, great ships, or Levanters in each, accompanied by despatch boats; plus a very large squadron of hulks and other storeships; and another large squadron of pataches and large fishing smacks; and a small squadron of four galleys and another of four galleasses.

The English fleet was organized in quite a different way; indeed, it was less organized, less military, more individual. But the qualifications for a naval officer, if he wished to command one of the smaller vessels, might prove too stringent for a modern officer-candidate, for he would be asked first to provide his own ship and then to find a crew for it. While the Armada lists declare its military organization the English list, certified correct by Roger Langford, reveals how the ships were raised and who paid for them; very interesting reading for a Chartered Accountant but somewhat lacking in technical detail. It contains all the information the editor of Jane's *Fighting Ships* would omit, and little else.

Thirty-four vessels were Royal, being listed as 'Her Majesty's whole army of the seas against the Spanish forces'. These were regular warships, of which thirteen were large (500–1,100 tons), eight were middling (200–400 tons) and twelve small (30–150 tons), plus one galley acting as Thames guardship. Another group of thirty-four were 'Merchant ships appointed to serve westwards under the charge of Sir Francis Drake', of which fourteen were middling (200–400 tons) and twenty small (14–160 tons). There were thirty 'Ships set forth and paid upon the charge of the City of London' – all small to middling (30–300 tons); and eight Merchant ships serving with Howard and paid by the Queen – again all small to middling (100–220 tons). There were ten ships and barks (20–186 tons) paid by the Queen; fifteen small victuallers (40–70 tons) which brought supplies to the main fleet at Plymouth; twenty Coasters (25–230 tons) under the charge of the Lord Admiral but paid by the Queen; another twenty-three Coasters (35–160 tons) serving under Admiral Seymour, some paid by the Queen but most paid by the port towns; and twenty-three 'Voluntary ships' which joined after the fighting had begun and so were paid by the Queen according to the time they had served. In all, 197 ships and 15,925 men.

The legend of the tiny English ships is seen not to be so false after all, for out of the 197 only some two dozen were sizeable warships, matching roughly the same number on the Spanish side; and a further three dozen or so were armed merchantmen large enough to go into the thick of the fight, matching a more or less equal number of armed merchantmen in the Armada. In numbers of heavy units, the two fleets were well matched, taking into account the fact that English tonnage figures are not consistent for individual ships and that the Spanish method of reckoning tonnage tends to exaggerate their size by about one third compared to the English measurements.

Many of the English ships had homely names or no names at all, and were simply called after their owners. Whereas some of the Spanish ships had liquid-sounding names, almost poetry; for instance, the *Nuestra Senora de la Rosa*, vice-flagship of Oquendo's squadron. Something like half of them had been named after Saints, or had religious significance, and there was even a small pinnace called *La Concepcion de Francisco de Latero*.

The names of the English ships had a hard, bright ring about them, like glittering golden coins – *Ark Royal, Bonaventure, Golden Lion, White Bear, Revenge, Victory, Dreadnought, Antelope, Triumph, Swiftsure, Swallow, Nonpareil*. Howard had moved out of the *White Bear*, owned by a relative, and was now flying his flag in the *Ark*. Originally owned by Raleigh, she had formerly been known as the *Ark Raleigh*; now that she was a Queen's ship, she became the *Ark Royal*. The great *Triumph* was Admiral Frobisher's flagship, the largest ship at sea in either fleet; high-charged, on the old carrack style of Henry VIII's time, of great 'majesty and terror to the enemy'. Drake's *Revenge*, half her size, was the first of a new class of warship; with a much cut-down superstructure (which caught the wind like sails which could not be furled) and probably much smaller draught; and certainly more manoeuvrable.

Among the large armed merchantmen were names like the *Galleon Leicester* (Leicester's galleon), *Merchant Royal, Roebuck, Golden Noble, Griffin*, and *Minion*. The smaller ships had names ranging from the poetic to the homely – the *Galleon Dudley*; *The Virgin, God Save Her*; the *Bark Bond* and the *Bark Buggins*; the *Diamond of Dartmouth* and the *Rat of Wight*; the *Heartsease, Speedwell, Bear Yonge, Chance, Delight*, and *Nightingale*. The *Bear Yonge* was the *Bear*, owned by Captain Yonge, so-called to distinguish her from similarly named ships such as the great *White Bear*. The English vessels are therefore easy to identify in the many contemporary narratives of fighting; not so the Spanish, where as many as a dozen different ships had the same name – *San Juan*, for instance, or *San Juan de Bautista* (St John, or St John the

Baptist); or, less frequently, *San Pedro* (St Peter).

In detail, we know little about the ships from documents or plans (the latter are almost non-existent). But several officers who, in their youth, served against the Armada in the Channel, penned general studies and conclusions which, although they tell us nothing about the 'trees', reveal a great deal about the 'wood'. In 1588, Admiral Sir William Monson was serving as a lieutenant in the pinnace *Charles*. Since Henry VIII's time there had been great changes in English shipbuilding, he wrote:

The marvel I speak of is, that notwithstand the apparent dangers and casualties of the sea aforesaid, yet not one of her Majesty's ships ever miscarried, but only the *Revenge*, which, in her voyage of 1591, was taken by the Spaniards by the unadvised negligence and wilful obstinacy of her captain, Sir Richard Greynville. If we compare these fortunes of the Queen's with those of her father's, who next to her had the greatest employment for his ships at sea, you will find great differences betwixt them, although we cannot properly call them voyages in King Henry VIII's time. For his ships were never so far from home but they might return again with a good wind in twenty-four hours' sail; as the others never expected to see the English shore, under four, five, or six months, and many times more.

Sir William listed the disasters to battleships which had occurred during the wars of Henry VIII, accident being at least a part-cause of the loss of the great carracks, *Regent* in 1512 by fire and explosion while grappling a French carrack, and the *Mary Rose* in 1545 by indiscipline and mishandling in battle, possibly allied to overloading. Of the latter vessel, Monson had personal experience: 'Part of the ribs of this ship I have seen with my own eyes; there perished in her four hundred persons.'

The difference between carracks such as the *Mary Rose* and the more modern battleship type, the galleon, was described by Sir Walter Raleigh:

We find by experience that the greatest ships are the least serviceable, go very deep to water, and of marvellous charge and cumber, our channels decaying every year. Besides, they are less nimble, less mainable, and very seldom employed. *Grande navio grande fatiga*, saith the Spaniard. A ship of 600 tons will carry as good ordnance as a ship of 1,200 tons; and though the greater have double her number, the lesser will turn her broadsides twice before the greater can wind once. The high charging of ships it is that brings them ill qualities, makes them extreme leeward, makes them sink deep in the water, makes them labour and makes them overset. Men of better sort and better breeding would be glad to find more steadiness and less tottering cage-work.

Necessarily the high castles of a carrack had to be lightly built, of clinker construction rather like a modern garden shed – this is what Raleigh meant by 'tottering cage-work'. The designer of a twentieth-century cruise liner has the same problem, which he solves in the same way but with modern materials. Nevertheless, at the time of the Armada the carrack still possessed many advantages in battle.

Majesty and terror to the enemy; more commodious for the harbouring of men; carry more artillery; of greater strength inboard and make the better defence; will over-top a lower and snug ship; the men cannot be so well discerned.

Unusually, a ship-builder's sketches of an Elizabethan galleon have survived. Dated 1586, two years before the Armada, they depict a smart yacht-like vessel; painted in Tudor green and white, the impression of rakish agility and speed would be even more pronounced. Elegant is the only word to describe her lines, which sweep down in a free-flowing curve from a high stern to amidships, where there is a weather deck, which sweeps up again into a neat and comparatively low forecastle.

Sir Arthur Gorgas, who served as a volunteer in the fleet against the Armada, was a kinsman of Raleigh and is known to be the author of several documents ascribed to Raleigh; in 1597 he was captain of Raleigh's flagship *Warspite*. The English still possessed the advantages they had displayed in 1588:

Namely for our swiftness in outsailing them, our nimbleness in getting into the weather of them, our little draught of water in comparison to theirs, our stout bearing up of our sides in all huge winds when theirs must stoop to their great disadvantage many ways, our yawness in staying well and casting about twice for their once and so discharging our broadsides of ordnance double for their single, we carrying as good and great artillery as they do and to better proof and having far better gunners . . .

He was clear as to the way these advantages should be used, a hand-to-hand battle being avoided at all cost.

Whereas we keeping aloof and in the weather of them, our great ordnance being all as good as theirs will have a great advantage of them. For we by getting into the wind may give them two broadsides for one, and then any stiff gale making them to slope turned up their keels towards us while we shoot them between wind and water and by their sloping to the lee side so turns up the mouths of their ordnance on the weatherside, which is towards us, as that they are found to shoot clean over our ships that lie low and snug as the mariners term it.

Gorgas then went on to describe in detail what the English would have done in 1588, if the Armada had actually attempted a landing, drawing a graphic picture of the laborious and difficult task of transferring men, guns, provisions and all sorts of army paraphernalia from the big ships at anchor to the small oared craft which must row them all ashore. The big English ships were to have attacked in the deeper water, holding the weather gauge, while the small English vessels were to engage the pinnaces and boats ferrying the army with its impedimenta to shore. Howard's dictum, 'We mean so to course them, as that they have no leisure to land', was here amplified by Gorgas:

Neither did they ever dare to land a man or fetch a barrel of fresh water on our shores in all that time they were here, so close did we still follow them.

But actually to defeat the Armada in battle, as distinct from frustrating its intentions, without closing to grappling distance, posed a problem for the English Admirals; and a knowledge of the Armada's defensive strength gave comfort to Medina Sidonia and his companions, as the signal fires blazed along the coast.

On Friday, 29 July, the bark *Golden Hind* commanded by Captain Thomas Flemyng had sighted the Armada, the wind being southerly or south-west; and, the news being brought to Plymouth, the English fleet had begun to warp out of harbour that night. There is no mention in surviving contemporary documents of a game of bowls being continued on Plymouth Hoe in spite of the news; but the story could be true: the way to get out, even in the teeth of a wind, is to wait for the tide to ebb and use boats to tow or 'huffle' the big ships into the centre of the outgoing stream where the current flows fastest. By three in the afternoon of the next day, Saturday, 30 July, most of the English fleet was clear of the potential ship trap of Plymouth Sound.

At dawn on Saturday, almost the whole Armada was close enough inshore for Medina Sidonia to have seen the 'fires and smokes' of the English invasion beacons carrying the news inland and along the coast. But the Duke saw no reason for haste.

I have all the Armada together, and I will set sail as soon as the flag galleass (the *San Lorenzo*) has been put in order, her rudder being broken. These craft are really very fragile for such heavy seas as these. The galleys have not appeared, nor have I any tidings of them, which causes me great anxiety.

So the Armada merely drifted, while the English laboured to get their ships to sea. They at any rate were under no illusions as to what might happen if the Armada, with its 19,000 soldiers, caught them in Plymouth Sound. Mr Marmaduke Darell reported of victuals left on the quayside:

The haste of my Lord Admiral was such in his setting forth upon Saturday morning, as that divers of his ships had not leisure to receive the full of their last proportions.

In his turn, Howard was able to report on the effort put forth by his crews:

Although the ships of the English army with that wind were very hard to be gotten out of harbour, yet the same was done with such diligence and goodwill, that many of them got abroad as though it had been with a fair wind.

The Duke showed no desire to press on and interfere with the English. It was evening before he even sent out a pinnace under Ensign Juan Gil to reconnoitre; it returned with a captured fishing boat and its crew of four men.

They said they were of Falmouth, and had that evening seen the English fleet go out of Plymouth under the charge of the Admiral of England and of Drake.

The Duke called a Council of War immediately, but kept very quiet about it in his official correspondence; we know about it only from the English interrogation of Don Pedro de Valdes after he was captured.

The same day the Duke called to council, being within 10 or 12 leagues from Plymouth, where, by the report of the fishermen whom we took, he had understanding that the English fleet was at anchor. It was resolved: we should make the mouth of the haven and set about the enemy, if it might be done with any advantage; if not, we should keep our course directly to Dunkirk without losing time.

The two reports of what the fishermen had said were not necessarily contradictory. Ships riding out of harbour on the ebb would anchor when the tide turned, so as not to lose the ground they had gained. Also, not all the ships could emerge simultaneously. Indeed, we know that of approximately 100 ships, only fifty-four got completely clear of the Sound that day. The Duke himself recorded in the war diary: 'In the evening many ships were seen, but because of the mist and rain, we were unable to count them.'

An enemy force always looks larger than it really is, and one Spaniard who made an estimate was wrong. He was Pedro Estrade, an infantry officer in the *San Marcos*, sailing in the same squadron as Medina Sidonia:

In the afternoon we discovered about 76 sail and knew them to be the English fleet; they did bear towards the east (i.e., downwind), the wind being SW. Then we amained until it was day and ran under our foresails only, which was a great oversight.

The accountant, Calderon, who was an admirer of the Duke, saw nothing wrong in doing nothing in a situation favourable for attack.

As it was already late, and the weather was thick, we could not reconnoitre the enemy's fleet. The Duke ordered Captain Uceda to go through the Armada during the night, giving instructions for the ships to be put into order of battle, as the enemy would be upon us in the morning. The Duke then gave orders for sail to be shortened, and remained awaiting him.

Medina Sidonia was now writing to the King for the second time that day. Clearly, something other than the pro and con of a decisive battle inside Plymouth Sound had been discussed at the Council of War that evening:

The object of the present letter is to say that I am obliged to proceed slowly with all the Armada together in squadrons as far as the Isle of Wight, and no further. All along the coast of Flanders there is no harbour or shelter for our ships. If I were to go from the Isle of Wight thither with the Armada our vessels might be driven on to the shoals, where they would certainly be lost. In order to avoid so obvious a peril I have decided to stay off the Isle of Wight until I learn what the Duke of Parma is doing, as the plan is that at the moment of my arrival he should sally with the fleet, without causing me to wait a minute.

Somebody at the council table must forcibly have put his finger on the weak point of the Enterprise, the difficulties of an actual junction with Parma, which the King had insufficiently considered. Parma himself had repeatedly warned that he could not come out unless the weather was calm and the Armada could protect his barges and flyboats from both the English fleet and the shallow-draught raiders of the rebel Netherlands fleet. Certainly, the Armada's safest option was to occupy the anchorages between the Isle of Wight and Portsmouth. The English were in complete agreement about this. A sober intelligence appreciation had already been circulated, giving cogent reasons why the Armada should attempt to capture the island and estimating that 8,000 men would be required. The French invasion of Wight in 1545 was a full-scale precedent, following many previous French raids in the area. If the Spaniards could set up a base in Wight, which they could 'easily' do, then, '. . . all the castles and sea towns of Hampshire, Sussex and Dorsetshire will be subject to be burnt.'

Therefore, from the evening of 30 July on, the entire

operational plan of the Armada changed; it became more practical. For the Spaniards the only unknown factor was the English fleet, and what it might do to prevent a landing in England direct from the Armada's own ships. For the English, there was no change. They already expected the Spaniards to attempt to force their way into Spithead and land troops.

At midnight the weather was as dismal as it had been throughout the day; but at two o'clock in the morning of Sunday, 31 July, the moon came out. The cold, silver light sparkled on the waves and the slow wake of the ships as, hardly moving, they dreamed through the night under the few rags of sail needed to keep them on course. Calderon, looking out across the water, could just detect in the gloom, inshore of the Armada and still downwind, five strange ships which must be part of the English fleet. They were all still there, he thought, still at a disadvantage; and would remain so tomorrow. That was comforting.

7

'Not Half of Them Men-of-War'

Somewhat to the westward of Plymouth, we had some small fight with them.

John Hawkyns to Walsyngham

In spite of the unseasonable weather, it was summer; the days were long. It was not completely dark until about ten o'clock, and it was growing light again between five and six. Consequently, at dawn on Sunday, 31 July, the Spaniards expected to sight the English roughly to the north-east, scattered between the Eddystone reef and Plymouth Sound, much as they had been the night before. But eastwards, the sea was bare. The only sign of the enemy was northwards, close in with the shore, where a small group of ships was tacking repeatedly, zig-zagging westwards into the teeth of the wind. The soldier, Estrade, noted that there were seven of them. The Duke's estimate was higher, as usual; he counted 11, 'amongst which were three great galleons that cannonaded some of our ships, and continued turning to windward, the wind having shifted to WNW.' The sullen thudding of cannon fire rolled across the sea, as the handful of English, outnumbered by more than ten to one, even by Medina Sidonia's estimate, passed close to the left wing of the Armada, methodically tacking; at each seaward reach, which brought them within gunshot of Recalde's Armada of Biscay, they contemptuously let fly at it. The reason for their confidence soon became apparent: these were better ships than the Spaniards'.

Actually, as they had only just come out, they were probably some of the more unwieldy English ships, perhaps including Frobisher's 'high-charged' 1,200-ton *Triumph*, impressively larger than any single ship in the Armada, and in direct line of descent from Henry VIII's monstrous, experimental *Great Harry*. But the most astounding thing that met the Spaniards' gaze was a cloud of sails astern and to seaward of the Armada, bearing down with arrogant ease on the four squadrons of armed merchantmen which formed the rear of its formation. The Spaniards regarded them with surprise and alarm. Medina Sidonia put their number at eighty. Calderon wrote:

The enemy's fleet, with the wind astern, bore down on us. They had 20 great galleons, from 500 to 800 tons burden, and 50 of from 200 to 300 tons, extremely well armed, rigged, and handled. They came towards us in very good order . . .

In haste, the Armada shook itself out into battle order, and the Royal Standard went fluttering up to the masthead of the fleet flagship, Medina Sidonia's *San Martin*. There was very little else he could do. The real striking force of the Armada, the warships of the Castilian and Portuguese squadrons, as well as the galleasses, were at the front, ready to bear the brunt of an action against an English fleet caught ahead of the Spanish might, downwind, where they should have been. Now, by some devil's trick, they had in the few hours of darkness reversed that position of disadvantage, and were attacking where the Duke could not get at them. The Armada was arrayed like an eagle: the two dozen real warships were the head and beak, poised to strike ahead; behind them came the body of the fleet, the ill-protected host of two dozen storeships; and attached to the body at the rear, like two great, drooping wings, trailed some forty armed merchantmen, the Armadas of Andalusia and Biscay echeloned out to the left, towards the shore, the Armadas of Guipuzcoa and the Levant staggered out to the right, to seaward. Except for their flagships, these squadrons were weakly armed; against them, the English gun superiority would be crushing. But how had they managed totally to outmanoeuvre the Spaniards?

As the English came steadily on, their ensigns and red battle flags flying for a fleet action, one answer became speedily apparent to the most arrant amateur in the Spanish fleet. The soldier, Estrade, wrote: 'The English had the vantage by reason of good powder, store of shot, and good ships of sail and by a wind.' The Duke noted:

The enemy's fleet, with Drake on board, number 80 sail as far as can be counted, some of them being excellent vessels, and all of them very rapid sailers. Their ships being very nimble and of such good steerage, as they did with them whatsoever they desired.

The impression of English superiority was overwhelming, when coupled with the dreaded name of Drake, the legendary pirate Admiral who had sacked their colonial cities, taken their treasure ships, sailed into Cadiz, and blockaded the Spanish coast. The man of blood and fire was upon them. Many were ready to panic without further ado.

The English ships came plunging on, not 80 sail but only 54, and bearing across the rear of the Armada to pick up the inshore group, now beating out to sea across the stern of the Spanish fleet to join them. When they were joined, they were still only 67. There were 40 ships still in Plymouth, and another fleet, equal in size, with some of the best of the new ships, hundreds of miles away blockading Parma's invasion army off Dunkirk. At this moment, the Armada outnumbered them two to one in ships; in fighting soldiers its superiority was overwhelming. The approaching English looked coldly out on their enemy, trying to gauge its strength from the forests of masts which stretched for miles across the sea. 'At our first meeting of them, which was within two miles of Looe in Cornwall,' wrote Richard Thomson, lieutenant of the 200-ton *Margaret and John* of London, 'they were 136 sail of ships and pinnaces, whereof 90 were very great ships, and the rest of smaller account.' Drake's experienced eye saw more clearly: 'The fleet of the Spaniards is somewhat above a hundred sails, many great ships; but truly I think not half of them men-of-war.' Howard's report was detailed:

About 9 of the clock in the morning, we recovered the wind of their whole fleet which, being thoroughly descried, was found to consist of 120 sail, great and small; whereof there are 4 galleasses and many ships of great burden.

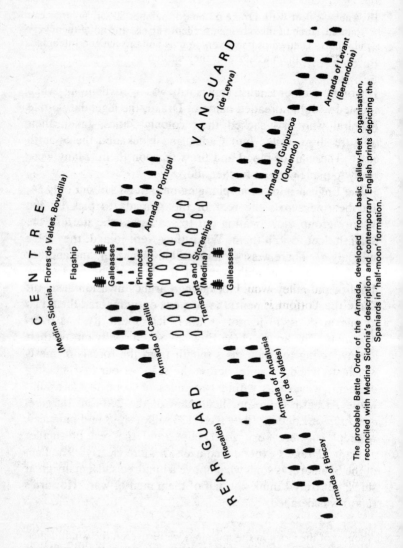

The probable Battle Order of the Armada, developed from basic galley-fleet organisation, reconciled with Medina Sidonia's description and contemporary English prints depicting the Spaniards in 'half-moon' formation.

VANGUARD
(de Leyva)

Armada of Levant
(Bertendona)

Armada of Guipuzcoa
(Oquendo)

Armada of Portugal

CENTRE
(Medina Sidonia, Flores de Valdes, Bovadilla)

Flagship

Galleasses

Pinnaces
(Mendoza)

Transports and Storeships
(Medina)

Galleasses

Armada of Castille

REAR GUARD
(Recalde)

Armada of Andalusia
(P. de Valdes)

Armada of Biscay

The actual numbers of the Armada varied somewhat, as swift pinnaces were despatched ahead with letters for Parma, or back to Spain with reports for the King; but it can have been little more than 120.

In none of the English narratives, diaries, and letters is there any clue as to how the English had so swiftly turned the tables on their enemies, and were now about to attack, instead of being attacked. Howard passes it off as, 'We did what we could to work for the wind.' Neither Drake nor Hawkyns, real seamen, even bothered to mention it. It must have been some commonplace trick, which any experienced mariner could manage in his sleep, if he had an English ship under him. The tidal stream in the Channel flows up to Dover, then turns and comes back; the times of the varying rates of flow at particular points are something that every seaman today knows by heart, since they can make a speed difference of four knots, and ships leave harbour timed exactly to catch a fast stream going in the right direction. Inside the great bays of the West Country there is little tide; it is necessary to go further out in order to pick up the current, and by sailing out beyond the Eddystone, as the English did, they would in fact enter the main stream. And since the bottom is not a flat desert, but on the contrary, a maze of submerged mountainous reefs reaching near, and sometimes above, the surface, some parts of the stream flow faster than others. The currents in the depths are very complex, but leave surface signs which can be read, all the way from Bolt Head to the Lizard. To mariners who had sailed all their lives out of Plymouth, getting to windward of a dozing Armada on their own doorstep would be elementary. Much easier, in fact, than trying to explain to Walsyngham how the trick was done.

Now they bore down, their sails bellying out with the wind, the spray racing upwards from their bows; with the creak of timber and the shouting of orders as the gun-ports were opened and the long guns run out. The powder had been poured in, the shot rammed home on top of it; now the gunners, slow-matches burning, waited for the huge-hulled targets to loom into view through the ports. They were riding into action, strung out in loose line ahead, for the first gun battle of all time; there was no precedent, no history, no well-thumbed book of rules behind them. The last major engagement of fleets had been a galley action, as standardized as a dance; won by boarding, by soldiers swarming across bulwarks on to enemy decks; won by the Spaniards, at Lepanto, long ago. Now they would try what sails and swift ships and gunpowder could do.

Howard was not fond of putting pen to paper, except for brief exhortations for more money, more food, more powder, more shot; Drake loathed marshalling arguments to prove points which he knew already to be plain and indisputable; John Hawkyns wrote only mild business letters, and those seldom. Only Raleigh had the gift of coldly summarizing essentials, and was spokesman for them all.

He wrote, contemptuously, for those who did not understand the new tactics:

Certainly, he that will happily perform a fight at sea must believe that there is more belonging to a good man of war upon the waters than great daring, and that there is a good deal of difference between fighting loose or at large, and grappling. To clap ships together without consideration belongs rather to a madman than a man of war; for by such ignorant bravery was (the Italian Admiral) Peter Strozzi lost at the Azores, when he fought against the Marquis of Santa Cruz. In like sort had the Lord Charles Howard, Admiral of England, been lost in the year 1588, if he had not been better advised than a great many malignant fools were. The Spaniards had an army aboard them, and he had none; they had more ships than he had, and of higher building and charging; so, that, had he entangled himself with those great and powerful vessels, he had greatly endangered this kingdom of England. For twenty men upon the defences are equal to a hundred that board and enter; whereas, contrariwise, the Spaniards had a hundred for twenty of ours, to defend themselves withal. But our Admiral knew his advantage and held it; which had he not done, he had not been worthy to have held his head.

His advantage was speed, mobility, range, gun power. And the fame of Drake and the English seamen. As the English galleons loomed larger and larger, effortlessly overtaking the Armada, the swift pinnace *Distain*, despatched by Howard, clapped on all sail and moved ahead. Into the great hollow half-moon formed by the two wings of forty armed merchant-men she came, all alone, among the slow-moving, high-castled Spanish ships; and her tiny pop-gun cannon roared out a defiance across the waves. Then the first group of English ships, not tight-packed in ranks like the Spanish squadrons, but sailing line ahead, in follow-my-leader style, came racing past the sterns of first, Bertondona's Levanters, and then Oquendo's Guipuzcoans, both under the general command of Don Alonso de Leyva, in charge of the right wing.

As the English guns bore, they fired. Livid yellow flame ran along the hulls, lighting up the gun-ports, and clouds of smoke poured out over the sea, wreathing the oncoming ships in a thick mist, and drifting down slowly on to the retreating Spaniards. The whistle and whine of cannon balls shrilling through the air followed the broadsides; white columns of water rose up from the waves, and collapsed; and the crash, the ship-shaking shock of hits, and the piercing screams of mutilated men, rent the disciplined calm of a moment before, upon which the sound of the discharge, seconds later, rode like a thunderclap.

By later standards, those broadsides were not so terrible. The English ships were passing a few hundred yards away, not lying gun-muzzle to gun-muzzle; the shot itself, when loaded, was not a close fit within the bore, was likely to come out at odd angles, so that the number of near-misses would be high. The propellant powder was coarse stuff, not as potent as it was to be later, and the cannons and culverins were of no great weight. But such a barrage as this, at sea, had never been seen or experienced before. The shock of a physical charge, by mailed foot or horsemen, was a thing to which the Spanish soldiers were well inured; it had behind it only the strength of men like themselves, or of animals easily frightened. But the shock of a fire-fight, the screaming, whining, roaring, nerve-shattering sudden impact of heavy battery after battery blazing away at a tightly concentrated target, this was something different. It was worse, far worse, than any cannon fire on land, playing on a wide front against a whole army – and, if truth be told, very often a private war between opposing batteries. It did not matter that, in this case, the guns were firing at masses of wood; for the men were tightly packed within, and they could see, with the approach of each English ship, twenty or more guns moving up to play upon them, and they shrank when the muzzles bore, feeling that each and every shot was intended for them alone.

The Duke very nearly lost his Armada there and then, despite his vastly superior numbers; for its great defensive strength, its rigid, near-perfect military formation was momentarily rent. The right wing (styled the 'Vanguard' in current military parlance) bulged and broke, despite de Leyva's efforts to rally them; or, as Calderon put it, 'certain ships basely took to flight.' In their efforts to get away, they fled before the wind and the rest of the oncoming English, and ran in amongst the ships on the other side of the half-moon formation, the left wing, under Recalde (styled the 'Rearguard' according to military usage).

This availed them hardly at all, because the English were faster, and, as they swept across the arc of the dissolving half-moon, the smoking, fuming guns were being swabbed out and re-loaded. And the same nerve-shattering barrage broke on them all, reinforced by the broadsides of another group of English ships approaching from nearer to the land. In his turn, Admiral Don Martinez de Recalde found his command disintegrating, partly from the stabbing thunder of the English broadsides, partly from the rush of fleeing ships from the shaken right wing. The armed merchantmen of Biscay and Andalusia suffered the unprecedented cannonading in horror and dismay. From their high castles, they could beat off with ease any attempt to board; were themselves only too eager to swarm over the English bulwarks and into the enemy ships, if they could get at them. But the English never closed the range, and it was clear to all that unless the English wanted to board, no Spanish ship would ever get alongside them. Nor could these armed merchantmen fire back with effect; their guns were light, they had not many of them, and they were lacking in range as well as hitting power. Only the squadron flagships were strong. De Leyva's *Rata Coronada*, almost alone of the fleeing right wing, was trying to fight back, aided by Admiral Oquendo's flagship; and shortly after, Recalde in the *San Juan* was merely an isolated rallying point for a small group on the left wing, of which the most prominent was another strong vessel, the *Gran Grin*, vice-flagship of the Armada of Biscay.

The Duke of Medina Sidonia's description of that first shattering attack of the outnumbered English, the first massed use of their revolutionary new methods and equipment, made dismal reading in the War Diary of the Armada.

The enemy's fleet passed, firing on our van (right wing) under the charge of Don Alonso de Leyva; which drove into the rear (left wing) under the charge of the Admiral Juan Martinez de Recalde, who stood fast and abode the assault of the enemy, although he saw that he was being left unsupported, for that the ships of the rearguard were shrouding themselves in the main body of the Armada. The enemy assailed him with great discharging of ordnance, without closing, whereby his ship suffered much in her rigging, her forestay was cut, and her foremast had two great shot therein. In the rear, supporting him, were the *Gran Grin*, with Don Diego de Pimental and Don Diego Enriquez, the son of the Viceroy of Peru. The *capitana real* (Medina Sidonia's flagship) struck her foretopsail and let fly the sheets, and coming to the wind, awaited the rear to gather it into the main body of the fleet.

According to Calderon, among the casualties in Recalde's powerful ship were Captain Pedro de Ycaina and other officers wounded; according to one of her crew, captured later, fatal casualties totalled fifteen.

The *San Martin*, the royal *capitana*, or fleet flagship, clumsily put her bluff bows round and began to work back, against the wind, towards the action raging in the rear, followed by some other galleons and the two galleasses which formed part of the 'main battle', the fighting head of the Armada. As they turned out of line, the tight-packed mass of storeships came slowly past them, with the wind behind, and following them close, the hapless fugitives from the right and left wings. These, reported Calderon, who was in the vice-flagship of the transport squadron, 'were peremptorily ordered by the flagship to luff and face the enemy.'

The Armada's meticulous defensive formation, in which lay its main strength, was coming apart, the disorder made more confused by the clouds of gunsmoke drifting slowly across the water, so that sometimes only the topsails of ships could be seen. No one witness can have seen the battle in its entirety, nor even half of it; nobody ever does, even when smokeless powder is used. Battle is essentially a personal experience. The witness is not looking at a game of chess, but at life and death; his life, possibly his death. Everything he sees is tinged with emotion, with the feeling of walking a deadly tightrope; no care for the future, for the future narrows down to now: will he, or will he not, survive the next five minutes? Or, worse even than death, will he, like Captain Priego's ensign in the flagship of Oquendo's squadron, lie mutilated, bloody and screaming on the deck, quivering with the shock of the hurtling iron ball that took off his leg? In many of the ships raked by the English fire, ploughboys, peasants and fishermen, conscripted for war, were hearing for the first time the horrible, animal howling, high-pitched and inhuman, of human beings terribly hurt.

Two separate engagements developed, cut off from one another by the gunsmoke. Howard's *Ark Royal* spearheaded one attack, and he was probably followed by his kinsmen in *Golden Lion* and *White Bear*, among others. He reported: 'The *Ark* bare up with the admiral (flagship) of the Spaniards wherein the Duke was supposed to be, and fought with her until she was rescued by divers ships of the Spanish army.' But this battered flagship, whoever she was, could not have been Medina Sidonia's *San Martin*, which was in fact leading the rescue force.

No less than three English flagships were taking part in a simultaneous action with another part of the disorganized Spanish rear, for Howard reported: 'In the meantime, Sir Francis Drake, Sir John Hawkyns, and Sir Martin Frobisher fought with the galleon of Portugal, wherein Juan Martinez de Recalde, vice-admiral, was supposed to be.' Ubaldino adds the detail that this 'Portuguese galleon was also accompanied by a squadron of several galleons of the same nation.' Recalde's flagship was a large Portuguese galleon, the *San Juan* of Oporto; and she was in fact rescued by two other Portuguese galleons, Medina Sidonia's *San Martin* and the *San Mateo*. Almost certainly, Howard was disappointed in his belief that he had fought Medina Sidonia, who seems to have been engaged with Drake, Hawkyns, and Frobisher.

Calderon, who was also present, identified a big English ship as the enemy fleet flagship, and noted:

She struck her foresail, and from the direction of the land sent four vessels, one of which was the vice-flagship (presumably meaning

Drake), to skirmish with our vice-flagship (Recalde's *San Juan*) and the rest of our rearguard (the Armada's left wing, commanded by Recalde). They bombarded her and the galleon *San Mateo*, which, putting her head as close up to the wind as possible, did not reply to their fire, but waited for them in the hope of bringing them to close quarters. The *Rata*, with Don Alonso de Leyva on board, endeavoured to approach the enemy's vice-flagship, which allowed herself to fall towards the *Rata*. But they could not exchange cannon shots, because the enemy's ship, fearing that the *San Mateo* would bring her to close quarters, left the *Rata* and bombarded the *San Mateo*. Meanwhile the wind forced Don Alonso de Leyva away, and he was prevented from carrying out his intentions; but he exchanged cannon shots with other enemy ships. Juan Martinez de Recalde, like the skilful seaman he was, collected all his ships whilst protecting his rearguard, engaging at the same time eight of the enemy's best ships. The Duke's flagship most distinguished herself this day, as she was engaged the greater part of the time, and resisted the fury of the whole of the enemy's fleet.

The soldier, Estrade, was somewhere there, amid the stabbing gun flashes and boiling powder smoke, in the Portuguese galleon *San Marcos*. He mentions some 'very good artillery which the *Rat* had', but implies she was Don Pedro's flagship instead of de Leyva's, as she actually was. But the formidably armed oared galleasses were unmistakable, and their arrival concluded the engagement:

The vice-admiral of the galleasses (the vice-flagship *Zuniga*) went putting himself into our horn of Don Pedro de Valdes; and the English when they saw the galleasses to enter, they retired and went away all that they could. And the artillery ceased and we did apart ourselves.

Howard reported that he broke off the action at one o'clock, but Estrade says that there was some cannonading going on until four o'clock; possibly some of the English ships, which were operating loosely in small groups, could not resist the opportunity to dash in now and again and have a nibble at the straggling disorganized Spaniards, who were stretched over so many miles of sea that from one part of the battlefield a brief attack in another would come only as a distant thudding of gunfire. Howard reported the conclusion of the main engagement:

The fight was so well maintained for the time that the enemy was constrained to give way and bear up room to the eastward, to stop their leaks, in which bearing up, a great galleon, wherein Don Pedro de Valdes was captain, became foul of another ship which spoiled and bare overboard his foremast and bowsprit.

Up to that time Don Pedro's Armada of Andalusia, being in a less exposed position than Recalde's Biscayans, had got off lightly. He wrote:

Our ordnance played a long while on both sides, without coming to hand stroke. There was little harm done, because the fight was far off. When it had ended, I sent a pinnace unto Juan Martinez de Recalde, to know whether he had received any harm. His answer was that his galleon had been sore beaten, and that his foremast was hurt with a great shot. He prayed me that I would come to relieve him, for that other-ways he should not be able to abide any new fight if we were offered it the same day.

Immediately Don Pedro turned out of the line and began to work back upwind to the battered and dismayed Biscay squadron, their nerves still shattered from the cannonading they had received. Indeed, both squadrons had now become intermingled, and were trying to sort themselves out, with Recalde's splintered flagship lying far to the rear.

As de Valdes began to tack westwards, hauled close to the wind, there drifted down upon him a mass of ships, some his, some Recalde's, sailing on converging courses and working their sails. A Biscay ship loomed ahead among the Andalusians, leaving no room between her and the other ships for Don Pedro's vessel, the *Nuestra Senora del Rosario*, to pass through the narrow gap; and no room either for him to turn away. As both ships swung under their helms, the bows of Don Pedro's big flagship smashed into the Biscay ship, destroying the spritsail and carrying away also one of her crossyards. The damage to the *Rosario* sent her partly out of control, for the steering of such heavy ships was done as much with the pull of the foresails as with the helm. As she pulled clear, a ship following the Biscayan loomed ahead, also on a collision course. She was the *Santa Catalina*, one of Don Pedro's own squadron, and her presence, behind instead of in front of a

Biscay ship, illustrated better than anything else the confusion and terror which had made most of Recalde's squadron 'shroud themselves in the main body of the Armada'. Now, however, there was no avoiding her, and she drove heavily into the crippled *Rosario*, breaking her bowsprit and bringing down the halyards and forecourse. Don Pedro's ship lay heaving on the waves, the rest of the Armada driving past her; and, as her crew took emergency measures to bring her under control again, Don Pedro fired a gun for help.

Hardly had it boomed out across the waters, and Medina Sidonia turned once again into the wind to wait for her, than an enormous cloud of black smoke, lightning lit by a brilliant yellow flash, poured up from the other wing of the Armada, where Oquendo's Guipuzcoans were re-forming. The thunder of the detonation followed seconds later. This was no cannon shot, it dwarfed even the roar of a broadside. Oquendo's vice-flagship, the *San Salvador*, had blown up. The hulk, reeking and streaming powder smoke, masts tottering, stern castles and galleries gone, upper deck blown to splinters, drifted sluggishly astern on the waves. From inside her came a low, persistent moaning, mixed with terrible screams, the agony of horribly burnt men.

It was now two o'clock, according to Calderon's very full and detailed diary – one hour after Howard had broken off the main action. An hour, with fast, modern ships, is a very long time; to re-impose order on straggling sailing ships, moving clumsily eastward at three or four knots, sixty minutes is a very short time. In spite of Spanish discipline, the Armada was not yet re-arrayed to the Duke's satisfaction. Preoccupied with re-forming his wings in battle order, he was confronted first with the crisis of the *Rosario* and, minutes later, with the shock of the *San Salvador* explosion. Both ships were drifting helplessly astern, and would be taken by the pursuing English unless he did something about it. Both ships were flagships, one commanded by an admiral; both contained treasure essential to the fleet if it had to put into a foreign port where supplies would have to be paid for. The *Rosario* had 52,000 ducats of the King's money, to be paid out on behalf of the Andalusian squadron, apart from private treasure and plate belonging to the noblemen aboard. The *San Salvador* had far more, for the Paymaster General was aboard her, and had under his eye the largest single amount of money in any Armada ship, much greater than the average 50–55,000 ducats held in the flags and vice-flags of the squadrons. The Duke was very hard pressed and, in the circumstances, did more for the *San Salvador* than for Don Pedro, who ever afterwards loathed him for it. He would hardly have succeeded, even there, had it not been for the galleasses which, with their banks of great oars, were independent of the wind, and were sufficiently heavily gunned to make the English careful.

Apart from these cares and preoccupations, he knew now for a certainty that his master, the King, in his fighting instructions, had been aware of only half the truth. He had been right when he warned that: 'The enemy's object will be to engage at a distance, on account of the advantage which they have from their artillery.' By one reckoning in the *San Martin*, the English had fired more than 2,000 rounds at them that day, to which the Armada had replied with 720 round shot, entirely without effect. No one even so much as claimed to have damaged an English ship, whereas there was splintered planking and dead men in many of the Spanish ships. True it was, too, that the Spaniards had tried to carry out their King's imperative command 'to close and grapple and engage hand to hand'. The *San Martin*'s consort, the *San Mateo*, had hopefully come up into the wind and held her fire, inviting Drake, Hawkyns and Frobisher to come alongside and helpfully hang about while the great Portuguese galleon poured down her hundreds of armed men into them. And all they had done was treat her as a battle practice target for their gunners, racing past her at a rate she could not match. And poor Don Alonso de Leyva, the Lieutenant-General of the whole Armada, accompanied by the flower of Spanish chivalry in the great *Rata Encoronada*, had not even been able to match the performance of the *San Mateo*, lumbering slowly after the nimble English vessels, for he had been unable even to come up into the wind; instead, when he had attempted to do so, he had simply drifted sideways in the opposite direction to the enemy. Whereas, as Medina Sidonia had noted, 'The English did with their ships whatsoever they desired.' This factor, the speed and handling qualities of the enemy's new vessels, had quite simply been left out of account by the planners back in Spain. There would be no grappling, unless the English desired it.

They did not. It would have been madness to press a close action, when less than half the English fleet was present, when time was on their side, when every day their numbers must increase. Indeed, even during the battle, reinforcements of men were being sent out from Plymouth by the Mayor, William Hawkyns, and hourly were being taken into the ships. The fight, as the Mayor reported to the Council in London, was in 'plain view' of Plymouth, 'which we beheld'. The knowledge that they were fighting under the eyes of their countrymen, and not mere ignorant Londoners, but the people of a mariner's town, inflamed some of the English captains to the point where they would have taken unpardonable risks, had Howard allowed it. Henry Whyte, captain of the 200-ton *Bark Talbot*, wrote angrily to Walsyngham some weeks later:

The majesty of the enemy's fleet, the good order they held, and the private consideration of our own wants, did cause, in mine opinion, our first onset to be more coldly done than became the valour of our nation and the credit of the English navy; yet we put them to leeward, kept the weather of them, and distressed two of their best ships, whereof Don Pedro's was one.

The panic of the rearward Spanish squadrons, the way they crowded each other in their efforts to escape the gunfire, the bumping and boring which disabled Don Pedro's flagship, and the plight of the stricken *San Salvador*, must have prompted many to believe that this was the moment to press right home into that great formation and really carve it up. Howard, risking the kingdom on it, thought the time was not ripe; he had not enough strength for a knockout blow. The Spanish superiority in infantry was appalling; any attempt to break into the great half-moon from the rear would mean enveloping his forces in double their number of Spanish ships, where they could be surrounded, grappled, boarded, and taken.

The really experienced fighting admirals regarded the day's events as a mere preliminary canter, an interesting and inexpensive experiment with the new methods. 'There hath passed some cannon shot between some of our fleet and some of them,' commented Drake coolly, aware that they had been bombarding the armed merchantmen and had yet really to test the best ships of the Armada bunched together. 'As far as we can perceive, they are determined to sell their lives with blows,' he added dryly. John Hawkyns, who was a businessman at sea, when doing business at sea meant fighting, was briefly business-like. He dismissed the battle, saying, 'We had some small fight with them in the afternoon.'

Howard had to be more forthcoming and justify his decision. 'The Lord Admiral, considering there were forty sail of his fleet as yet to come from Plymouth, thought good to stay for their coming before he would hazard the rest too far.' To Walsyngham, he wrote: 'We durst not adventure to put in among them, their fleet being so strong.' And he added, bearing out Drake's old warning that the ammunition allowance was good for about a day and a half: 'Sir, for the love of God and our country, let us have with some speed some great shot sent to us of all bigness; for this service will continue long; and some powder with it.' These, together with the lack of victuals, and the comparatively small number of English vessels present, were probably the 'wants' referred to by Whyte of the *Bark Talbot*.

Howard then flew the flag for council and the admirals came across to the *Ark Royal*,

where his Lordship's considerate advice was much liked of, and order delivered unto each captain how to pursue the fleet of Spain; and so, dismissing each man to go aboard his own ship, his Lordship appointed Sir Francis Drake to set the watch that night.

8

'A Voice in Spanish Calling Us'

Many eyes in the English fleet must have been looking hungrily at the two distressed Spanish vessels, strong and important units of their respective squadrons. Don Pedro's *Rosario* was the *capitana*, or flagship, of the Armada of Andalusia; the *San Salvador* was the *almiranta*, or vice-flagship, of Oquendo's Armada of Guipuzcoa. The crippled *Rosario* was now moving again, limping slowly towards the rear of the retreating Armada, while the *San Salvador* was surrounded by Spanish vessels trying to take her in tow. No doubt some bold and rash spirits among the English, such as Whyte of the *Bark Talbot*, thought it 'coldly done' when Howard made no move to interfere, but instead hoisted the flag for council. Yet, when it was over, Howard was able to record that his 'considerate advice was much liked of'. What had been talked about, and what had been decided, and why was it more important than the two potential Spanish prizes?

There are enough clues scattered about to make it plain. Ubaldino, the confidant of both Howard and Drake (and also Don Pedro), records that Howard's decision not to press the attack until he was no longer outnumbered was ratified. This was plain common sense and, in the light of what the English actually did during the following week, can probably be summed up as: 'We can afford to wait, because we shall grow progressively stronger; by the time we reach the Straits of Dover, and join with the fleets of Seymour and Wynter, we shall have actual superiority; that will be the time to smash them.' A vital factor in this decision must have been the serious inroads into the stocks of powder and shot caused by the brief action off Plymouth. Drake had forecast this situation exactly, and we know from many reports, mostly clearly expressed in

Hawkyns' letter to Walsyngham, how large this problem loomed in their minds and how perilously close they came at times to complete impotence, from lack of ammunition. Their new methods of gun-fighting, instead of grappling, were too new; the industrial complex to support such intensive cannon-ading did not exist. Gunpowder then was as scarce and secret as uranium was recently, and master gunners as important to war then as nuclear scientists now; indeed, for security reasons, master gunners, at this moment, were not allowed to leave the country. The Armada, as yet, had no such worries; it had been stored and ammunitioned for a long campaign of many months, from the resources of a power far more wealthy than England, and controlling most of the existing powder factories. The English were going to be ammunitioned from hand to mouth, and from day to day, literally by whatever could be scraped from the bottom of the barrel and brought out to them from the shore.

A word from Howard, and the rhythm of the following week's fighting, tells the rest of the story. 'We mean so to course the enemy as that they shall have no leisure to land,' he wrote next day. The English would fight only in defence of possible invasion objectives, of which there were three to come after Plymouth. There were Torbay and Portland, mentioned in the November 1587 invasion estimates, and the Isle of Wight, also listed but much the more likely objective for the Spanish army. The Spaniards would have to be 'coursed', come what might, off all three places. How was this to be done? Again, common sense and the week's events give a plain answer. Somebody would have to keep inshore of the Spaniards, while the rest put in 'spoiling' and 'fixing' attacks; that dangerous inshore station would have to be given to Frobisher, whose vast *Triumph* was eminently defensible, aided by the older, higher-charged English ships, particularly those of Howard and his kinsmen. The easily taken but nimble new galleons of Drake and Hawkyns would be better employed where there was plenty of sea room, out to sea. As this is exactly what happened, and as the two coming battles were virtually duplicates of each other, and as, on each occasion, all the English leaders played and replayed the same distinctive roles, recognizable one from the other, an overall battle plan may be assumed. It could hardly have been an accident, when it makes so much sense; remembering also that the men who attended Howard's Council of War were the cream of the fighting seamen of their time. They had good reason to be content when they went down the side of the *Ark Royal* and into their boats. Here, despite the English 'wants' in munitions and in numbers, was a workable scheme.

The Spaniards were much less happy; indeed, they had had a shock. They had expected the English artillery superiority, but had not been too worried because a little cannon fire was thought unlikely to sink a ship, or even cause many casualties. What they had not bargained for was the deadly combination of superior gun-power with superior speed and mobility, which meant that they would have to take continual punishment without effective reply. Not suspecting the English ammunition shortage, which would effectively curtail the cannonading, they foresaw a bleak future. Although outnumbered two to one, the English had panicked the rear of the Armada and endangered the whole Spanish formation; when the English fleet grew to its full strength, what could stop it? At the moment, the Duke was a little too busy with his cripples to give the matter effective thought, but he was to do so next day, when the Armada's battle formation was to be drastically altered and the ultimate disciplinary measure – death – threatened to any ship captain who emulated that disgraceful panic off Plymouth. Prisoners taken in the next twelve hours, their recollections fresh, were to supply the background to the Duke's decisions. Ubaldino reported, having talked to some of them:

After meeting the English fleet and seeing it get under sail so easily through the skill of the English, versed as they were in sea matters, and seeing that, with the type of ships they had which were a good deal smaller than the Spanish, they were able to get very near to the much larger ships and fight against them to their own advantage, the Spaniards confessed themselves greatly surprised and admitted that they had lost much of their hope in the victory of their fleet.

Normally, it is wise not to take the depositions of prisoners at exact face value, but the events that evening, and the decisions taken next day, show that this was no great exaggeration.

At first, however, it seemed that the Duke had the situation in hand, and that there would be no prisoners. His own flagship stood by the burning *San Salvador*, while four pataches man-oeuvred alongside, got a line across, and began to tow her after the Armada. The fire on board was put out, and an unsuccessful attempt made to remove some of the wounded to the hospital ships. But the great carrack was such a reeking shambles inboard that the task defied all human effort. Calderon, who was in another *San Salvador*, which helped to take off survivors, reported:

Both after decks were blown up. More than 200 men were killed, including Ensign Castenada, who was on watch; and the ship was rent in both bow and stern. Many of the men jumped into the sea and were drowned, but the four pataches saved the principal persons, including Paymaster Juan de Huerta, with his staff papers, and some money in his charge.

Captain Juan de Villaviciosa, Vice-Admiral of Oquendo's squadron and the senior naval officer on board, had burns; Captain Pedro de Priego, commanding a company of ninety-four soldiers, was badly burnt; the other two infantry captains, Don Francisco de Chaves, with 133 men, and Geronimo de Valderrama, with ninety-two, were unhurt. As there were in addition sixty-four seamen in the ship, she had therefore suffered more than sixty per cent fatal casualties at one blow. The shattered decks were littered with dreadful travesties of men, blackened and pock-marked as if soot had been driven into their flesh, their clothes still smouldering; flesh had run from their faces and hands as if it had been liquid; some were still alive, and moaning, but if anyone attempted to lift them, the skin and meat came away at the touch, leaving the white bone showing. For such wounds as these, the Armada was not prepared at all, let alone in such overwhelming numbers. How had it happened? Sabotage, it was whispered.

Calderon, who next day reported that he had 'received on the flag-hulk Captain Villaviciosa and about 34 burnt men,' had the opportunity to question survivors, including those who had been in the vicinity of the explosion. He wrote:

It is said that Captain Priego had beaten a German artilleryman, who went below, saying that one of the pieces had got wet, and would have to be discharged. He fired the piece and then threw the port fire into a barrel of powder.

A party of fourteen Dutch mariners then serving in the Armada, who later deserted when off the coast of the Netherlands, had heard much the same story, presumably from other survivors taken into different ships in the fleet.

She was set on fire by reason of the captain falling into a rage with the gunner and threatening to kill him if he shot no righter. The gunner cast fire into the powder barrels and threw himself overboard. In this ship, they say, was the treasure and five ensigns of Spaniards.

Apart from minor detail, these two first-hand stories are identical. But when Ubaldino came to write his history, there were two versions of the gunner's motive in circulation.

An army captain (i.e., Priego) had insolently beaten a Flemish gunner, it is not known whether on account of his work or of the wife of the gunner who was with him, as is the custom of his country; whereupon the poor wretch, despairing of his life and that of his wife, and perhaps even more of her honour, and that of his daughter, set alight to a barrel of gunpowder, thus avenging himself and his dear ones.

Ubaldino was merely reporting the two versions then current, both of which could conceivably be true; the gunner may well have had a double motive for his drastic action. It was with this very point in mind that Medina Sidonia had included in his Fleet Orders the instruction: 'As it is an evident inconvenience, as well as an offence to God, that public or other women should be permitted to accompany such an Armada, I order that none shall be taken on board.' Consequently, another historian, writing nearly four centuries later (Professor Mattingly, *The Defeat of the Spanish Armada*), roasted Ubaldino for his credulity in believing that there might have been women in the Spanish ships; disdainfully, he dismissed the possibility as 'poetic licence'. What he was doing, in effect, was to lecture a sixteenth-century historian on the customs of the sixteenth century.

But poor Ubaldino was at least as conscientious in his

research as his American rival and he was better informed. He
knew what the English had found in the ruin of the *San
Salvador*. A few Spaniards, mostly of 'the common sort', for
the senior officers had been rescued, plus 'two Frenchmen, four
Almains, and one Almain woman'. Here, possibly, was the
wife or daughter of the 'German artilleryman' beaten by
Captain Priego, according to Calderon, for the official inven-
tory of the *San Salvador*, certified to the Council by George
Trenchard and Francis Hawley, justices of the peace for Devon,
still survives, in one of the two main source works for the
Armada campaign. Among the living, they found this 'one
Almain woman'.

While the treasure was being taken out of the *San Salvador*,
Don Pedro de Valdes had brought up near the rear of the
Armada, to repair the damage to the *Rosario*; and was soon
totally, instead of partially, disabled.

While I was in this case, the sea did rise in such sort that my ship,
having struck sail and wanting her halyard of the foremast, being
withal but badly built, did work so extremely as shortly after, and
before it could be remedied, her foremast brake close by the hatches,
and fell upon the mainmast, so as it was impossible to repair that hurt
but in some good space of time. I did again send word thereof several
times to the Duke, and discharged three or four great pieces, to the
end all the fleet might know what distress I was in, praying him either
to appoint some ship or galleass to tow me ahead, or to direct me what
other course I should take.

And all the fleet did take note of his distress. Don Jorge
Manrique, Inspector-General of the Armada, later coldly
reported to the King: 'The Armada passed on, leaving her
behind in sight of the enemy; and what subsequently became
of her and her crew is not known.' Estrade, writing when more
had been learnt, recorded:

Then again she shot off four pieces, but there were none that came to
succour her, for that the wind did blow much, the sea was grown, and
the English did follow us. At prayer-time we left her, for that the
Duke of Medina did shoot off a piece with a bullet by which we
proceeded on our way. After, we understood that she was boarded
with five galleons, who did much harm unto Don Pedro and slew all
his people.

There were seven Englishmen in the *Rosario*, and knowing what their fate would be, if captured, four of them got into the pinnace which Don Pedro sent to the *San Martin* to ask for aid; but three remained behind, taking their chance. In the pinnace also went the friar, Bernado de Gongora, who had to stay in the Duke's ship and watch the final desertion of his friends.

The Duke continued on his course, leaving them in the power of the enemy, who always followed a league astern; and in the ship was good old Vicente Alvarez, the captain, and what has been done with them God knows.

The rage among the Spaniards may be imagined, directed, not at the English, but at Medina Sidonia and his advisers in the *San Martin*. But their fury was as nothing to Don Pedro's.

Nevertheless, although he was near enough to me, and saw in what case I was, and might easily have relieved me, yet would he not do it; but even as if we had not been Your Majesty's subjects nor employed in your service, discharged a piece to call the fleet together, and followed his course, leaving me comfortless in the sight of the whole fleet, the enemy being but a quarter of a league from me.

The Duke's version of the affair is rather different; it records a half-hearted attempt to save the disabled flagship and her treasure. Half-hearted because, the Duke was advised, he would risk losing the whole Armada if he tempted another battle with the English so late in the day.

As it was now night, Diego Flores told the Duke that if he took in sail and stood by her the rest of the Armada would not perceive it, as most of the ships were far in advance, and he would find himself in the morning with less than half the Armada. Diego Flores was of opinion that the Duke ought not to risk the whole of his force, as he was sure that if he stood by he would lose the day.

Personally a brave man, but quite unable to judge the technical merits of the case, and impressed as they all were with the alarming effectiveness of the English fleet, Medina Sidonia gave way.

In face of this advice the Duke ordered Captain Ojeda to stand by Don Pedro's flagship, with four pataches, Don Pedro's vice-flagship,

Diego Flores' flagship, and a galleass, to attempt to pass a hawser on board and tow her, or else take the men out of her.

The attempt failed, and Medina Sidonia fired the recall gun. Don Pedro was left behind, in the night, to the mercy of the English. Two hours later, recorded Calderon, out in the darkness over the heaving black waters behind them came the sullen rumble of gunfire, three or four shots only. Then silence. 'Nothing further is known of Don Pedro,' Calderon wrote.

In the mind of every man was shame, coupled with the knowledge that Don Diego Flores de Valdes was the cousin of Don Pedro de Valdes, that they were known to dislike each other, and that it was Diego Flores who had advised that his kinsman be left to his fate.

In fact, Medina Sidonia, in his War Diary, exaggerated both the size of the force he sent to help the *Rosario* and the urgency of the English threat; at any rate, only one ship made for the crippled Spaniard, the rest swept on after the Armada with silent guns. This lone vessel was the *Margaret and John* of London, 200 tons, ninety men, Captain John Fisher. Her master was John Nash and her lieutenant was Richard Thomson, who probably did the actual composing of their joint petition for a share in the prize money. Thomson must have been a smart man for, within a week, he took part in the capture of two Spanish flagships. The *Nuestra Senora de Rosario* was his first.

We only, with our ship, as all the fleet can testify, bare romer with the (Spanish) ship, being accompanied neither with ship, pinnace, or boat of all our fleet. At our approach, we found left by her, for her safeguard, a great galleon, a galleass and a pinnace, with order either to help her repair her masts, and so follow the Spanish army, gone before, or else to bring away the men, treasure and munition thereof, and to fire or sink the ship; all which three, upon the sudden approach of our ship, only forsook Don Pedro, leaving him to the mercy of the sea. And this much hath Don Pedro himself confessed, condemning and exclaiming much upon those that were left for his comfort, in that they forsook him, upon the coming of one small ship.

About 9 of the clock the same evening we came hard under the sides of the ship of Don Pedro, which by reason of her greatness and the sea being very much grown, we could not lay aboard without spoiling our own ship. And therefore, seeing not one man shew himself, nor any light appearing in her, we imagined that most of the people had been taken out; and to try whether any were aboard or not, we discharged 25 or 30 muskets into her cagework, at one volley, with arrows and bullet. And presently they gave us two great shot, whereupon we let fly our broadside through her, doing them some hurt, as themselves have and can testify.

After this we cast about our ship, and kept ourselves close by the Spaniard until midnight, sometimes hearing a voice in Spanish calling us; but the wind being very great, and we in the weather (upwind), the voice was carried away, that we could not well understand it, but were persuaded by our mariners, to be the voice of one swimming in the sea; whereupon we put off our ship boat with 8 oars, to seek, call, and take them up; but found nobody.

It must have been an eerie experience, locked alone on the night sea with the great blacked-out Spaniard, her high castles towering above them, and all inside as quiet as death. Obviously, Don Pedro had doused every light, in the hope of being unmolested, so that he would have time to repair the damage and perhaps rejoin the Armada. The *Margaret and John* left him shortly after midnight, to follow Howard. Drake, in the *Revenge*, had the post of honour that night, leading the pursuit throughout the hours of darkness. Very shortly, however, the glow of his stern lantern vanished abruptly, as if wiped off the face of the night with a duster. Howard, puzzled, moved up to find out what had happened, but could see in the gloom no sign of his Vice-Admiral. Then the moon came out. On all the sparkling expanse of silver sea ahead and around, there was no ship that could conceivably be the *Revenge*, only the huddled forests of masts and white sails in front that was the Armada. Howard closed up to within culverin shot of them, followed at some distance by the *White Bear* and the *Mary Rose* (the second *Mary Rose*, of 500 tons, built 1555, ten years after the loss of the first Royal ship of that name), and sailed on steadily through the night, just out of range of the enemy's guns.

At dawn next morning, Monday, 1 August, Howard found himself alone on the waters off Berry Head, by Torbay, with only these two English ships, and the Armada, for company. Far astern, half-mast high, came the next English ship; and the rearmost was quite out of sight. Still, there was no sign of the *Revenge*. One of the first ships to come up with Howard's *Ark*

Royal was the *Margaret and John* of London; she must have had a very pretty turn of speed. As Thomson wrote afterwards:

We went aboard the *Ark*, and certified his Lordship in what distressed state we had left the ship our enemy; praying leave that we might be permitted to return to finish our attempt; or that his Lordship would send a pinnace to Dartmouth or Plymouth, that some shipping might be set forth to fetch her in.

While they were making their report, with one eye on the prize money, no doubt, a fast pinnace came creaming up from astern, the water sheering back from her bows; and she also came alongside the English flagship. Out of her came Captain Thomas Cely, jubilant, less conscious of that 'patched carcase' of his, the souvenirs of his time in the Spanish prisons and the galley at St Mary Port less than ten years before. Curiously enough, Puerto Santa Maria, with its groves of orange trees, was where the Duke of Medina Sidonia had his estates. Cely's news would not please him. 'Up came one Captain Cely,' wrote Thomson, 'certifying his Lordship that Sir Francis Drake, staying behind the fleet all night, had taken the said ship of Don Pedro de Valdes, with 460 men in her, full of artillery, munition, and treasure.' So that was where Drake had got to – cunning beggar!

Howard, accepting that Drake always had uncanny luck where treasure ships were concerned, reported simply: 'Our own fleet were disappointed of their light, by reason that Sir Francis Drake left the watch to pursue certain hulks which were descried very late in the evening.' If he had seen strange sails to seaward, it was certainly his duty to find out what they were; and if he had to do it personally, with the flagship, to extinguish his stern light before he turned off course, in order not to lead the rest of the fleet astray. Other people, notably Martin Frobisher, the sanguine Yorkshireman who commanded the *Triumph*, were not so easily satisfied with the truth of the story; or if true, that it was the whole truth. It was not until some weeks later that Frobisher had the satisfaction of telling one of Drake's officers, to his face, what he thought of Sir Francis.

The officer, Matthew Starke, deposed that Frobisher's diatribe had gone as follows:

Sir Francis Drake reporteth that no man hath done any good service but he; but he shall understand that others hath done as good service as he, and better too. He hath done good service indeed, for he took Don Pedro. For after he had seen her in the evening, that she had spent her masts, then, like a coward, he kept by her all night, because he would have the spoil. He thinketh to cozen us of our shares of fifteen thousand ducats; but we will have our shares, or I will make him spend the best blood in his belly; for we hath had enough of those cozening cheats already.

Then he demanded of me if we did not see Don Pedro over night or no. Unto which I answered: 'No.'

Then he told me that I lied; for she was seen to all the fleet. Unto the which I answered: 'I would lay my head that not any one man in the ship did see her until it was morning, that we were within two or three cables length of her.'

Whereunto he answered: 'Ay, marry', saith he, 'you were within two or three cables length; for you were no further off all night, but lay a-hull by her.'

Whereunto I answered: 'No, for that we bare a good sail all night, off and on.'

Then he asked me to what end we stood off from the fleet all night. Whom I answered that: 'We had descried three or four hulks, and to that end we wrought so, not knowing what they were.'

Then saith he: 'Sir Francis was appointed to bear a light all that night; which light we looked for, but there was no light to be seen; and in the morning, when we should have dealt with them, there was not above five or six near unto the Admiral, by reason we saw not his light.'

Then saith he: 'I have no more to say unto you; you may depart.'

The phrase 'when we should have dealt with them' was significant; for on the morning of 1 August, the Armada was off Torbay, one of the listed possible objectives. Clearly, the English had intended to give battle; but Drake's attention had saved their powder, for the Armada kept steadily on. Now there were only two possible invasion points left – Weymouth, by the Bill of Portland, and the Isle of Wight.

9

'Hang Any Captain . . .'

The first man into the *Rosario* was Nic Oseley, civilian, businessman, and spy. Among the English State Papers are accurate reports concerning the mobilization of the Armada; some of these were the work of Oseley, who under cover of his business as a merchant in Spain, took on in 1588 the adventurous task of riding from port to port to gain information, in spite of the fact that he was known as an English agent, having previously been imprisoned for it. On his return to England with the latest news, just before the coming of the Spaniards, Walsyngham had sent him to Lord Howard. But it was Drake who took him on board, as up-to-the-minute adviser on the Armada, and it was Drake who put to use his knowledge of Spanish, on the morning of Monday, 1 August. And he was, of course, much the best person to put to the commander of this powerful ship Drake's terms of surrender. 'Aboard they had much evil order, as I did see,' reported Oseley, 'who by Sir Francis' commandment was the first went to them.'

Don Pedro recorded the events as follows:

Finding myself in so bad case, void of all hope to be relieved, and Sir Francis Drake, admiral of the enemy's fleet, bearing towards me with his ship, from whom there came a message that I should yield myself upon assurance of good usage, I went aboard him, upon his word, to treat of the conditions of our yielding.

According to Ubaldino, who had it first-hand from Sir Francis, Drake's offer was brusque and brutal: 'Surrender unconditionally or give battle.' There was a pointed reference to 'the rules of war', and 'that they should surrender to his will, because otherwise he did not wish to waste his time, and perhaps lose sight of his fleet.' The rules of war, then, were that mercy was shown to an opponent, by land or by sea, only if he laid down his arms without fighting. Once blood had been shed, no quarter was given to men of the 'common sort'; the senior officers, however, could expect to survive because of their ransom potential. Therefore, Don Pedro's own life was not in question, nor that of his officers, but only those of his men. He had a high-charged ship, which would give the English some trouble to take; he could delay Drake and keep him out of the fight for a little time, and there was his own honour at stake. But the gaping gun-ports of the *Revenge*, and the 'hurry up, no bloody nonsense' attitude of her admiral, decided him. The crippled *Rosario* would not last long. Drake would simply lay the *Revenge* across her bow or stern, from which only a few Spanish guns could reply, and batter her with his broadsides until half her men were dead or dying. As for his honour, no one could be ashamed of surrendering to the most famous fighter then at sea; indeed, there was even a certain distinction in it.

Therefore, wrote Don Pedro,

the best conclusion that could be taken was the safety of our lives and courteous entertainment; for performance whereof Sir Francis Drake gave us his hand and word of a gentleman, and promised he would use us better than any other that were come to his hands, and would be a means that the Queen should also do the like; whereupon I thought good to accept of his offer.

The promise was carried out to the letter, and ten days later Don Pedro and his senior officers found themselves guests in the house of Richard Drake, a kinsman of Sir Francis; 'about forty of the better sort besides bestowed in divers men's houses in London', the rest remaining in the captured ship. Even as prisoners, however, the Spaniards could still do some good for Spain. The men Nic Oseley questioned told him, straight-faced, that the Armada numbered 150 sail. And Don Pedro, 'talking courteously and in a familiar way' to Ubaldino, presumably at Richard Drake's house, stated that the number was 142, of which, of course, he quickly added, a mere 110 were fighting ships. To make these estimates more credible, he gave a number of details – the presence of hospital ships, the detaching of the galleys, and so on – which were accurate, but of no particular value to the English.

In fact, before surrendering, he had given most probably a quick security briefing to his men, guessing that they would be thoroughly interrogated, as in fact they were. Drake, having just reported the Spanish fleet as 'somewhat above a hundred sails, not half of them men-of-war', no doubt smiled politely. For, 'after having conversed together a brief space, Vice-Admiral Drake expressed the wish that Don Pedro should always eat at his table, thus honouring him as a foreign friend, and he desired him to sleep in his cabin.' To make even greater show of hospitality, Drake, adds Ubaldino,

allowed no violence to be done to the persons of the Spaniards on board the prize, nor did he allow anything to be taken or touched of the goods belonging to Don Pedro. Of course the money that was found there, amounting to 50,000 escudos, belonging to the Royal Treasury of Spain, was taken and later given to the Lord Treasurer of England.

And therefore it came about that Don Pedro, although a prisoner, did not miss the fighting after all; indeed, he was to be in the thick of it throughout, watching the defeat of the Armada from the stern cabin of Drake's flagship – a grandstand seat if ever there was one.

Of course, Drake's main motive must have been the sheer interest of being able to talk to someone on the opposite side who was nearly, if not quite, in his own class, for Don Pedro was an Admiral of reputation who had held high command in the Portuguese campaign. At the same time, he had put his opponent into a good humour and could hardly help picking up information of importance. But that cut both ways, and the English Government were alarmed when they heard of it, thinking that some of the 'secrets of the services' might be revealed. Consequently, they ordered Don Pedro out of the *Revenge* and into house arrest in custody of Richard Drake. There, on 14 August, he was examined according to a carefully drawn-up questionnaire headed *Articles to be ministered to Don Pedro de Valdes and his associates*. Don Pedro fenced delightfully with his interrogators.

'What was the end and purpose of the King of Spain his sending so great an army by sea into these parts?'

'The King sent this armada to the Prince of Parma for to clear the way, so as he might land in this kingdom and conquer it,' replied Don Pedro, blandly.

'With what honour and conscience could the King do the same?' enquired the interrogator, with a touch of English self-righteousness.

'It lieth not with me to answer if the King did well or ill, being a subject, and unable to judge the actions of his prince,' replied Don Pedro, making a point which may still be debated.

But these were only sighting shots. The Government's main preoccupation was with the potential, and perhaps mythical, fifth-column. 'What princes Catholics were parties to this enterprise, and what support did they look for out of France, from whom, and from what place?' Don Pedro shook his head. He knew nothing about that, he said. 'Which were their two places where they should have made their descent here in this realm; and what party did they look for here?' pressed the interrogator. But Don Pedro would say only that the selection of a landing place was left to the Duke of Parma, except that they intended to anchor at the Isle of Wight, if necessary, to repair damage. He knew nothing of any support to be expected from Englishmen. The interrogator came back to that point a few minutes later: 'Which of the Englishmen in the army were privy to the secrets of the enterprise?' 'None of them,' replied Don Pedro. On military matters he definitely tried to mislead them, but not so grotesquely as would make it apparent. There were in the Armada, he said, about 140 ships, and 29,000 men; and the Duke of Parma had 36,000 horse and foot. On the *Rosario*'s treasure, he went the other way, and underestimated. 'Near 20,000 ducats, as also vessels of silver worth another thousand,' he said. Perhaps he had made a little under-the-counter bargain with Drake; we shall never know. We know only that, when facing his interrogators, Don Pedro de Valdes was still fighting for Spain.

Most of the Spanish prisoners seem to have maintained the same unbroken front. Vicente Alvarez, captain and owner of the *Rosario*, stated that the Armada had consisted of 152 sail when it left Corunna, and had been depleted only by the four galleys and two pinnaces despatched to carry letters. But he gave away the 'River of London' as the invasion objective, and stated that 'it was commonly bruited amongst them that a third part or one half of the realm of England would join to their aid so soon as they should enter on the land.' He admitted that seven or eight Englishmen had been serving voluntarily in the *Rosario*, some of whom had been captured with her, but 'the rest, William Stucley, the pilot of the ship, Richard Brierley, and one more, passed forth of the ship before they were taken, promising to fetch them more aid.' The English renegades serving in the Armada knew, naturally, what their fate would be, if taken, and escape was probably the main motive of these men. Alvarez put the King's Treasure at 52,000 ducats, more than double Don Pedro's estimate.

A much more detailed and accurate report came from Gregorio de Sotomayor, who stated that his family were well-off Portuguese: 'Trade or occupation, we have none; but do live by our goods and rents.' Medina Sidonia's worries about deserters are partly explained by his statement that: 'when the Spaniards embarked themselves, they commanded 2,000 Portingals to go aboard upon pain of death.' He did not know of any traitors in England, but, 'as a good Portingal', would gladly have helped the Queen by naming them, had he known. The treasure, he said, was in the various flagships, naming them; particularly rich was 'a Venetian ship in whom came for general Don Alonso de Leyva; this ship brought great store, for there came in her the Prince of Ascoli, and many other noblemen.' He concluded this voluntary confession, which was additional to the questionnaire, by giving a most important piece of information:

I declare further that King Philip did command that the fleet should be victualled for 6 months, but Luis Hezar and Francisco Duarte of Cadiz did victual them but for 4 months, and with that which was nought and rotten. For which occasion the King commanded them to be apprehended; and so they remained prisoners in Portugal at our coming away. And this is the very truth.

It was. On the day he was taken, it hardly mattered, but within a few days of his being questioned, it was vital. And by that time there was independent corroboration.

Drake's *Revenge*, when she closed with the *Rosario*, had been accompanied by the *Roebuck*, 300 tons, 120 men, under Captain Jacob Whiddon, one of the armed merchantmen of the Western Squadron. Whiddon was told to take the prize into Dartmouth, but the crippled *Rosario* would not go in that direction, which was dead into wind, and Whiddon therefore brought her into Torbay. A colourful description of the scene eventually reached the King of Spain from his agents in England.

Two English couriers, who embarked at Rye on 26 July, report as follows: After they had left port they fell in with some fishermen, who told them that shortly before a large Spanish ship, with many oars on each side, and full of Englishmen, had passed. They said she bore a banner of Santiago, and another flag of the Queen of England over all. The people on board had spoken with them, and had told them that the English fleet had encountered the Spanish fleet on Sunday, and fought it. They said they had fought, but did not say whether they had been victorious, or were beaten. The English ambassador is troubled, as it is thought that their fleet is defeated . . .

The Spanish official who interpolated this piece of wishful thinking was only one of many to make the same mistake; the Armada may not have been invincible, but the optimism of its supporters was.

Before the *Rosario* had even reached Torbay, it was first come, first served. Whiddon had out of her ten of the best brass guns for his own vessel, muskets and calivers for his own men, barrels of wine and oil for everybody; he had some of the powder and shot, too, but no one could prove it afterwards, because he blued that on the Spaniards. A Plymouth pinnace, which encountered her next, sent by Howard to get the powder and shot out of her for use in the English fleet, came away with two fine brass guns as well. The *Samaritan* of Dartmouth, 250 tons, 100 men, had to be content with a single brass gun, ten muskets, and ten calivers. Then she came into Torbay, and the natives swarmed over the bulwarks.

When the Deputy Lieutenants of Devon, Sir John Gilberte and George Cary, hot-footed it down to Torbay to take over the prize and make an inventory, an appalling spectacle met their eyes – rows of empty gun carriages in a looted ship. Many of those guns which remained were old-fashioned iron types, not worth the lifting. Cary wrote bitterly to Walsyngham:

I was never much experienced in these causes before this time; but now I find that all these sea goods are mixed with bird-lime; for no man can lay his hands on them, but is limed, and must bring away somewhat. Watch and look never so narrowly, they will steal and pilfer.

The remaining stock of small arms they had moved to the shore, 'lest it be embeaselled away'.

However much it may have annoyed those two gentlemen at the time, it is obvious in retrospect that the seamen were performing merely their strict patriotic duty, to defeat the civil service at any cost, and the Spaniards, too. For Gilberte and Cary received a request from Mr Carew Raleigh, brother of Sir Walter, for six of the guns to be placed in his footling fort at Portland; and passed it, for action, to the Council. The place for the guns, now, was in the ships fighting the Armada at that moment; the seamen had a use for them and the land men had not. However, Gilberte and Cary did their main job, which was to despatch eighty-eight barrels of fine-corned Spanish powder and 1,600 Spanish round shot to Howard's munition-starved ships.

A month later, they had got the *Rosario* into Dartmouth at last, under tow of eight boats, and, by now, were sincerely regretting Drake's promise to the Spaniards 'for the safety of their lives and courteous entertainment'. Cary grumbled to Walsyngham: 'We would have been very glad they had been made water spaniels when they were first taken.' The *Rosario*'s own store of provisions was rotted already: 'their fish savours, so that it is not to be eaten, and their bread full of worms'; and 'the people's charity to them (coming with so wicked an intent) is cold; so that if there be not order forthwith taken by your Lordships, they must starve.' He added an interesting comment: 'The pilot of the ship is as perfect in our coasts as if he had been a native born.'

Of the Englishmen taken in her, he said nothing; but another report by a Spanish agent tells their story: 'Don Pedro has been captured, and two Englishmen with him, one of them named Browne, have been hanged.'

The capture of the *Rosario* was an unexpected windfall for the English, helping to make good the laggard processes of government by which they were starved of ammunition. But what turned the tide was the taking, a few hours after her capture, of the damaged *San Salvador* also, complete with another great store of powder and shot. In fact, the Duke was thoughtfully re-ammunitioning his enemies. All he rescued from the *Rosario* were a few frightened English traitors, before he abandoned her 'in sight of the enemy', in Don Jorge Manrique's ominous phrase. Now, he did it again. The precipitate abandonment of this second flagship, in something like a panic, is made clear by Calderon's diary, for he was very closely concerned:

She continued her voyage with great difficulty, until Monday (1 August), in the morning, when the Duke ordered the people to be taken out of her and the ship sunk. The captain, however, was badly wounded, and the men in a hurry to abandon the ship, so that there was no one to sink her; besides which, she had many wounded and burnt men on board, who could not be rescued as the enemy was approaching.

This latter phrase was pure loyalty, for the English fleet, that morning, consisted of Howard's *Ark Royal* and about half a dozen other ships, the rest having been scattered and delayed by Drake's much-debated gambit which had resulted in the capture of the *Rosario*. Howard's own report was: 'Very many were out of sight, which with a good sail recovered not his Lordship before it was very late in the evening.' There was therefore no good cause for the panic, except the battering the Spaniards had taken the previous day off Plymouth. The *San Salvador* was not even obviously sinking, for Calderon hazarded: 'It is believed that the enemy will have put a hawser on board and towed her to a port on the coast.'

The Duke, of course, covered himself (and Diego Flores de Valdes) by entering in the War Diary: 'At eleven o'clock the captain of Oquendo's vice-flagship came and informed the Duke that the ship was foundering, and had become unmanageable.' Actually, she was still afloat nearly four months later, albeit with ten men continuously working the pumps, and not

in a very seaworthy condition, for then she sank at last, in a
November gale, 70 miles further up-Channel, taking with her
part of her prize crew and some of the men who had sailed her
from Spain. However, the men in the Armada did not know of
these little military deceptions; they saw only, as Estrade did,
that 'We left her, and the English went to her, shot off a gun,
and went aboard.' 'In sight of the Armada she was captured by
the enemy,' wrote the historian of the galleass *Zuniga*. 'Abandoned in sight of the enemy,' reported Don Jorge Manrique to
the King. Knowing how small the English fleet was at that
moment, it must have been a distressing sight for the Spaniards.

The first English vessel alongside her was a small skiff from
the *Victory*, Hawkyns' flagship; in it was Hawkyns himself and
Lord Thomas Howard, of the *Golden Lion*. 'They saw a very
pitiful sight,' wrote the Lord Admiral:

the deck of the ship fallen down, the steerage broken, the stern blown
out, and about 50 poor creatures burnt with powder in most miserable
sort. The stink in the ship was so unsavoury, and the sight within
board so ugly, that they shortly departed.

They had found, to their relief, that she had been abandoned
in such haste that her ammunition stores were intact; and the
Bark Flemyng, presumably the ship of that Captain Flemyng
who had first sighted the Armada, was ordered to tow the
reeking derelict into Weymouth. That is to say, she was to
follow the Armada and the handful of pursuing English on
their 'headland to headland' course across the wide mouth of
Lyme Bay. The Spaniards, therefore, had the unexpected
pleasure of seeing the *San Salvador* still keeping on her course
up-Channel, but under English management. However, she
soon lagged behind, because Flemyng's ship was only of fifty
tons, and the *San Salvador* by English estimation 600 tons (958
tons by Spanish reckoning).

Her munitions were so vital to the English (and soon were to
be equally needed in the Armada), that Howard sent a message
ashore to Richard Pitt, Mayor of Weymouth and Melcome
Regis, ordering him to tie up the loose ends. Pitt therefore
wrote to all mayors along the coast:

His Lordship hath taken two great carracks or ships from the enemy, sent to the shore, wherein great store of powder and shot in either of them; and requireth that all the said powder and shot be sent unto his Lordship with all possible expedition, for that the state of the realm dependeth upon the present supply of such wants. These are, therefore, in her Majesty's name, straitly to charge and command you, forthwith, upon receipt hereof, you make diligent enquiry to what place the said carracks or ships are gone . . .

That was on Wednesday, 3 August, and received a prompt reply from the Mayor of Lyme Regis:

Received this same day by 9 of the clock in the morning, and have sent out for the same purpose to seek out the same ships; and we see one great ship alone to lie in sight of this town of Lyme, and we think it is one of the ships. John Jones, Mayor.

The Government, however, was much slower off the mark here than they had been in the case of the *Rosario*; a full week passed before their representatives, George Trenchard and Francis Hawley (the latter was deputy vice-admiral), boarded the *San Salvador* to compile an inventory. They complained that they had been

greatly delayed by reason of the far distance of the ship in the bay from this town of Weymouth, and by high winds . . . the carrack is so great that she cannot be brought into this haven. We think it also part of our duties not to conceal from your Lordships the notable spoils that were made upon the ship; the disorder growing so far, as we could very hardly repress it ourselves, the great repair from all places being such. The bolting out of particularities our commission reacheth not unto, but, surely, in the stealing of her sails and cables, etc., the disorder was very great. It is credibly thought that there were in her 200 Venetian barrels of powder of some 120 pounds weight apiece, and yet but 141 were sent to the Lord Admiral. This very night some inkling came unto us that a chest of great weight should be found in the forepeak of the ship the Friday before our dealing; and all search hath been made sithence our coming, but no treasure can be found, and yet we have removed some part of the ballast. We find here no Spaniards of any account, but only one who calleth himself Don Melchor de Pereda, and nine others of the common sort; two Frenchmen, four Almains, and one Almain woman; and since their landing here, twelve more are dead. We humbly beseech your Lordships to give some speedy direction what shall be done with them, for that they are here diseased, naked, and chargeable.

The revenge of the 'German artilleryman' had not even yet run its full course; the *San Salvador* still had many lives to claim.

Medina Sidonia, patient, well-meaning man that he was, had been concentrating during that disastrous Monday of 1 August on what he thought were major issues, beside which the loss of two flagships, shameful though it was, seemed unimportant. The panic and disorder into which the attack of only some seventy English ships had thrown the rear of the Armada, was a clear warning to re-organize and re-impose discipline. His advisers produced a theoretical formation much better able to deal with such attacks in future; he approved it, and had it distributed round the fleet, for 'action that day'. With the order, went the hangmen. The Armada's War Diary records:

The Duke summoned the whole of the sergeant majors (senior military policemen), and ordered each one to go in a patache, and take his instructions round to every ship in the Armada, specifying in writing the position which they should respectively occupy. Orders were also given to them, in writing, to immediately hang any captain whose ship left her place, and they took with them the Provost Marshals and hangmen necessary for carrying out this order.

As the Armada re-grouped in this new formation, Nic Oseley, for one, was impressed.

They are divided, as I do see, twelve in a squadron, and do keep such excellent good order, that if God do not miraculously work, we shall have wherein to employ ourself for some days.

It was a brave threat, and a brave piece of work, from a timid and vacillating leadership; which that night put in a timid and vacillating attack on the English. 'The night fell very calm,' wrote Howard,

and the four galleasses singled themselves out from their fleet, whereupon some doubt was had lest they might have distressed some of our small ships which were short of our fleet, but their courage failed them, for they attempted nothing.

He was now content, for thanks to Medina Sidonia and the advice of Diego Flores, the English were sure enough of their ammunition supplies to mount a battle in the morning, and to 'course' the Spaniards safely past Portland.

10
'Forced to Flock Together Like Sheep'

Athwart of Portland, we had a sharp and long fight with them, wherein we spent a great part of our powder and shot.

John Hawkyns to Walsyngham

Hawkyns had dismissed the Battle of Plymouth, during which the Spanish rear had panicked under the new-style bombardment attack, as 'some small fight'. But the Battle of Portland, he said, was 'sharp and long'. Hawkyns had been a professional fighting businessman all his life, a slave trader among other things; even the excellence of the English ships was mainly his work. His cold verdicts on the Armada battles are not those of an excited tyro, nor are they separated in time, for they all occur in his brief report on the campaign, written for Walsyngham's benefit, on 10 August. He meant exactly what he said, neither less nor more. He could have told much more, of course, which would have been very helpful to historians; but he got paid for fighting, not writing. And, with Drake, his former protégé, he was in the thick of the fighting, timing his attacks to perfection. But in his report he mentioned only those points which seemed to him vital; and in his brief summaries, the ammunition state, the 'powder and shot', is emphasized after every battle, except the first one at Plymouth. Clearly, it was the limiting factor in three out of the four battles. Despite their numerical inferiority, the English could have done much more at Portland, had they not had to hoard ammunition, not knowing how many battles they had yet to fight. The stores of the *Rosario* and the *San Salvador*, 1,600 round shot in the former alone – nearly as much as was expended by the whole English fleet off Plymouth – enabled them to fight one more battle more than they had expected; but how many battles were still to come? On the morning of Tuesday, 2 August, when the Battle of Portland began, the bulk of the captured powder and shot had not yet arrived, or been distributed; but it was money in the bank against present expenditure. The Lord Admiral could afford to loose the reins a little, and allow his men to fight.

Frobisher and associates, the great *Triumph* leading, began to beat up for Portland Bill, working their way inshore into the teeth of the dawn land breeze. They intended to work the fast-flowing Portland 'race' against the Spaniards, and to hold them off from any attempt to get into Weymouth Bay. Howard and kinsmen, plus Hawkyns, also in powerful ships, stood east-wards, parallel to the general lie of the land, but at right angles to the giant dragon's back of the jutting Bill of Portland; they were headed for the heart of the Armada, to 'fix' it, hold it in position, while Frobisher made his difficult and dangerous cast shorewards. The 'old firm', Drake and the fast ships of the Western Squadron, went racing out to sea, aided by the north-east wind, ready to swing round when the wind steadied, and put in at the exactly calculated moment a 'spoiling' attack on the seaward wing of the Armada, 'rolling it up' shorewards in increasing confusion. In fact, a fairly standard and formal sort of plan on military lines, confusing only to naval students long afterwards, obsessed by the semi-comic impasse of two fleets trying to fight each other in 'Fleet Line Ahead'. But that was still very much in the future, and no one engaged off Portland that day had ever heard of it. If anyone had suggested any such thing, they would have dismissed it as irrelevant. The English, in their reports and correspondence, refer with perfect indiffer-ence, sometimes to the Spanish 'army', sometimes to the Spanish 'navy', meaning in both cases the Armada; and they talk indifferently of the English 'army' and the English 'navy', meaning in both cases the English sea forces. In fact, they made no distinction: to them, war was indivisible.

So it was to the Spaniards also, although they were a little old-fashioned, behindhand in taking hold of the new-fangled artillery weapon; they still placed much of their faith in 'conventional' forces – horse and foot. Whereas the English, with no great military tradition to hinder them, were experimenting with the new 'hardware', to see what it would do and how it could best be used. To the more hidebound of the Spaniards, the artillery was an 'ignoble arm', uncolourful, unmanly, and not really fair. Now, having had a taste of it at sea, they had hurriedly revised their formation; but it was still military.

As originally planned, back at Lisbon, and as actually used off Plymouth, it was standard stuff, consisting of the two basic formations used by any formed body of troops: 'Marching Order' and 'Battle Order'. This explains the (to us) infuriating habit of the Spaniards, when they refer to their rear as the 'Vanguard'. Their nomenclature was based on the 'Marching Order' and not the 'Battle Order'. What happened in land operations was this: the army was strung out along a road in four divisions, the Vanguard leading. Behind it came the Centre, or 'Main Battle', including the army commander's HQ, the support weapon groups, and so on. Behind that coiled the baggage train, sometimes a siege train, too, and in the rear, where it ought to be, the Rearguard. As armies spent most of their time marching, not fighting, everyone thought of this formation as the normal one. Then, from up front, came the shout: 'Enemy ahead – under effective fire!' or whatever the current jargon was for that exciting moment. Immediately, three things happened. The Centre, or 'Main Battle', on the word of command, came to a crashing halt on the left foot. The Vanguard about turned and doubled back, inclined out to the right, to take post on the right of the Centre, so forming the right wing. Simultaneously, the Rearguard came up at the double from behind, inclined out to the left, and took post on the left of the Centre, thus forming the left wing. The baggage, or siege train, shuffled to a halt behind the Centre, and looked scared. The army was now arrayed in Order of Battle.

This, with modifications, was what the Armada did off Plymouth on the Sunday, when Medina Sidonia hoisted the Royal Standard to his maintop. The main modification was one imposed by sea warfare (or desert warfare, for that matter); there wasn't a front or a rear in reality. Instead, there was 'All Round Defence', familiar phrase. The Spaniards knew there was one English fleet at Plymouth, and another off Dover; they expected to be between them, and to have to fight facing both ways. Therefore, although the baggage train (the storeships) was in the middle, the Centre, or 'Main Battle', under Medina Sidonia, remaining in position ahead of it, the Vanguard and Rearguard both went to the rear, inclined outwards and backwards in echelon, theoretically able to hold off the Plymouth fleet.

In the event, they were able to do no such thing; and began streaming away in panic and confusion from the English cannonade, so that Medina Sidonia, leading the 'Centre' (which now was actually the head of the fleet), had to double right round to the rear with some of his best ships before he could bring pressure to bear where it was needed. It was this long detour which the new formation, worked out on the Monday, was designed to avoid; it was more compact, very much more 'All Round' in its defence capabilities. The Plymouth formation was described by the English as a 'half-moon', an apt picture of the backward sloping right and left wings formed by the Vanguard and Rearguard respectively. The formation from Portland on, they called a 'plump', or 'roundel', again a descriptive term.

What had been forced on the Spaniards was a total reorganization. The store ships remained in the middle, as before, but everything else was changed, with the main weight of the Armada at the rear instead of at the front. There were two compact fighting divisions now, in place of three separate, loose formations. There was, at the rear, what we may call the 'Battle Group Alonso de Leyva', composed of both the former Vanguard and Rearguard, stiffened by three of the galleasses, plus four strong ships – *San Mateo*, *San Luis*, *Florencia*, and *Santiago* – detached mainly from Medina Sidonia's own squadron. The rest of the fighting ships of Portugal, plus Diego Flores' Castile squadron, and one galleass, remained in front, under the Duke, forming what we may call the 'Battle Group Medina Sidonia'. Don Alonso's appointment was temporary, for he was not an admiral but a general, the Land Forces Commander of the Armada; Recalde was the senior seaman, but his flagship had been so battered by the English off Plymouth that she could not go into action that day, at any rate. De Leyva commanded, wrote the Duke, 'pending the repair of Juan Martinez de Recalde's ship.' The actual positioning and alignment of the ships is not stated, nor does it matter; the main point was to be able to bring a strong force to bear, at the right place, at the right time. And that was the intention of the English also.

The actual processes of the battle are bloated and distorted, in the two main narratives, those of Howard and Medina Sidonia, because neither really knew what he was doing (both were acting under instructions from their juniors), and because they had neither of them been in such an action before. The real fighting experts had their coats off and were working away frenziedly, too busy to write reports, so that the flights of description were left to the amateurs. Consequently, the Duke and the Lord Admiral, thrilled to the core at their own courage, tell their tales on the level of, 'There was I, upside down, at 40,000 feet'. There is a happy, patriotic optimism about them that smacks of the first despatch from the front by a brand new war correspondent.

Few of the eminent scholars who have tried subsequently to find a pattern to the battle have had much success; most of them approvingly quote Camden's baffled, 'It was managed with confusion enough'. Largely, this was because they were looking backwards from the standpoint of fully developed sailing ship warfare between nearly identical fleets, instead of looking forwards with the Elizabethans to a very different problem, solved on military lines. The essence of the tactics developed later was for rival fleets to sail in line ahead past each other; two rulers, placed parallel on a table, would represent that formal encounter. Such battles were rarely decisive, because the fleet which turned in towards the other lost the advantage of its broadside guns. Nelson broke this impasse by going back to the first principle of war – overwhelming numbers at the point of attack. His method varied with the nature of each particular problem, but the object was the same, and it was sound.

The Elizabethans had a particular problem, quite different from any set Nelson, but when the moment for decisive battle came, they used exactly the same principle as he did. But the

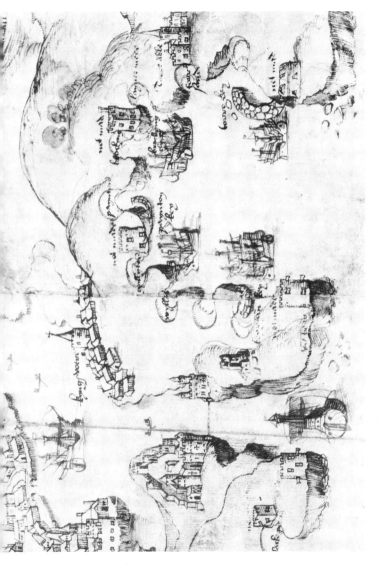

The Port of Plymouth in Henry VIII's time, showing carracks entering or at anchor and the land defences against seaborne attack, which were mainly his work. *Photo: British Library*

Queen Elizabeth I of England. *Photo: National Maritime Museum, Greenwich*

King Philip II of Spain. *Photo: National Maritime Museum, Greenwich*

Mary Rose, a 700-ton pre-Armada carrack built 1509-10, sunk by accident 1545, search begun by the author 1965, found 1966, raised 1982, seen here in 1986. The starboard stern castle is preserved to a maximum height of some 13 metres (42 feet) above the 32 metre (105 feet) long keel. The wreck was found crammed with guns, ammunition,

ABOVE: A miscellany of continental shipping in 1561, described as depicting Spanish carracks and galleons. The two on the left are certainly carracks, one having more guns than the other, including a very large piece amidships. The two vessels on the right are clearly cargo ships, ill-armed or unarmed. The distant ship in the centre is a galleon. The Armada was recruited from vessels as diverse as these and probably very like them. *Photo: Science Museum*

BELOW: The galleon *Ark Royal,* formerly the *Ark Raleigh,* Howard's flagship. Although she retains the high stern castle, the formidable forecastle of the old carrack type, which served as an emplacement for infantry, has been eliminated. The rig remains the same – square sails on fore and main masts, lateen sails on the mizzen and bonaventure-mizzen masts. A better sailer but less defensible. From a line engraving by C J Visscher. *Photo: National Maritime Museum, Greenwich*

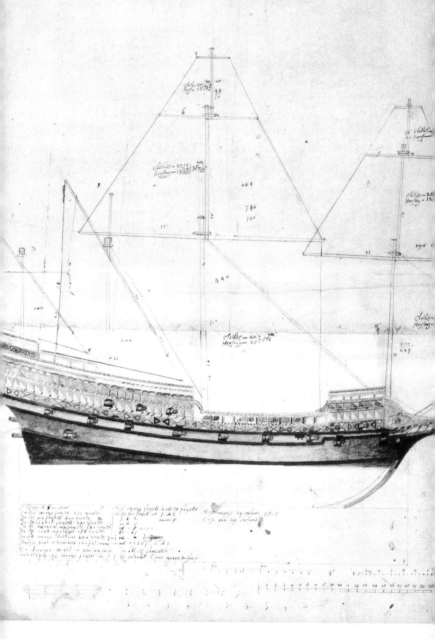

The new-type English galleon which beat the Armada. This draught and sailplan was drawn by Matthew Baker in 1586. Compared to the towering carrack, she has the lines of a racing yacht. Drake's flagship, the *Revenge,* was of this design.

Photo: By permission of the Master and Fellows of Magdalene College, Cambridge

ABOVE: *Vasa,* a post-Armada galleon built 1625-8, sunk by accident 1628, search begun by Anders Franzén 1953, found 1956, raised 1961, intact almost to the upper deck. This is the lower battery deck soon after recovery, showing the success of the 17th century salvors – all the guns bar three were removed from their carriages by divers working from a primitive bell. Some two dozen skeletons of crew members and passengers were found in and around the wreck. *Photo: Vasa Museum*

BELOW: The upper deck of the *Vasa* in 1973, looking aft past the knightheads and capstan to the stern castle, with workmen replacing some of the deck planks which had been torn off by anchors during her three centuries underwater.
Photo: Alexander McKee

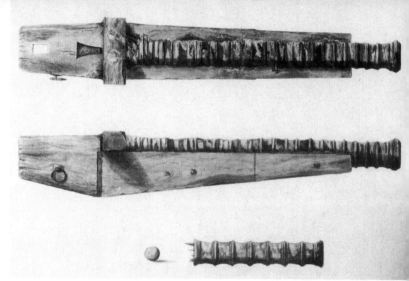

ABOVE: A wrought-iron breech-loading 'port piece' of 1545, found in the *Mary Rose* by John Deane in 1836. A number of Armada ships included such obsolete weapons among their armament in 1588.

Photo: Alexander McKee

BELOW: John Deane also raised three different types of bronze gun from the *Mary Rose,* recording them in a portfolio of water-colour drawings. This illustration shows: Top, a Cannon Royal, a short gun firing a large iron shot (bore shown right in bottom row); Centre, a Culverin Bastard, a small, shortened version of the long-range heavy culverin (bore shown centre in bottom row); Below, a Demi-Cannon, a heavy gun but firing a lighter shot (bore shown left in bottom row) than the Cannon Royal. All were still in use at the time of the Armada and for long afterwards. *Photo: Alexander McKee*

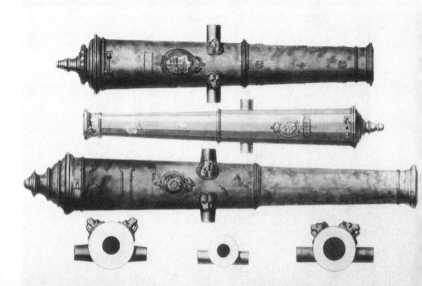

ABOVE: Lord Charles Howard, Earl of Effingham. From an oil painting by D Mytens. *Photo: National Maritime Museum, Greenwich*

ABOVE: Sir Martin Frobisher. From a line engraving by C van de Passe. *Photo: National Maritime Museum, Greenwich*

BELOW: Sir John Hawkyns. From an oil painting by an unknown artist. *Photo: National Maritime Museum, Greenwich*

BELOW: Sir Francis Drake. From an oil painting by an unknown artist. *Photo: National Maritime Museum, Greenwich*

The Battle of Plymouth, showing the small English Western Fleet harassing the Armada, which is sailing in crescent formation. The artist has inserted at lower left the later incident of the capture of the *Rosario* by the *Revenge*; one of the small ships here is possibly Captain Cely's. From a line engraving by J Pine after

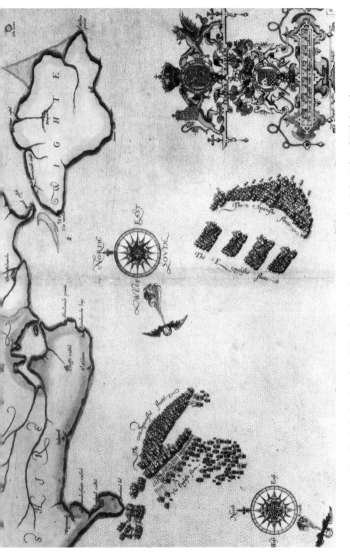

On the left the Battle of Portland and, centre, south of the Isle of Wight, the Armada still in crescent or 'half moon' formation but the English fleet now divided into four or more manageable squadrons, according to Adam's Chart No. 6, a contemporary document. *Photo: National Maritime Museum, Greenwich*

DVNE. NOSE

The Battle of the Isle of Wight under Dunnose cliff, the English ships being towed and manoeuvred by their boats in a dead calm, and the two Spanish galleasses rowing to the rescue of the *Duquesa Santa Ana*, bottom left. From a

Launching the fire-ships against the Armada off Calais, with the scratch crews returning in rowing boats to the now reinforced English fleet. From a line engraving by J Pine after C de Lempriere. *Photo: National Maritime Museum, Greenwich*

The fight for the flag-galleass *San Lorenzo* off Calais. Boats and pinnaces attack the stranded enemy in the shallows, while Howard waits further out in deeper water. From a line engraving by J Pine after C de Lempriere. *Photo: National Maritime Museum, Greenwich*

ABOVE: *Santa Maria de la Rosa*. The inscription 'Matute' on the edge of a pewter plate which finally identified the wreck. Francisco Ruiz Matute was a captain in the Sicilian *tercio,* who was known to have sailed in this ship. *Photo: Colin Martin*

BELOW: *La Trinidad Valencera*. A gun carriage wheel, for use on land with the siege train of the Spanish Army, lying on the seabed off Donegal, where the ship broke up. Some heavy guns did go with the Armada, but it was difficult to emplace them in the ships on their ordinary field carriages, and most were probably carried below in the hold. The *Mary Rose* mounted her heavy guns on purpose-built shop carriages, but large wheels like this one, for use ashore, were stored below in the fore part of the carrack. *Photo: Colin Martin*

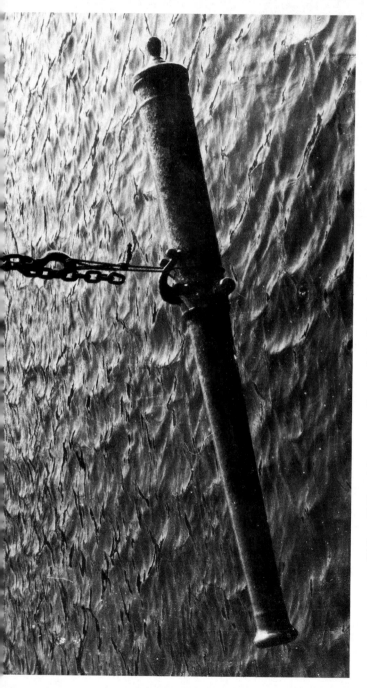

El Gran Grifon. A bronze *media sacre* being hoisted ashore at Fair Isle. Although this ship was armed only with such light guns, she was in the forefront of the fighting. Many English musket shot, part-flattened by impact on her hull, were found at the wreck site; and more than half of her listed ammunition was never fired at her enemies, being found by the divers nearly four centuries later.

Channel encounters were not meant to be decisive. The English object was to knock the Spaniards off balance at the right moments and so prevent landing. And the method they used was the orthodox military one of beating the enemy, not so much by fighting, as by disorganizing him. Even the finest troops in the world lose most of their effectiveness when some are jammed tightly together, others are scattered, and all cohesion is lost. One way of doing this is by deep penetration, separating front from rear. Another, equally classic method, is the 'Cannae' – the double-envelopment. The enemy's attention is held or 'fixed' in the centre by a dummy attack, while his flanks are rolled up by simultaneous attacks on both wings; if this comes off, his formations are so jammed together that they cannot fight effectively and, if the pressure can be kept up, eventually become a mere struggling mob. Viewed in this light, which was a normal one for Elizabethan times, both the Portland and Isle of Wight battles suddenly make sense; the obvious confusion is explained.

Naval historians normally fall back upon the weather as a cause for confusion; their narratives explain this move or that by reference to an unexpected change in direction of the wind. This extreme capriciousness of their wind lends excitement and drama to the story, as they describe how so-and-so found himself in consequence in some unexpected and intolerable situation. Poor Frobisher is blackguarded right and left, and Drake seems somehow a magician, always in the right position at the right moment, as if he had a crystal ball handy. In fact, of course, he had; they all had. It is only the scholars who find the repeated changes in wind direction unexpected.

The truth, less suspenseful perhaps, but more satisfying, is that summer winds in the Channel form a pattern which is about ninety-eight per cent predictable. Yachtsmen tend to put off at the last civilized moment, between 9 and 9.30 in the morning, with the last of the land breeze from the north. Then they expect a spot of calm lasting for half an hour or an hour, before the standard south-westerly gets up. Motorized amateur divers study wind force and direction, too, because these are vital factors in predicting probable underwater visibility and may mean the cancelling or diversion of a previously planned expedition. And all along the line from Looe, in Cornwall, to Brighton, in Sussex, their logbooks record the present-day facts: twice only, perhaps, was the prevailing wind from the north, the best direction for diving; on every other occasion the wind was in the southern arc, usually south-west. Steadily, monotonously, infuriatingly from the south-west. Just as it was for the Armada. Absolutely standard. You could bet on it.

Obviously, Drake bet on it, too. He probably had an alternative plan as well, but as it turned out, he had no need to use it. The usual interchange of warm land air with cold sea air took place as the sun rose, and a gentle breeze blew from the north-east. Theoretically, that gave the Spaniards the weather-gauge, for what it was worth; actually, it gave the galleasses a chance to see what they could do, light winds or dead calm being their designed operating conditions. The English fleet split into three, and then four sections; the whole fleet first stood north-west, across wind, towards the shore. The Armada obediently followed, upwind of the English; the Spaniards were chasing the English, the English were running! The crowd of under-employed spectators in the Spanish fleet, from Medina Sidonia to Estrade, began to get excited. Then orders crackled in the English fleet, sails flapped momentarily, they spun round in their tracks in a large reversal of course, and approached the Spaniards at an angle, luffed very close to the wind. There was going to be a battle! They were going to be able to board! They were going to wipe out the disgrace of Plymouth!

The Duke was urging on his men in a surge of happiness he had not believed possible. Bertondona was the first favourite. There he goes in the great *La Reganzona*, 1,249 tons; he's closing their flagship, yes, he's got her, she's turning away, he's pressing alongside, no, he isn't, oh well, he got quite near anyway. Ah, here come the rest, they'll catch her! *San Marcos, San Luis, San Mateo, La Rata, Santa Ana, San Felipe, San Juan de Sicilia, Florencia, Santiago,* the *San Juan* of Don Diego Enriquez (newly appointed to command Don Pedro's old squadron) and, straining along in the rear, the giant Levanter *La Trinidad Valencera*, flagship of the Battle Group Don Alonso de Leyva. The Duke's heart swelled with patriotic Spanish pride, as the great galleons and carracks, with their high castles and glistening, glittering paintwork, bellying sails and stiff banners snapping in the breeze, bore down on the enemy flagship; he noted the names of them all, as they went down to the attack as if in review, and the battle smoke went bellying across the sea from the mouths of a hundred guns.

They were broken, the English! There was a group of them, huddled under the land, cut off from the rest of their fleet. Prey for the galleasses! They could be boarded and taken, every one! He was going to win a naval battle, he, the quiet gentleman who preferred the land! But he would deserve it! He would intervene! He had a personal direction sent at once to Hugo de Moncada's flag galleass *San Lorenzo*, to get that great English ship, probably a Portuguese Indiaman, cut off there with her consorts under the land. And he waited with feverish impatience for de Moncada to run her alongside, and let the Spanish infantry swarm up over her insolent bulwarks, and have that English flag run down.

The excitement of the action infected everyone on the Spanish side, for the English ships in the centre were accepting battle, close battle, and the scene was constantly shifting. Wrote Estrade enthusiastically, in the *San Marcos*:

We gave chase to the enemy, the galleasses with some other ships wearing into them, playing with their ordnance, turning in the wind from the south-west to the south-east, fighting with us, and there was great store of cannon shot. The flagship of Juan Martinez de Recalde came entering in from the south-east, and with him and Juan Gomez de Medina, in the *Gran Grifon*, flagship of the hulks, and other ships, we came so nigh unto the enemy Vice-Admiral that with one piece of cast-iron we shot two bullets into the Vice-Admiral of the English, and there was great shot of ordnance.

Even the storeships were fighting the English! It was incredible! In fact, so excited were the Spaniards that two gunners in one of the hulks forgot their gun drill, neglected to sponge out the gun after firing, and shoved the fresh powder bag down the hot muzzle, still reeking with fragments of blazing powder. They lived, but were badly burnt. Two gunners in Calderon's ship, the vice-flag hulk *San Salvador*, did the same thing, and the resulting explosion killed both of them.

In fact, the 'holding' force in the centre, under Howard and Hawkyns, had done its job and 'fixed' the bulk of the de Leyva Battle Group. *Ark Royal, Golden Lion, White Bear, Elizabeth Jonas, Victory*, and *Nonpareil*, firing with better guns far better served, gave better than they got; and with their speed and mobility, even in light winds, ran the Spaniards close alongside without allowing them to board. Drake was not present; he was going fast out of it, seaward under cover of the southward drifting gunsmoke of the main battle. Soon, fifty English ships, shrouded in the clouds of smoke from the cannonading, had gone out to sea with the last of the land breeze.

Meanwhile, the battle under Portland Bill had been going on for an hour and a half, and de Moncada had achieved nothing. Frobisher had got himself into a position from which he could block any Spanish attempt to break into Weymouth Bay; apart from the *Triumph*, he had five of the London ships with him, including the *Margaret and John*. The four galleasses, urged by the Duke to get alongside them with 'both sail and oar', had now been backed up by a horde of great ships – Gaspar de Sosa's *Florencia*, Oquendo's *Santa Ana*, Garibay's *Begoña*, Maldonada's *San Juan Bautista*, and Don Alonso de Luzon himself in *La Trinidad Valencera*. The furiously impatient Medina Sidonia could see the galleasses swept by the racing, boiling current very close to the *Triumph*, their oars flailing the water, but never actually closing to board. In fury and disgust, he had the bows of the *San Martin* turned in that direction and bore down to give a hand himself, but it was too late. That night, he sent a written reprimand to Don Hugo de Moncada: 'A fine day this has been! If the galleasses had come up as I expected the enemy would have had his fill.'

But de Moncada was a galley man, which was why he had been chosen to command the Neapolitan galleasses squadron, and he was used to tideless smiling seas. What Frobisher had made him try to negotiate was Portland Race which, on a high spring tide, runs up to seven knots. It can be done, of course, but to 'work' it as Frobisher was doing required local knowledge of a highly specialized kind, and a good deal of cold nerve. Given understanding of its mechanism, a 'race' and its accompanying 'eddy' gives effortless power of movement in two opposite directions; in fact, it was to Frobisher at least as helpful as a bank of oars either side of the *Triumph*. If one can imagine three moving roadways, the outside one doing two knots in one direction, the middle one doing seven knots in the same direction, and the inside one doing one knot in the opposite direction, one sees the possibilities. But to penetrate the powerful, driving curtains of water – for they descend vertically with sharply defined faces – is initially intimidating. Further, the eddy and the race are linked like the tracks of a tank, and the speed difference between them is absorbed by circular 'boilings' which are the opposite of whirlpools, boiling up in the centre, sliding under at the sides. To venture a heavy ship into that, within a stone's throw of a rocky shore, would be enough to make a stranger catch his breath. Frobisher could do it because he knew for certain that he had deep water close inshore. Today, the sides of Portland Bill slope down very steeply underwater, covered with large rocks and boulders fallen probably from the cliffs above, to a depth of between sixty and seventy feet and, eventually, out in Weymouth Bay, merge into a flat, sandy bottom; in Frobisher's time it was probably much the same. De Moncada cannot have understood, for Frobisher repeated the trick two days later, and got away with it again.

Sir Arthur Gorgas, looking back on the lessons of the battle that day between Frobisher's ships and the oared galleasses of de Moncada, wrote:

Our towboats may aid us to wind about [aim] our broadsides and so can bestow our great ordnance for our own defence and in offence of them.

According to the diarist of the galleass *Zuniga*, which was engaged against Frobisher, they first went into action at eight o'clock. According to Howard, the galleasses 'were very well resisted by those ships (Frobisher's) for the space of an hour and half, when at length certain of her Majesty's ships bare with them, and then the galleasses forsook them.' The diarist of the *Zuniga* agrees:

While we were attacking the great ship of the enemy and two other ships, five of the enemy's galleons bore down upon our galleasses; the

wind at this time having suddenly shifted, so that the enemy had it
astern whilst we had it against us, and consequently none of our ships
could come to our aid. The galleasses therefore had to run and join
the rest of the Armada.

According to Calderon, 'at ten o'clock the wind shifted to the
south'; i.e., at the usual time for the wind change.

   Howard agrees:

The wind then shifted to the south-eastwards and so to SSW, at what
time a troop of her Majesty's ships and sundry merchants' assailed the
Spanish fleet so sharply to the westward that they were all forced to
give way and to bear room.

Captain Vanegas, an Armada witness, agrees:

The enemy's *capitana* with fifty other ships got the wind of us, and
that they could well do because of their extreme nimbleness and the
great smoke that came from the artillery; and they charged upon the
right wing of our Armada.

   There it was, then, the standard land battle fought at sea, in
the standard wind conditions of the English Channel. The left
wing (Frobisher) working round the enemy's inshore flank, to
prevent him edging into Weymouth Bay; the centre (Howard
and Hawkyns) fixing the enemy with a close battle which
sucked in most of his best ships and held them there for ninety
minutes; while Drake and 'the merchant ships appointed to
serve westwards under his charge' escaped under cover of the
smokescreen provided by the battle in the centre, and were
ready, when the wind swung round to south-west, to put in a
spoiling attack on the enemy's seaward flank and roll it up.
Which it certainly did, in spite of Medina Sidonia's brave and
desperate efforts to stop it.
   This was the final phase of the action, in which Howard and
Medina Sidonia at last encountered each other gun muzzle to
gun muzzle but not, as the Duke hoped, quarterdeck to
quarterdeck. The immediate cause of their encounter was that
the left wing of the double-envelopment – Frobisher's ships –
was nothing like strong enough for that classic task, and
probably the English had nothing so ambitious in mind. He was

to act merely as 'longstop', a kind of sliding longstop, riding up and down on the race or the eddy, able to go sweeping into Weymouth Bay at high speed simply by moving twenty yards from one current to the other, if he so desired. Anyway, at this moment, as Drake's seaward attack developed and began to roll up the right wing of the Armada shorewards, Howard thought Frobisher hard-pressed. So, in order to take the pressure off him, and simultaneously 'fix' the centre of the Armada so that Drake's move could have maximum effect, he attacked directly eastward at the centre of gravity of the enemy fleet. He did not go directly towards Frobisher; that would be 'wet hen' tactics. And as this was the decisive moment, which would crumple up the Armada and remove any threat to Portland, he made clear that the punch must have weight behind it.

His Lordship called unto certain of her Majesty's ships then near at hand and charged them straitly to follow him, and to set freshly upon the Spaniards, and to go within musket-shot of the enemy before they should discharge any one piece of ordnance.

There is always a tendency, at first, to fire too soon in a blaze of happy optimism. That the English leaders had already realized this and were trying to check the tendency, Ubaldino makes clear, for after paraphrasing Howard's order to close to musket-shot range, he adds, what he must have learned from Drake and Howard: 'because that was the true method of helping friendly ships with the greatest damage to the enemy.' There was one other good reason for really closing with them at that moment. If a lucky Spanish shot should disable an English ship now it did not matter in the least; the Armada would soon be in no position at all to snap her up as a prize. Had that happened earlier in the morning it would have mattered a great deal.

Howard's close-fight orders were, he recorded, 'very well performed by the *Ark*, the *Elizabeth Jonas*, the *Galleon of Leicester*, the *Golden Lion*, the *Victory*, the *Mary Rose*, the *Dreadnought* and the *Swallow* – for so they went in order into the fight.' They must have made a brave sight – Howard was obviously stirred – as the great English galleons, heeled over to

port under the pull of their stiff-bellying sails, slid through the
waves with the silver spray creaming back under their bows and
tumbling astern; for the breeze was stiffening, and the English
ships worked best under these conditions. Compared to the
Spaniards, they looked like racing yachts. There the comparison ended, for the green and white paint of their sides was
abruptly broken by double rows of gun-ports, heavy guns on
the lower deck, lighter pieces on the upper deck. That threat
did exactly what it was intended to do. 'Which the Duke of
Medina perceiving,' wrote Howard 'came out with 16 of his
best galleons, to impeach his Lordship and stop him assisting
of the *Triumph*.'

Medina Sidonia's own narrative shows how it looked to the
other side:

Soon afterwards, the enemy's ships returned, with the wind and tide
in their favour, and attacked Juan Martinez de Recalde in the
rearguard. Don Alonso de Leyva reinforced him, and my flagship,
which was in the midst of the main squadron, sailed to the support of
those ships of the rearguard which were mixed up with the enemy's
rearguard (Frobisher and his reinforcements) and were separated from
the mass of both fleets.

The Armada was in a fine old tizzy, with the Battle Group
Medina Sidonia forced to help de Leyva, who was helping
Recalde, who was soon in bad trouble.

The Duke ordered Captain Marolin de Juan (the Armada's fleet
navigator) to go in a feluca and try to guide the vessels which were
near the Duke's flagship to the support of Juan Martinez de Recalde.
When this was effected, the enemy left Juan Martinez, and attacked
the Duke's flagship, which was isolated and on her way to the
assistance of the said ships.

By now both sides had got their enemy's flagships sorted out;
they now knew roughly who was who, whereas, off Plymouth,
any large and important looking ship was judged to be the
enemy leader. So when Howard's battle group left Recalde and
bore down on the *San Martin*, the Duke knew that here was his
chief opponent, a nobleman of his own rank and station, who,
judging from the closeness of the action, might let him grapple
and board; but he was terribly disappointed.

When my flagship saw that the flagship of the enemy was leading towards her, she lowered her topsails, but the enemy's flagship passed her, followed by the whole of his fleet, and shot at her, ship by ship, as it passed. Our guns were served well and fast . . .

'The *San Martin* returned their fire with so much gallantry,' wrote Don Jorge Manrique, 'that from one side alone she fired off 100 shots, and the enemy did not care to come to close quarters with her.'

She was reinforced by Oquendo's flagship, which managed to join her and help her gallantly in her brave fight [wrote Calderon]. The *San Martin* fired over 80 shots from one side only, and inflicted great damage on the enemy. The latter shot at the Duke at least 500 cannon balls, some of which struck his hull, and others his rigging, carrying away his flagstaff and one of the stays of his mainmast.

'The galleon *San Martin* did bear room with us, and played with her cannon almost with all the whole English army in such sort that for more than one hour we could not see her for smoke,' wrote Estrade, enthusiastically.

'My flagship was in the hottest of the fight,' wrote the Duke; and although she was eventually reinforced by Recalde, de Leyva, Oquendo, and the Marquis de Penafiel in the *San Marcos*, he added, complacently, 'they did not come up until the hottest fury was passed.'

The Lord Admiral was always in the hottest of the encounter [wrote Howard proudly, of his own part in the action], and it may well be said that for the time there was never seen a more terrible value of great shot, nor more hot fight than this was; for although the musketeers and harquebusiers of crock (manning heavy muskets on a mounting) were then infinite, yet could they not be discerned nor heard for that the great ordnance came so thick that a man would have judged it to have been a hot skirmish of small shot, being all the fight long within half musket shot of the enemy. At which assault, after wonderful sharp conflict, the Spaniards were forced to flock together like sheep.

The plan had worked, and Drake's seaward attack had rolled up the right wing on the centre, but Howard singled out for praise only one man: 'William Coxe, captain of a small pinnace of Sir William Wynter's, named the *Delight*, showed himself most valiant in the face of his enemies at the hottest of the encounter; he afterwards lost his life in the service with a great shot.' Of course, this happened under Howard's own eyes; the battle smoke was so dense that the whole scene, so terrible and novel to these men, could not be made out by any one witness. They were stunned, deafened, utterly weary with the day-long cannonade and the continuous work and excitement, the typical nervous drain of battle. That was the end of the action, except for a small Spanish sortie in the evening, by four or five ships, which was beaten back by the *Mayflower* of London and some other ships showing, as Ubaldino remarked, 'great daring, tempered with prudence'. The rest, with that strange joy that comes of being still unexpectedly alive after passing through an inferno of shrieking, howling, whining missiles, had leisure at last to discover, as usual, that the damage, for all that, was relatively light.

Don Jorge Manrique, Inspector General of the Armada, reported: 'The enemy retired, without having inflicted any notable damage on us.' The Duke claimed, doubtfully: 'The enemy admiral shortened sail, having as it seemed to us, sustained some damage.' The main English preoccupation, however, was not with damage, but the ability in the future, the very near future, to inflict it again on the enemy. For, Hawkyns grumbled, 'We had spent a great part of our powder and shot, so that it was not thought good to deal with them any more till that was remedied.' They had 'coursed the enemy' off from all chance of landing in Weymouth Bay, had he intended to do so; in so doing, they had shot away most of their ready-use ammunition; and the Armada was now within very close distance of the Isle of Wight, where a landing must definitely, not just possibly, be expected. A month ago, Howard had warned: 'The Spanish fleet may come to the Isle of Wight, which for my part I think they will attempt.' In fact, on this very day, Admiral Seymour in the Narrows, having just received a report from Drake of the Battle of Plymouth, written in haste immediately afterwards, was himself writing to the Council:

I do send your Lordships Sir Francis Drake's letter, by the which you shall understand the state of the Spanish army, how forward they be;

and as to our opinions here, we conjecture still their purpose may be to land in the Isle of Wight, to recover the same – which God forbid. Thus humbly praying your Lordships to send us powder and shot forthwith, whereof we have want in our fleet, and which I have divers times given knowledge thereof, I humbly take my leave. From aboard the *Rainbow*, at anchor a quarter seas over against Dover, the 23rd of July [2 August], 1588, at 11 of the clock at night.

The ammunition state was critical, not merely in Howard's part of the fleet, but in those squadrons also which lay still ahead of them, blockading Parma.

11

'To Win an Honourable Death'

On Wednesday, 3 August, there was a lull. The winds were light, the English almost out of ammunition. The two fleets drifted slowly eastwards along the coast of Dorset, until at evening the southern cliffs of the Isle of Wight were visible ahead. The moment of decision was approaching. Dorset was almost frighteningly rugged: great, grey cliffs reared up hundreds of feet, the lines of the rock strata distorted into a crazy pattern of arcs smeared here and there with green patches of vegetation; great natural arches sprang straight out of the cold, clear depths. Inland, the hills were high and forbidding. There was no landing here. In the distance, the chalk cliffs of the Isle of Wight shone white; there was no landing there, either. The anchorage and the landing place were beyond the island, between its northern coast and the mainland at Portsmouth. Therefore, the Armada kept 'the direct trade', the headland-to-headland course that led from the seaward tip of the dragon-backed Bill of Portland to the looming bulk of Dunnose height, higher even than the white cliffs below it that formed the southern cape of the island. Exactly 352 years later, in July, 1940, the radar station on Dunnose was picking up the first Luftwaffe formations to venture into the area on business; and four days after the anniversary of the Armada fight, another desperate battle took place under Dunnose, as the roaring formations surged in and, one by one, like high-divers plunging from a board, the *sturzkampfers* of Richthofen's Fliegerkorps peeled off and went screaming down on a battered British convoy, until all the water south of the Wight, for many miles, was littered with strange wreckage. And above, the thunder of the guns, the white puffs of blossoming smoke, the shrill whine of diving fighters and the drum-roll of machine-gun batteries. But the fighter pilots who went down that day on the bombers, and the seamen caught in the exploding chaos of an erupting sea, fought with Drake and Hawkyns and Howard behind them. They fought for an inviolate island that had never been conquered, and would not be, even now.

But Drake, and Hawkyns, and Howard, and Frobisher, too, had no such tradition behind them. Instead, they had a tradition to reverse – that England fell easily into the lap of a conqueror, and that the Isle of Wight was especially vulnerable. It was only forty-three years since, in King Harry's time, a French fleet had penetrated into St Helen's Roads. Many times the towns of Portsmouth and Southampton, and villages without number that lay inland of the easy, sandy beaches of the low-lying coast to the eastward, had been stormed, sacked, and burnt by soldiers landing out of enemy ships. And dead men lay in the ditches, where they had been cut down by the invaders, merciless enough in the swift and brutal way of soldiers; but not followed, as the new Spanish professionals would be, by black-garbed torturers guided by renegade Englishmen, perhaps even helped by Englishmen ashore. Sir George Carey, commander of the Wight garrison, with his headquarters centrally placed at Carisbrooke Castle, had his watchers out on the southern cliffs to look for their coming, and the troops of this most important outpost camped and assembled, ready to 'impeach' a landing. The mainland opposite was held by Henry Ratcliffe, Earl of Sussex, styled 'Constable of Portchester Castle, Warden and Captain of the town, castle and isle of Portsmouth.'

Reluctant as they were to strip their forces to the point of impotence, both responded to Howard's appeals. Two days later, Sussex was to write: 'I have sent him so much powder and shot as that I have altogether unfurnished myself.' As he was Howard's first cousin, he probably replied to the appeal more readily than is usual in modern times. Carey had sent Howard 'four ships and a pinnace sufficiently furnished with mariners and soldiers' on the very day of the Battle of Portland, and the following day, 3 August, sent 'another pinnace unto him with an hundred men; but he returned them unto me with great thanks, willing the captain to tell me that he had as many men as he desired or could use.'

In London, the Council directed, 'that in the county of Kent a good number of the best and choicest shot of the trained bands in the said county should be sent forthwith to the seaside, that they be brought out to double man the ships.' The Council wanted prizes, they wanted to hear of captured Spanish vessels, so they were sending Howard the pick of the coastal Home Guard, whom Howard in due course returned, with thanks, as he had Carey's company sent out in the pinnace.

In fact, war fever was running high. Leicester, with 4,000 men, was at Chelmsford, north of the Thames, ready to repel a landing on that side of the estuary; the Thames boom was being hurriedly strengthened to prevent the heavy Spanish ships from breaking it by ramming. Great events were imminent, threatening the very capital of England. So intense was the feeling of standing in the open on a great stage, for which the play was even now being composed by a more than human dramatist, that all sorts of people suddenly began stampeding for the footlights. The most surprising characters succeeded in joining the fleet. On 3 August, Sir Horatio Palavicino, a Genoese banker high in the confidence of the Government, and personal friend of the chief Spanish intelligence agent in London, wrote to Walsyngham that he no longer wished to serve with the Earl of Leicester, declaring:

The greatness of my zeal, which desireth to be amongst those who do fight for her Majesty's service and for the defence of her kingdom, doth constrain me, with an honourable company, to depart as this night toward Portsmouth, there to embark and join the Lord Admiral, where I hope to be present in the battle, and thereby a partaker in the victory or to win an honourable death . . .

And so Sir Horatio, with his 'honourable company', rode through the night towards the battle and, before they even reached Portsmouth, must have heard the sound of the guns, thundering out in the Channel.

While the citizens of London prepared their leather firebuckets, with which each household had been provided – for the 'fire' in 'fire and sword' was no idle word – the worthies of

Torbay watched Spanish soldiers marching through the town, the brown-burned men of the *tercios*, or regiments, a word as ominous as 'Panzer Division' was to be 352 years later. Women watched them, old men, children – but hardly any Englishman of martial age; for the men of Torbay were mariners, and every mariner that England had, be he ocean explorer or inshore fisherman, was with the fleet. In fact, the *Rosario* was being worked into Torbay by her Spanish crew, under armed guard; there were not enough English seamen left to do it. But the marching Spanish soldiers were received with hatred. George Cary of Cockington, the Devonshire Cary, not to be confused with the Hampshire Carey who was holding the Isle of Wight, reported to the Council the 'greatest discontentment of our countryside, that a nation so much disliking of them, our vowed enemies, should remain amongst them.' Don Pedro de Valdes, however, later testified that many of the 'said poor people were raised by them and were their neighbours, and came in this employment for the love and zeal that they bear unto them', which was doubtless true. The English, however, were in no mood to consider why the Spaniards had come, but only that they had come.

From the Bill of Portland to the Isle of Wight is forty miles, but the Needles Channel is narrow, and the Armada was making for the Spithead entrance by St Helen's, a distance of a further twenty-five miles. With light winds lasting all day on the Wednesday, 3 August, and the rival fleets making less than two knots, anyone who cared to could have kept easy pace with the ships by walking along the cliff tops from Lulworth to Swanage, or obtained a grander panorama from along the crest of the Purbeck Hills; and doubtless, many did. From the heights of Chale, Bonchurch and Dunnose, in the Wight, the coming of the Spaniards could have been seen for half the day.

But there was very little to see, apart from a brief flurry of gunfire at first light, when some English ships made a dawn attack on the rear of the Armada, in which Medina Sidonia claimed hits on an enemy flagship. He gives details, but Howard reported merely:

There was little done, for that in the fights on Sunday and Tuesday much of our munition had been spent, and therefore the Lord Admiral sent divers barks and pinnaces unto the shore for a new supply of such provisions.

He also, as we know, sent back Carey's pinnace and its one hundred men; and was to reject in turn the soldiers of the trained bands of Kent. We know that he was short of victuals, as well as powder and shot, and he probably thought both food and powder would pay better dividends if fed to his mariners and gunners than if shared out also among a host of semi-trained soldiers. But this was to get him into trouble at Court, later on. Just as Lord Dowding had to face a court of enquiry after winning the Battle of Britain, so Howard had to face his accusers after he had beaten the Spaniards. In both cases, London expected too much. They wanted annihilation; and they did not get it. The Luftwaffe was beaten, but still in being, after the Battle of Britain; the Armada was beaten, but still in being, after Howard, Hawkyns, Drake and the rest had finished with it. But only numbers can annihilate; and by order of the Council, a substantial group of formidable English ships were being deliberately immobilized, 'half seas over from Dover'. Howard was still outnumbered. Even if he had not been, a handful of half-trained infantry did not allow him to board a fleet of high-charged ships carrying something like 18,000 soldiers, 10,000 of them highly trained professionals. England had no such force, nor could she afford one.

Both sides made use of the pause on that peaceful Wednesday, for a re-organization. The Spaniards, Recalde's *San Juan* having been made battle-worthy again, divided their rear into two squadrons – one commanded by de Leyva, the other by Recalde, but with Recalde in overall command; Medina Sidonia still commanding the battle group at the head of the formation. The Armada was now divided, so to speak, into one powerful battle group under the Duke, with two 'Don Columns' of twenty ships each in the rear. The English, on the other hand, rationalized their three existing, untidy battle groups – Frobisher and some of the London ships; Drake and the Western Squadron; and Lord Howard and kinsmen, with Hawkyns in close attendance to see that he did not do anything foolish. Howard had obviously passed the test now, for they ceased holding his hand, and formed four squadrons.

We know Frobisher commanded the inshore squadron, we know that Howard had sole command of the next squadron in line, we know that Hawkyns was next to him and to seaward, therefore Drake was on the extreme seaward wing, as far away from Frobisher as they could get him, and also in the most vital position from the point of view of the intended battle plan. Very probably also, Frobisher, an explorer with nothing like the fighting experience of Drake and Hawkyns, had special tidal knowledge and could make best use of the various 'races' in which this stretch of water abounds. Once again, the personal factor had to be considered; as it obviously was by the Spaniards, in allowing de Leyva to retain part of his temporary command. He had great prestige as a chivalrous soldier, and had serving with him in the *Rata Encoronada* the pick of the younger sons of the nobility of Spain.

The English must have been satisfied with the success of their battle plan, as it had worked off Portland, for they now intended to employ it off the Wight, but with greater weight on the right wing. Adams's Chart No. 6, published in 1590 to illustrate both the Battle of Portland and the re-organization of the English fleet into four squadrons on the following day, shows clearly what it was; indeed, it is obvious enough already, from a study of the combined English and Spanish narratives, and the chart serves merely as additional confirmation. Great stress has been laid on the 'military' organization of the Armada, derived, obviously, from the parade-ground manoeuvres of galley fleets. But the plan which the English are using is military also; as indeed it would have to be, given the tough hedgehog formation for all round defence into which the Armada had been re-organized after Plymouth.

It is the typical double-envelopment plan, familiar to military students from Hannibal on, and still used at all levels, from Army Group to platoon. It has survived all weapon changes, because it works – given sufficient force. If the force available is somewhat weak, the result is not annihilation, but a crowding together of the enemy's ranks which makes it very difficult for him to manoeuvre. Put in at the right moment, when the Armada was preparing to land troops on defended beaches – an operation requiring exact spacing and timing of the assault formations – the landings would be thrown completely out of gear and could not in fact be attempted without the risk of complete disaster. The particular variant of the plan used by the English was the obvious one, when one flank of the enemy is jammed up against an immovable or impassable obstacle; in this case, the English cliffs with a tide race at their foot. Then, the main weight is directed at the other, exposed flank, so that the enemy is squeezed laterally against this immovable obstacle. In this context, a 'right hook'. A Spanish witness off Portland thought the right hook had fifty ships in it, but he probably exaggerated in his excitement – large formations always look much larger than they really are. The Adams's Chart of the battle shows the main weight employed in the centre by the holding force; he is probably right, for at Portland the centre consisted not of Howard's group alone, but Hawkyns's as well. No doubt, after that battle, and with the far more vital battle of the Wight still to come, Drake and Howard must have said, with von Schlieffen: 'Keep the right wing strong!' The new formation for four squadrons would allow that: Frobisher taking up the 'stop' position under the cliffs, Howard attacking in the centre with the holding force, and not less than two squadrons, those of Drake and Hawkyns, combined to deliver the all-important roll-up punch from seaward – the 'right hook'. All perfectly possible, provided the wind kept to the routine pattern of the Channel. But it did not, and because the fate of England might hang on this conflict, the English had to resort to desperate measures to get the battle going as planned.

In fact, the wind died away altogether on the night of 3–4 August, thus frustrating an English night attack which was to have been put in by twenty-four armed merchant ships – six from each of the four squadrons. This, if it could have been done, would, at minimum risk and cost, have kept the Spaniards on the jump all night and so have facilitated considerably the main assault early next morning.

When the sun rose up behind the hills of Wight on Thursday

and drove away the shadows from the gently stirring sea, both fleets, with flapping sails, and in no great order, lay motionless on the waves for many miles, stretching southward from the island almost out of sight.

12
'South of This Island Six Leagues'

By the occasion of the scattering of one of the great ships from the fleet, which we hoped to have cut off, there grew a hot fray, wherein some store of powder was spent.

John Hawkyns to Walsyngham

'This morning began a great fight betwixt both fleets, south of this island six leagues,' wrote Sir George Carey at dusk on the night of 4 August. 'It continued from five of the clock until ten, with so great expense of powder and bullet, that during the said time the shot continued so thick together that it might have been judged a skirmish with small shot on land than a fight with great shot on sea.' Carey was in a hurry when he scribbled that note to the Earl of Sussex, and neglected to make his meaning crystal clear. 'Stretching as far south of this island as six leagues', would have been more correct, fitting the statements of witnesses and also a contemporary picture, showing Frobisher close in under Dunnose. Or perhaps he meant that the opening phase of the battle took place far out to sea, which it did. The immediate cause of the action was the lagging behind during the calm of the night of two Spanish ships.

According to Estrade, 'at the break of day, the hulk of Pedro Meras was so nigh unto the enemy that more than twenty came shooting at her very strongly, but none of them did lay her aboard, although they were very near.' The list of the Andalusian Squadron shows a number of large vessels classed simply as 'ships', including the ill-fated *Rosario* herself, plus one 'patache', one 'galleon', and one 'hulk' owned by Pedro Meras, the 900-ton *Duquesa Santa Ana*. The patache was for scouting and for conveying orders and messages; the role of the 'hulk' is not really clear. She may have been a storeship attached to the squadron, or just a particularly tub-like merchant vessel, but she did carry 280 soldiers, more than any other vessel in that squadron, except for the lost *Rosario*, which had 304. In fact, there were more soldiers in just this one Spanish squadron than in the whole of the English fleet.

Although Estrade mentions only one hulk in distress, Calderon says there were two: 'The weather was calm, and the hulks *Santa Ana* and *Doncella* fell astern. The enemy attacked them with some of their ships, which they towed within range.' The *Doncella* is the only 'hulk' listed in Oquendo's Guipuzcoan squadron, the rest being described as 'ships'; she was of 500 tons and carried 156 soldiers. The Duke, however, wrote: 'The hulk *Santa Ana* and a galleon of Portugal had fallen somewhat astern, and were fiercely attacked by the enemy.' Such discrepancies are not terribly important, illustrating merely that, after five thundering hours of confused battle, memories are liable to err a little and that, often, a witness could describe with fair confidence only what happened in his own immediate vicinity. In this battle, for instance, Howard's report concerns mainly the doings of his own squadron, and has only fringe references to Frobisher and Hawkyns, and none at all to Drake by name; which means that Drake was operating at some distance from him, on the seaward wing, possibly some six leagues out to sea, if we can accept Carey's estimate. That would be about nine miles south of some point of the island, which is diamond-shaped.

Howard reported that one of the lagging Spanish ships was to seaward of him, opposite Hawkyns.

There was a great galleon of the Spaniards short of her company to the southwards. They of Sir John Hawkyns his squadron, being next, towed and recovered so near that the boats were beaten off with musket shot. Whereupon three of the galleasses with an armado issued out of the Spanish fleet.

The 'armado' was presumably de Leyva's flagship *Rata Encoronada*, being towed into action by the galleasses for the sake of her extra gun power; both the Duke and Calderon mention her as engaged. The diarist of the *Zuniga*, who was present, wrote:

The English would certainly have captured the hulk *Santa Ana* if the three galleasses, *San Lorenzo, Zuniga*, and *Girona* had not at once gone to her rescue. In order to save her, they had to engage over thirty of the enemy's ships . . .

While Hawkyns was having his ships towed into action by their boats, into the fierce musketry fire of the soldiers massed behind the bulwarks and castles of the *Duquesa Santa Ana*, Howard strove to cover him by engaging the oncoming galleasses, their oars rhythmically beating to froth the oily calm of the heaving sea. The *Ark Royal* and the *Golden Lion* also launched their longboats, and began to tow the two big ships into action, a fairly desperate measure. The Spanish rowers were under cover, the Englishmen in the open boats were not; the galleases were the most heavily armed ships in the Armada, mounting fifty guns each, any one of which was capable of knocking a longboat into splinters. At the last moment, the boats hauled round hard, to bring to bear on the galleasses the broadsides of the *Ark* and the *Lion*. Wrote Howard:

There were many good shots made at the galleasses in sight of both armies, which could not approach, it being calm, for the *Ark* and the *Lion* did tow to the galleasses with their longboats. They fought a long time and much damaged the galleasses, that one of them was fain to be carried away upon the careen; and another, by a shot from the *Ark*, lost her lantern, which came swimming by, and the third his nose. At length it began to blow a little gale, and the Spanish fleet edged up to succour their galleasses, and so rescued them and the galleon, after which time the galleasses were never seen in fight any more, so bad was their entertainment in this encounter.

The 'little gale', that freshening sea-wind which usually breaks up a calm in these waters, and was doubtless expected, enabled the English to get their battle plan moving faster; and this day, they took extreme risks. Frobisher went inshore, as he had at Portland, to work the tide race under the cliffs; Howard pressed the Spaniards hard in the centre; and the squadrons of Drake and Hawkyns swung round to deliver the 'right hook' from seaward. Overall, the plan was the same as that which had worked at Portland, but complicated and made difficult by the peculiar wind and tidal conditions of the Isle of

Wight area; yet possibly paying a much greater dividend if matters could be managed right. The whole of the English movements, from dawn onwards, show a desperate desire to get things moving at almost any cost. The expedient of towing their ships into action is alone sufficient indication. Obviously, the Armada had to be in such-and-such a position, in a given state of disorganization, at a definite time.

Although the two fleets were motionless, relative to the sea, they were not motionless relative to the land; the east-setting current was drifting them steadily north-east, parallel to the cliffs, towards Bembridge Foreland. The Armada had only twelve miles to go; then it could sweep round Bembridge Ledge and into St Helen's, anchoring between there and Spithead in a great arc, from behind the cover of which the boats could put away for the shore with the assault troops. Any wind from the southern arc would be favourable all the way, for, when it hits the barrier of the Isle of Wight, it divides and flows round the island and into Spithead. So, too, does the tide, at the right time; but there is a period when the Channel tide continues east along Bembridge Ledge, and meets there a tide race setting outwards from St Helen's, and also, a little further east, a fast, south-east-going stream consisting of the mass of water previously locked up in Southampton Water and the three wide harbours of Portsmouth, Langstone, and Chichester. That stream runs three to four knots; so long as it was running near its peak speed, the Armada could not make headway against it, being tied to the speed of the slowest of the hulks. If the English could hustle the Spaniards past the Spithead entrance at the right time, the Armada would never have a chance to get into the anchorage, but be drifted away beyond the submerged tip of Selsey Bill. If the Spaniards tried too hard, the English might even get some of them embayed inside the wide sweep of Hayling and Bracklesham, or at any rate on the barely submerged remains of the Selsey peninsula.

This coast, which both fleets were now approaching, was completely different in character from anything they had passed before. The West Country cliffs are high and steep, rising from comparatively deep water and a rocky bottom; very clear, cold water. But the coasts of the Hampshire/Sussex border are low-lying and sandy; for many miles from the shore there is, at low tide, no water to float a ship of any size. Two hundred years before, much of it had been dry land; then the floods of the thirteenth and fourteenth centuries, caused by a drastic change in sea level, had inundated large areas, including villages and churches. The old rivers, both those which had existed in prehistoric times when the Wight was not yet an island, and those which had largely disappeared from sight after the inundations of the late Middle Ages, were still there, grooves in the seabed, and formed the intricate network of undersea channels which ships used to come into the harbours; but the average low tide depth over the greater part of the area is today often no more than ten to fifteen feet, less than the draught of many Armada ships. In fact, it was the same sort of coast that the Spaniards were to meet again off Dunkirk, with the same built-in hazards to an unwieldy fleet. In addition, it had the most complicated set of tides, unlike any others in the British Isles, caused by the setting of the Isle of Wight, diamond-shaped, off a mainland which followed its contours. The result is that slack water occurs in some places at high tide, in others one hour before and one hour after high tide, and others again, at low tide; to use the waters of this notoriously difficult area as part of their defences, would be an obvious measure. Depending on exact timing.

But if the English did not get the Spaniards past Bembridge Ledge on time, the tide would work for the enemy, taking them easily and directly to their intended anchorage, with the assistance also of the wind. Hence the English attacks from dawn onwards. These had the effect of holding back the Spaniards and delaying them, for Medina Sidonia himself was sucked into the fighting, together with his ships of the vanguard group. It had the additional effect of disrupting the Armada, so that, if anything went wrong with the timing and the enemy was in fact able to turn into the anchorage off St Helen's, it would do so off-balance. Any attack, if caught in the forming up area short of the start-line, will waver and may collapse, and doubly so if it is a landing operation launched from ships against defended beaches. No one then alive had more experience of amphibious operations than Drake and Hawkyns, who were therefore the two men best fitted to deliver the blow against one. In the absence of a complex signalling system (on land or at sea), greater responsibility devolved on individual commanders, without noticeable loss of cohesion; and in any case, there was nothing that Howard could profitably tell Drake or Hawkyns; indeed, it was a providential mercy that primitive communications prevented Walsyngham from conducting the campaign at long range from a London office.

All that Howard had to do, this morning of Thursday, 4 August, was to get stuck into the centre of the Armada and bring on such a battle as would suck into it the fighting ships at the head of the enemy formation, as well as their rear. Once he had done that, once the enemy centre was firmly held, Frobisher could try to get round their shoreward flank close under Dunnose, while Drake and Hawkyns carried out their enveloping manoeuvre out to sea. And it went off like clockwork. Even Howard's narrative, focused on the battle in the centre, shows that the two wing movements were near enough simultaneous. The diarist of the *Zuniga* makes it more than plain. He says: 'Some of our ships got mixed up with the enemy's fleet, and there was a great deal of fighting *on all sides*, as the English had assumed the *half-moon formation*.' An admirably brief appreciation of the situation.

The English moves followed on as a result of the counterattack by Howard on the three galleasses, *San Lorenzo*, *Zuniga*, and *Girona*, lying somewhat to seaward of centre; during this action, the wind freshened and enabled Howard to dispense with the boats which had been towing his ships. 'The Duke's flagship, with the vanguard, came to their assistance,' wrote Calderon, tactfully omitting to mention that the Duke himself was absent, having got separated from his own battle group, and was near the shore, close under Dunnose, accompanied only by the fourth galleass. 'Finding the flagship alone, except for the galleass *Patrona*, and to windward of the line of battle,' writes Calderon without a blush, 'the enemy selected some of the best ships in his fleet to deliver a combined attack on the flagship, the rest of his vessels being left to engage the rearguard.' The latter was Howard's group, the 'combined attack' on the *San Martin* being led by Frobisher in the *Triumph*, at the head of the inshore, left-flanking squadron.

The plan would have succeeded if Oquendo had not kept so close a luff, and sailed towards the flagship with other vessels following him, and thus covering her and receiving the chief brunt of the attack, which was very heavy.

'They came closer than on the previous day,' wrote Medina Sidonia, 'firing off their heaviest guns from the lowest deck, cutting the trice of our mainmast, and killing some of our soldiers.' A number of the Spanish ships rallied to their distressed leader, including Recalde and Don Diego Enriquez, and two of the stronger galleons. There is no doubt about where they were, for the Duke recorded that: 'Oquendo placed himself before my flagship, as the current made it impossible for him to stand alongside.' Frobisher was working 'race' tactics again, using this time the notorious St Catherine's race, which can reach eight knots on a spring tide and pours, heaped and heaving, down past Dunnose to join the Bembridge race at right-angles. Once again, as at Portland, Medina Sidonia thought he had got Frobisher; and, once again, he was vastly mistaken; and this time he had no one but himself to blame.

The Spaniards, seeing Frobisher's *Triumph* apparently pinned by the wind to leeward of them, came down confident of the kill; in fact, by the odd way she was moving, they thought they had crippled her. 'This enemy flagship had suffered considerable damage,' wrote the Duke, 'and had drifted to leeward of our Armada.' 'Her rudder was injured and useless,' said Calderon, and the Duke went on:

My flagship then turned upon her, supported by Juan Martinez de Recalde, the *San Juan de Sicilia*, the flagship of the galleons of Castile, the *Gran Grin*, and the rest of our ships. To windward of us was the enemy's fleet coming to support his flagship, which was in such straits that she had to be towed by eleven longboats, lowering her standard and firing guns for aid. My Royal flagship and vice-flagship were gaining on her so much that the rest of the enemy's vessels stood towards her, to support her, and we were sure that at last we should be able to succeed in boarding them, which was our only way to victory.

Calderon thought so, too:

Ten longboats from the other ships took her in tow, and, the wind freshening, our flagship and other ships sailed towards her; but she got out so swiftly that the galleon *San Juan* and another quick sailing ship – the speediest vessels in the Armada – although they gave chase, seemed in comparison to her to be standing still.

Captain Vanegas added: 'We had already got the enemy flagship almost within musket shot, when nine launches got her under way and conveyed her out of our hands with such rapidity, that it was a thing of wonder.'

These phrases are usually quoted to show the superior sailing qualities of the English fleet as a whole; but the *Triumph* was one of the old-fashioned high-charged ships, not a low-built galleon like the *Revenge* or the *Victory*. In fact, the description reads perfectly for what happens when a ship, or for that matter a swimmer, moves into a tide race or eddy – and suddenly goes sliding smoothly away without effort. The change from one sliding roadway to the other is made by going diagonally across the stream, and through the 'boilings', a matter of twenty yards or so; which is probably what Frobisher was using the boats for. The Duke's description of Oquendo's ship being unable to come alongside him, due to the rushing power of a current which was moving a 1,000-ton ship like a log of wood, makes it virtually certain.

And there, on that note of near-victory over Frobisher's flagship, the official Spanish record of the battle abruptly ends. Medina Sidonia (or was it Diego Flores?) entered her in the War Diary as Howard's flagship, knowing perfectly well she was not, for the *Ark* had already been correctly identified off Portland. Don Jorge Manrique, reporting later, knew this, for he described her as 'the largest ship in the enemy's fleet', not as the English fleet flagship.

But it was not the end, not even of this particular phase of the action, for the English fleet flagship, Howard's *Ark Royal*, was bearing down steadily on the *San Martin* and the other Spanish ships fruitlessly chasing Frobisher. He wrote, having described vaguely some action of the Drake and Hawkyns squadrons going on simultaneously:

During which time, over against Dunnose, the Lord Admiral, espying Captain Frobisher with a few other ships to be in sharp fight with the enemy, and fearing they should be distressed, did, with five of his best ships, bear up towards the admiral of the Spanish fleet; and so breaking into the heart of them, began a very sharp fight, being within two or three scores paces one of the other, until they had cleared Captain Frobisher and made them give place.

Neither Medina Sidonia nor Calderon care to describe this; instead they sing out in unison, like trained song-birds.

Seeing that in the proposed assault the advantage was no longer with us, and that we were now near the Isle of Wight, the Duke discharged a gun and proceeded on his course, the rest of the Armada following in very good order, the enemy remaining a long way astern.

This was how Medina Sidonia put it. And Calderon piped up with: 'This being seen by the Duke, and the weather being fair, he proceeded on his voyage.'

In what 'proposed assault' was the advantage no longer with him? The chase after Frobisher? On the contrary, the assault was that outlined in the Duke's letter to the King, dated off Plymouth:

I have written to Your Majesty clearly, and the object of the present letter is to say that I am obliged to proceed slowly with all the Armada together in squadrons as far as the Isle of Wight, and no further, as all along the coast of Flanders there is no harbour or shelter for our ships.

Something had happened to cancel that assault, and as the assault anyway was against the King's orders, it would be best to let the matter lie, and not put himself in the ridiculous position of admitting failure to carry out a forbidden enterprise.

In fact, the Frobisher action was widely hailed as a victory, and much heartened the Armada; the *Zuniga* diarist wrote: 'It was asserted that during the day the enemy suffered much damage, especially their flagship. They had at this time 90 vessels all told . . .' The master of a Seville ship wrote:

Off the Isle of Wight, we found the wind fair and were aweather of them, going very near of them and they flying. We had them broken and the victory three parts won, when the enemy's *capitana* turned upon our Armada, and the galleon *San Mateo* which had the point of the weather wing gave way to it, retreating into the body of the Armada.

The 'weather wing' of the Armada was, of course, many miles out to sea, virtually out of sight of Howard, who refers merely to the *Nonpareil* and the *Mary Rose* striking their topsails 'very bravely' during the extrication of Frobisher; these ships were of Drake's and Hawkyns's squadrons respectively, and this meagre hint is all the information he gives us about the progress of the 'right hook'. The Seville captain is more informative. When the seaward wing of the Armada was driven in by it, the *San Mateo*, one of the genuine warships, being hustled into the body of the fleet, there was a general attack.

Seeing that, the enemy took heart and turned with his whole fleet or the greater part of it, and charged upon the said wing, in such wise that we who were there were driven into a corner, so that if the Duke had not gone about with his flagship, instead of conquerors that we were, we should have come out vanquished that day. Seeing that, those of his Armada that had been cut off, bore up to rejoin.

It is not clear what he means by 'driven into a corner', but the success of the Drake/Hawkyns 'right hook' is clear; the seaward wing of the Armada was rolled up more effectually even than at Plymouth, when the Spaniards 'were forced to flock together like sheep'. For, in this case, the Armada had actually been cut in two – and by an inferior force of some ninety ships. This could easily have happened, if the Spanish formation had been pressed in close against the coast, for then the inshore ships would be in a faster current than those offshore; the current itself would tend to tear the Armada apart. In the jostling confusion, some of the ships might have been in danger of running on to the submerged rock ledges which stretch out a long way seaward between Culver Cliff and Bembridge Foreland; and perhaps this is what the Seville captain meant by a 'corner'. On the other hand, once well clear of the tip of Bembridge Ledge, there would have been little, tide permitting, except their own disorganization to prevent the Spaniards from bringing up to their anchors inside the Spithead anchorage. It is more likely that they were swept past the point of Bembridge Ledge in some confusion, and there found themselves being jammed, not against a coast, but against a fierce, outgoing current, and then, as they tried perhaps to come in, were swept bodily away by the main south-east-going stream towards the long arc of the Selsey peninsula. That would certainly fit the description of a 'corner', particularly if Drake and Hawkyns were continually pushing them northwards at this time, for the whole battle would then drift very fast to the north-east, and Medina Sidonia would certainly have to 'go about with his flagship', or have most of his Armada put on to Cymenes-ora, the then recently submerged Bill of Selsey, now known as the Owers banks. If this was the idea, it was not a new one, for the English shipmasters had made just this suggestion to the Lord Admiral, Lord Lisle, in July, 1545. Speaking of the French fleet then anchored off the Wight, they had stated:

If we come under sail towards them they must loose anchor and abide us under their small sails; and once loosed, they could not with that strainable wind fetch the Wight again and would have much ado to escape a danger called the Awers.

But the westerly wind of 1545 had died away into another unnatural calm, and the plan was never tried.

The Armada navigators must have realized early that they had been out-manoeuvred, for they were soon back on course to clear the tip of the Owers, so that Sir George Carey could conclude his letter:

The fleets kept the direct trade and shot into the sea out of our sight by three of the clock this afternoon; whereupon we have dissolved our camp wherein we have continued since Monday. And so praying your Lordship to send this enclosed by post, I humbly commit you to God. From Carisbrook Castle, this 25th of July [4 August], at 8 hours in the night.

The soldiers of the Wight garrison could now stand down with safety; the Armada's last port of refuge was gone.

13

'A Device of Firing of Ships'

Near to Calais, my Lord Admiral, with firing of ships, determined to remove them.

John Hawkyns to Walsyngham

Administratively, as the two fleets cruised past the Sussex beaches that evening after the battle, the Lord Admiral and the Duke thought as one: reinforcements and more ammunition. The cast of their thought was, however, quite different. Howard looked forward with confidence to the junction of his four squadrons with the two additional squadrons off Dover, which would at last give him numerical superiority, and to receiving fresh supplies of powder and shot. He wrote:

Now, forasmuch as our powder and shot was well wasted, the Lord Admiral thought it was not good in policy to assail them any more until their coming near unto Dover, where he should find the army which he had left under the conduction of the Lord Henry Seymour and Sir William Wynter, knight, ready to join with his Lordship, whereby our fleet should be much strengthened, and in the meantime, better store of munition might be provided from the shore.

This was no idle expectation, for he had written such a letter to the Queen, that Walsyngham had been rocketed into action.

On Friday, 5 August, while both fleets lay becalmed all day off Hastings, Walsyngham noted:

I find a letter written from my Lord Admiral unto her Majesty that, for lack of powder and shot, he shall be forced to forbear to assail and to stand upon his guard until he shall be furnished from hence. There is 23 last of powder sent unto him with a proportion of bullet accordingly. There are letters sent to the Lord Wyllughby,[1] and in his

---

[1] This is the same Lord Wyllughby as the hero of the anonymous poem quoted at the start of Chapter Six.

absence to Sir William Russell, to send over 1,000 of their best shot for the furnishment of the ships. I hope there will be an 100 sail of Hollanders and Zealanders at the least to assist the Lord Admiral within these three days.

As a result, Howard was able to report:

All this day and Saturday, 27th July [6 August], the Spaniards went always before the English army like sheep, during which time the justices of peace near the sea-coast, the Earl of Sussex, Sir George Carey, and the captains of the forts and castles alongst the coast, sent us men, powder, shot, victuals and ships to aid and assist us.

Some of the ammunition taken from the two captured Spanish ships also arrived. In fact, Howard celebrated Friday the 5th as a victory already. He staged a ceremony in his flagship, knighting Hawkyns and Frobisher, his own kinsmen Lord Thomas Howard and Lord Sheffield, also Roger Townshend and George Beeston, a venerable officer of the regular navy. This was 'in reward of their good services in these former fights, as also for the encouragement of the rest.' Apparently, he was very pleased at their success in having hustled the Spaniards past the Isle of Wight, when his force was so small.

In the Duke's letters, however, there is a distinct note of anxiety. For the first time the Spaniards were beginning to be worried by shortage of ammunition; not powder, they still had enough of that, but cannon balls. They had been provided with enough to last for six months of operations, including a land campaign, and had shot most of it away already in three sea battles. The reason was that they had expected to win by boarding, after only a brief, preliminary cannonade to cow the enemy; and, at that, they had expected only one sea battle to take place, for the English would hardly fight, they had thought, until both their fleets were united off Dover. In the evening of 4 August, immediately after the Isle of Wight battle, Medina Sidonia sent a fast pinnace on ahead to Parma, with letters and a liaison officer, Captain Pedro de Leon of the *tercio* of Sicily, to arrange for the junction of their two forces. In the covering letter, the Duke explained how he had done his best to induce one of the enemy's ships to grapple and so begin the fight; but all to no purpose, as his ships are very light, and mine very heavy, and he has plenty of men and stores. My stores are running short with these constant skirmishes; and if the enemy continues his tactics, it will be advisable for your Excellency to load speedily a couple of ships with powder and balls of the size noted in the enclosed memorandum, and to despatch them to me with the least delay.

Having slept on it, the Duke sent away yet another pinnace to Parma, pleading for help. He wrote:

Friday dawned calm, the fleets being in sight of each other; and the Duke despatched a pinnace to the Duke of Parma with the pilot Domingo Ochoa, to obtain from him shot of four, six, and ten lbs, because much of his munition had been wasted in the several fights; praying him also eftsoons to send 40 flyboats to join with this Armada, that he might be able with them to close with the enemy, because it had been impossible to come to hand-stroke with them.

The Duke must have been a very worried man. The Armada's planned role had been to convoy Parma across the sea to England; now, the Armada was asking the army commander, not only for powder and shot, but for ships as well, with which to hold off the English and enable it to keep the sea . . . It was a very strange reversal of roles, for which, naturally, Parma was neither prepared nor equipped. He had told the King, time and again, that his 'fleet' consisted of Dutch canal barges, which might just be able to stagger across the Channel on a very calm day, if protected by the Armada. But the Duke had persuaded himself, or been persuaded by someone else, that the answer to the English fleet was flyboats, and that Parma had them. Flyboats were not the answer; and Parma did not have more than a dozen of them anyway, for the bulk of the flyboats serving on that coast were sailing under the flag of the Dutch rebels – the '100 sail of Hollanders and Zealanders' mentioned by Walsyngham. They were keener even than Medina Sidonia to see Parma's 'fleet' come out; but their motives were rather different, for they confidently expected to be able to sink the lot. As Parma very well knew.

The Duke's demand in his memorandum for 'shot of four, six and ten lbs' to replace his wastage gives a hint that many of the Spanish ships were lightly armed; although the flagships, and some of the others, also seem to have had heavier guns, judging by their performance and the way the English avoided them. The 'good artillery' of the *Rata Encoronada* is a case in point. But precisely what those guns were we do not know from documents.

Broadly speaking, there were two main classes of bronze, muzzle-loading battery guns: the cannon-type and the culverin-type. The cannon was a short, heavy gun firing a large, heavy iron shot; the culverin was a long-barrelled heavy gun firing a much lighter iron shot at a higher velocity and for a greater distance; but at short range, the smaller shot would have had an impact rivalling that of the heavier cannonball. The two types had developed in land warfare: the cannon as a castle-cracking implement, the culverin as a counter-battery gun firing from the castle, to harass and smash the cannon before they could be emplaced. A demi-cannon was a cross between the two, a very heavy gun indeed.

In both classes, there were smaller guns, each with its own name; and there was an entire range of wrought-iron guns, large and small, each with its own name; and some cast-iron guns; and no standardization. Further, the 'proof' to which the guns were tested varied, the English apparently being superior; and the propellant, the gunpowder, varied also in its power and in the amount loaded at individual whim. So, 'broadly speaking' it must be. And it seems that the English at sea favoured the culverin class, in Elizabeth's time, whereas her father's ships had a mixed heavy armament of bronze cannons, demi-cannons and culverins, plus great wrought-iron breech-loaders firing for the most part stone shot rather than iron shot. The armament of the Spanish ships has been a matter of academic argument over the last one hundred years.

There is, however, a non-technical sequence of explanations for the apparent indecisiveness of the first three battles, which, moreover, has the all-important support of the people who actually took part in them. Firstly, the English were outnumbered initially but knew that the odds would shift to their side once they reached Dover and the fleets of Seymour and Wynter. Secondly, the English offensive power was limited throughout by shortage of ammunition. Thirdly, they dared not risk being boarded, because of the overwhelming superiority of the Spaniards in infantry. Fourthly, the English (and the Spaniards, too) were overestimating the effective ranges, from sheer inexperience of such fleet fighting. This recalls Lord Dowding's ruling, for the 1940 Battle of Britain, that the guns of the Spitfire and Hurricane fighters were to be synchronized at 450 yards, which was soon disregarded by the pilots, who set them to create a cone at 200 yards instead, but even then regarded that as the distance for a sighting shot; the kill was not to be made until at fifty yards you could 'see the rivets'. At first, many of the Elizabethan seamen must have tended to Lord Dowding's error. Ubaldino implies it, and a Spanish witness reported little damage done in the Channel because 'they shoot very far off'.

Further, what all the contestants thought of as rapid fire was not really rapid at all; probably less than ten rounds per gun per hour. Even so, the guns would heat up and have to be allowed time to cool.

Lastly, the effect of heavy gunfire on the main hull of a heavy ship, even at short range, was structurally not very dramatic. The modern theorists tend to write of 'ship-smashing' or 'ship-killing' guns; but this is a misnomer. It is most unusual, even today, for a battleship actually to be sunk by gunfire. The German *Bismarck* is a case in point. Half the British fleet failed to sink her by gunfire (although they pounded her upperworks into a wreck). The *Hood*, sunk by the *Bismarck*, is not a case in point, because although large, she was a battle-cruiser – a ship in which armour protection had been sacrificed to speed and gunpower.

Anything substantial succumbs, if at all, only to underwater explosions – to torpedoes, for instance. And not just one torpedo, but a salvo; or even several salvoes. The giant Japanese battleships *Yamato* and *Musashi* are examples. The Elizabethans did have the equivalent of a torpedo spread – wind and tide being right, they could loose a salvo of fireships at the enemy; but this standard weapon of the time could not be used in a mobile battle, only against a fleet at anchor. A development of this device so recent and so terrible that it ranked virtually as a 'secret weapon' was what the top level Spaniards called the *maquinas de minas* (the 'mine contrivance'), which was referred to by the lower ranks as, simply, the 'Antwerp hell-burner'. The King's warning to Medina Sidonia about the English 'offensive fireworks' seems to refer to something else: normal incendiary devices shot out of guns or muskets.

The Antwerp hell-burner, devised by the Italian engineer Giambelli for use against the investing Spanish forces on the Scheldt estuary, was not a simple incendiary device, it was explosive. A small ship was loaded with gunpowder barrels; a covering of heavy stones was placed on top of the barrels; and a time mechanism, consisting of clock-operated flintlocks, was laid. When the fire reached the powder, after the set interval, the resulting explosion was virtually that of a 'block-buster', made far more deadly by the sharp fragments of stone which spewed across a wide area like shrapnel. The Spaniards before Antwerp had lost a thousand men, and Parma himself had been wounded, from the explosion of just one such weapon. That was largely from the surprise effect – they had crowded round the apparently harmless ship and were standing up, in the open, when the explosion occurred; consequently, like others since, the new secret weapon had instantly acquired a reputation more terrible even than that warranted by the facts. Giambelli was known to be in England in 1588, but his talents were being unproductively employed in strengthening the Thames defences. The preparations being made at Dover were for simple fireships.

The men of the Cinque Ports, mostly fishermen from Rye and Hastings, sent thirty boats to the Queen's representative at Dover Castle, Rychard Barry, together with bundles of brushwood and barrels of pitch. Barry outfitted nineteen of them as fireships, loading as well an additional seventy-two barrels of pitch sent down to him for that purpose by Walsyngham.

This work was going on in Dover harbour, in anticipation of the Armada coming to anchor off the opposite coast, some twenty miles across the water, when, on Saturday, 6 August, both fleets were seen in the Straits, moving slowly off Boulogne towards Cap Gris Nez with the south-west wind which had sprung up again after the calm of the previous day. Ammunition boats were also being loaded, ready to go out to Howard's ships, and one of the more peculiar passengers who went aboard was an Irish student from Armagh, a Catholic sympathizer who, by the aid of his compatriots at Oxford University, had obtained a passport to go to France. The sailors told him they were bound for Calais, so he took their word for it, and next day was transferred to Howard's flagship, together with the powder and shot, and was consequently a spectator of what the English did to what he called 'our Armada'.

Similarly placed, of course, were Don Pedro de Valdes and the other Spanish guests in Drake's *Revenge*, about whom the Government was becoming restive, in case they should learn 'the secrets of the services intended'. Spectators gathered on both sides of the Straits, a natural amphitheatre, in anticipation of a battle, as they were to do again in 1940. On this occasion, one of them was the Governor of Calais, Monsieur Gourdan, who drove down to the shore in a coach with his wife, in order to have a grandstand seat for the affair.

The Spanish fleet, now on the French side of the Channel, passed close under the looming bulk of Cap Griz Nez and, sailing a few miles further on towards the open roadstead off Calais, suddenly came to double anchor like a squad of soldiers halting on a single word of command. Richard Thomson, of the *Margaret and John*, recorded what happened.

We kept the wind of them, which is a very great advantage and special safety for the weaker part. By that means, to the great annoyance of our enemies, we have so daily pursued them at the heels, that they never had leisure to stop in any place alongst our English coast, until they came within two miles of Calais, where in the evening, very politicly, they came all upon a sudden to an anchor, purposing that our ships with the flood tide should be driven to leeward of them; but in happy time it was soon espied, and prevented by bringing our fleet to an anchor also in the wind of them.

The Armada had now arrived at the point of no return. The Straits of Dover are the meeting place for the tides which sweep in from the Atlantic and divide to pass round the British Isles, one stream going past Scotland and so down into the North

Sea, the other flowing up-Channel. To pass from one stream to the other, in the Straits, is very tedious and, with the prevailing south-westerly winds, awkward indeed for sailing ships. Medina Sidonia reported that

there were divers opinions as to whether we would anchor there off Calais or go on further; but the Duke, understanding from the pilots who were with him that, if he went on further, the currents would carry him out of the English Channel and into the North Sea, he resolved to anchor off Calais, seven leagues from Dunkirk, from whence the Duke of Parma could join with him.

The Armada had boxed the compass of English history; history past, and history still to be. It had fought a battle off the Isle of Wight, in the very same waters where the dive-bombers were to destroy an English convoy in a battle equally decisive; it had then passed, beaten off from a landing, through the fringes of 'Piccadilly Circus', the junction of the roadways of steel ships which were to pass to and from Normandy like a conveyor belt in the summer of 1944; and it had anchored now exactly under the cliffs where the German command post was to be hastily sited at Wissant (in an old omnibus fitted out with telephones) for the Channel battles of 1940, in preparation for another proposed invasion which failed. And, 'seven leagues' distant, was Dunkirk, then a little fishing haven; but in 1940 to be wreathed with the black plumes of burning oil tanks, under which the Royal Navy and a host of amateur-manned auxiliary craft ferried off a trapped and defeated army from the beaches.

Another point also was different, and this was to be the turning point for the Armada; Dunkirk was held by Parma, but France was neutral. There was no shelter for the Armada on that coast; Parma had to come out quickly, or not at all. The Duke wrote at once to Parma:

The enemy's fleet is on my flank, and able to bombard me, whilst I am not in a position to do him much harm. I beseech your Excellency, if you cannot at once bring out all your fleet, to send me the 40 or 50 flyboats I asked for yesterday, as, with their aid, I shall be able to resist the enemy's fleet until your Excellency can come out with the rest, and we can get together and take some port where this Armada may enter in safety.

The Duke sent his secretary, Arceo, in a pinnace with the letter and a verbal message that Medina Sidonia 'could not tarry there off Calais without endangering the whole fleet.' None of this was the Duke's fault, nor was it Parma's; it was solely the responsibility of the King, who had failed to think out the problem in sufficient depth, or had perhaps thought that the Armada could easily brush aside English opposition at sea. But now, it was less than ever able to do so.

The English fleet was no longer 'the weaker part' numerically; it was now the stronger. Admiral Sir William Wynter, in the *Vanguard*, had brought his squadron into the Downs, hoping that there would be time to revictual his ships, which had rations only for three days more, when a pinnace arrived from Howard, ordering a rendezvous off the French coast.

We forthwith made sail and gat out [wrote Wynter], and by the time we could recover over, which was about seven of the clock in the afternoon, the Spanish army was anchored to the eastward of Scales Cliffs, very round and near together, not far from the shore.

Admiral Lord Henry Seymour, in the *Rainbow*, received the same message and led his squadron to the rendezvous with Howard, 'and met with his Lordship off Scales Cliffs, about eight in the evening, where both the armies anchored against the other, and we somewhat to the westward.' The little force of sixty-seven ships which had met the Spaniards off Plymouth had grown to something over a hundred before reaching the Straits, and now, anchored off Calais, numbered more than 140. Many of them were small private ships, volunteers, like those which, centuries later, were to help evacuate the BEF from Dunkirk; but nevertheless, a formidable sea force was gathered to windward of the Armada that Saturday night. Calderon thought there were 160 of them; the soldierly Estrade thought not so many:

So this day, with such ships as came unto them along the coast there were above 150 sail, yet in that which I did see and others likewise there were but 18 good galleons, or 20, of 300 tons, and the rest small, which did amaze me. The English did well accomplish their business (but with the secrets of God).

To the Spaniards, this quiet massing of force seemed very ominous; the English, now, had nearly three times as many ships as they had had a week ago, and the Armada was the weaker by two flagships. A gentleman of Medina Sidonia's household, Don Luis Miranda, wrote:

We rode there all night at anchor, with the enemy half a league from us, being resolved to wait, since there was nothing else to be done, and with a great presentment of evil from that devilish people and their arts. So too in a great watching we continued on Sunday all day long.

The strain was too great for some in the Armada. There began that evening the first of a series of desertions from the doomed Spanish force. The first to go were Simon Henriquez and Juan Isla, master and pilot respectively of the hulk *San Pedro el Menor*, which had taken part in the only victorious battle the Armada had ever fought – that off the Scillies, against the two little barks, Scottish and Irish, back in June.

But to some of the English, particularly those whose first sight of the Armada this was, the assembly of high-charged ships, grouped closely round the hulks and pinnaces like a protective wall, seemed immensely strong and hard to breach. Wynter wrote:

Immediately, so soon as my Lord Admiral's ship was come to an anchor, he sent his pinnace aboard my ship for me, commanding me to come aboard his Lordship, which I did; and having viewed myself the great hugeness of the Spanish army, did consider that it was not possible to remove them but by a device of firing of ships. His Lordship did like very well of it, and said the next day he would call a council and put the same in practice. His Lordship and I were reasoning of this matter in his Lordship's cabin, when there did drive with the tide aboard my Lord's ship her Majesty's ship the *Bear* and three others, who were all tangled together, so as there was some hurt done by breaking of yards and spoil of tackle.

Estrade and Miranda might have amended somewhat their opinion of the 'devilish arts' of the English, had they seen this accident, involving the Lord Admiral and his noble kinsmen; and what Drake and Hawkyns thought about it may be imagined. Medina Sidonia saw only the fact of the powerful reinforcements, under Seymour and Wynter, which he thought were commanded by John Hawkyns, who ranked second only to Drake as a Spanish legend. 'The enemy's fleet was reinforced by 36 sail, including five great galleons,' he wrote in the War Diary. 'This was understood to be the squadron which Juan Acles had under his charge before Dunkirk.' He sent Captain Heredia ashore to the Governor of Calais, to explain why the Spaniards had anchored in French waters, and Heredia shortly returned, having found Monsieur and Madame Gourdan sitting in a coach by the beach, waiting for the battle to begin.

But nothing happened that night, except the first trickle of desertions from the Armada; and nothing happened all next day, Sunday, 7 August, except a continual coming and going of pinnaces and small boats, among the English fleet, and between the Armada and the shore. The Duke was becoming desperate, as well he might, with the whole enterprise hanging in the balance. Monsieur and Madame Gourdan sent out to him a present of some fruit, and a message that the Armada's anchorage 'was extremely dangerous, because of the strong cross currents of the Channel.' Captain Don Rodrigo Tello, sent ahead in a pinnace by Medina Sidonia three days after the Armada had left Corunna, so as to give Parma plenty of warning, now rejoined with news of the invasion preparations.

He reported that the Duke of Parma was at Bruges, where he had visited him, and although the Duke expressed great joy at the arrival of the Armada, he had not come to Dunkirk up to the night of Saturday, when Tello had left, nor had the embarkation of men and stores been begun.

That evening, the Duke's secretary, Arceo, reported in similar terms from Dunkirk: 'Parma had not arrived there, the stores were still unshipped, and he, Arceo, thought that everything could not be ready under a fortnight.' During the day, a stream of messengers left the Armada for the shore. First, a provision party with 6,000 ducats to spend in Calais; and lastly, the Inspector-General of the Armada in person, Don Jorge Manrique, to stir up Parma's headquarters and get him to come out at once with his invasion barges to engage the English fleet and

sail across the Channel to the mouth of the Thames. The
Duke's last letter to Parma, written late that day, read:

I represent to you the urgent need of providing a port for the Armada,
without which it will doubtless be lost as the ships are so large. Besides
that, it is impossible to continue cruising with this Armada, as its great
weight causes it always to be to leeward of the enemy, and it is
impossible to do any damage to him, hard as we may try.

Clearly, the Duke was at the end of his tether, predicting
disaster, a few hours before the process actually began.

But Parma was sitting tight. He was not going to be involved
in the ruin of the enterprise. He made his explanations, not to
the Duke, but to the King that same day from his HQ at
Bruges:

The enemy has a large force of armed vessels on this coast to oppose
our coming out, but doubtless they will depart when the Armada
arrives. But to judge from what the Duke says, it would appear that
he still expects me to come out and join him with our boats, although
it must be perfectly clear that this is not feasible. Most of our boats
are only built for the rivers, and they are unable to weather the least
sea. It is quite as much as they can do to carry over the men in
perfectly fair weather, but as for fighting as well, it is evident they
cannot do it, however good the troops in them may be.

In the English fleet, the movements of boats were between
the squadron flagships and Howard's *Ark Royal*. Wynter wrote

Upon Sunday, being the 28th day,[2] my Lord put out his flag of
council early in the morning; and after the assembly for the council it
was concluded that the practice for the firing of ships should be put in
execution the night following, and Sir Henry Palmer was assigned to
bear over presently in a pinnace for Dover, to bring away such vessels
as were fit to be fired, and materials apt to take fire.

Wynter apparently did not know that the fireships had already
been prepared, and probably still thought the idea was his, the
discussion with Howard the previous evening having been so
rudely interrupted. But, in the event, they were not used. On
Sunday, at midnight, there would be a spring tide running

[2] 28 July by the English calendar.

strongly down from the west towards the Armada; and the wind was still from the west, gusty, with rain, as it had been for the last two days. Conditions then would be almost perfect for the firing of a fireship salvo at the Spaniards. We do not know who pointed that out, but after Palmer had left for Dover in the pinnace, Wynter recorded, 'it was seen he could not return that night, and occasion would not be over slipped, it was thought meet that we should help ourselves with such shipping as we had there to serve that turn.'

Captains Yonge and Prouse were given charge of the preparations, and among the eight small ships they selected were Yonge's own 140-ton flyboat and the 200-ton *Bark Talbot*, commanded by Henry Whyte, the captain who had been critical of the Plymouth attack as 'more coldly done than became the value of our nation and the credit of the English navy.' Thereafter, he allowed:

our fleet increased daily; and as men and ammunition came, we plied them every day with more courage than other, until they came to an anchor before Calais. There it was devised to put them from their anchor, and ships were allotted to the fire to perform the enterprise; among the rest, the ship I had in charge, the *Bark Talbot*, was one; so that now I rest like one that had his house burnt, and one of these days I must come to your Honour for a commission to go a-begging.

Such stores as could be got out were removed; but the guns were loaded so that they would explode in due course with the heat. Incendiary material was placed and the skeleton crews still aboard waited for the gun shot which would be the signal for the attack to begin. At midnight, with the tide pouring relentlessly down towards the tight-packed Spaniards, it came, as Wynter recorded:

About twelve of the clock that night, the ships were brought and prepared with a saker shot, and going in a front, having the wind and tide with them, and their ordnance being charged, were fired; and the men that were the executors, so soon as the fire was made they did abandon the ships, and entered into five boats that were appointed for the saving of them.

In close line-abreast, fire flickering up their rigging and the roar of the flames beginning to burst from their decks, they drove down on the anxious, sleepless Spaniards. Medina Sidonia wrote in his diary:

At midnight two fires were seen kindled in the English fleet, which increased to eight; and suddenly eight ships with sail set, and fair wind and tide, were seen coming straight for my flagship and the rest of our fleet, all burning fiercely.

'They came towards us all in flames,' wrote Calderon, 'burning furiously in the bows, with the mainsails and foresails set, and the rudders lashed.' The flames heated the metal first of this gun, then of that, and the powder began to explode; flaming, thundering, they rode down on the Armada. 'Spurting fire and their ordnance shooting,' wrote another Spaniard, 'which was a horror to see in the night.' There was not a single witness in the Armada, so far as we know, who took them for ordinary fireships. 'Fire machines or mines,' thought Medina Sidonia. 'Artificial fire,' judged Don Balthasar de Zuniga. 'Artificial machines,' wrote both Calderon and Manrique. The boom of the explosions, and frightful gout of flame when the deck of one of the fireships fell in, convinced them – these were floating mines, the hell-burners of Antwerp come again!

The Duke had put out a screen of pinnaces under one of his own officers, Captain Antonio Serrano, for just such a contingency as this. Serrano, a notably brave man in a gallant company of soldiers, had the desperate task of flinging grapnels on to the fireships and towing them aside, risking both fire and explosion while he did it. But the captains of the Armada did not wait to see what luck he had; they did not even stay for the capstans to get their anchors out of the ground; they simply cut their cables and ran, drifting with tide and wind in hopeless confusion all the way from Calais down to Dunkirk. A Spanish witness reported:

The eight ships, filled with artificial fire and ordnance, advanced in line at a distance of a couple of pikes' lengths between them. But by God's grace, before they arrived, while they were yet between the two fleets, one of them flared up with such fierceness and great noise as were frightful, and at this the ships of the Armada cut their cables at once, leaving their anchors, spreading their sails, and running out to sea; and the whole eight fireships went drifting between the fleet and the shore with the most terrible flames that may be imagined.

In the confusion, some of the unwieldy ships crashed into each other; Don Hugo de Moncada's flag galleass *San Lorenzo* was rammed by one of his own squadron, the *Girona*, and by Don Alonso de Leyva's flagship, *Rata Encoronada*. The crippled *San Lorenzo*, her rudder smashed, began to creep towards the shore. An angry Spanish officer snarled:

Fortune so favoured the English, that there grew from this piece of industry just what they counted on, for they dislodged us with eight vessels, an exploit which with one hundred and thirty they had not been able to nor dared to attempt. When the morning came they had gained the weather gauge of us, for we found ourselves scattered in every direction.

And bearing down on them, for the kill at last, came the six fast squadrons of the united English navy. Howard, Drake, Hawkyns, Frobisher, Seymour, Wynter. Heeling over before the wind, their flagships led the last attack. *Ark Royal, Revenge, Victory, Triumph, Rainbow, Vanguard*. Behind them their squadrons and, eager to be in at the death, all the little ships and pinnaces, too. *Pippin, Scout, Moon* and *Nightingale*; the *Bark Bonner* and the *Bark Buggins*; the *Rat of Wight* and the *Virgin, God Save Her. Pansy, Prudence, Jewel, Lark, Dolphin, Distain*. Crowding down came the *Brigandine, Black Dog,* and *Hearty Anne*, the *Handmaid of Bristol*, the *Crescent of Dartmouth*, the *Greyhound of Aldborough*. Timbers groaning, guns run out, musketeers manning their sides, white bow waves bursting from the heaving seas, they went racing down to the battle off Dunkirk. This day, there would be no holding back.

14

'Fourteen Chests of Very Noble Spoil'

The most surprised man, on the morning of Monday, 8 August, was the Prince of Ascoli, reputedly King Philip's natural son, who found himself at dawn in a Biscay fishing smack, in the middle of the English fleet streaming down to attack the Spaniards. He was one of a group of trustworthy officers whom the Duke despatched during the night, in light, fast vessels which the Spaniards called zabras, to carry orders to the scattered ships of the Armada. Having delivered the instructions, Ascoli returned to the *San Martin*, to find the Duke's flagship no longer there, nor any other Spanish ship, for that matter; but only the hulls of the eight fireships, still blazing on the shore. And as the grey light of the new day revealed his dangerous isolation, and the English did not bother to turn aside for so trivial a prize, he very shortly found himself in the rear of both fleets, completely cut off from his friends. Soon afterwards, he saw a Spanish pinnace in the same plight for much the same reason; she carried two members of the provost staff who had been sent round the Armada to give the captains the order to rally. As she was a better proposition from the fighting point of view, he transferred to her and followed in the wake of the battle. And ran straight into trouble, from a cause which he could not have foreseen.

The order of the English attack had been decided the previous day. Howard, the titular leader, was to go in first with his squadron; followed by a big battle group under Drake, which included the squadrons of both Hawkyns and Frobisher; followed by the two squadrons of Seymour and Wynter, Seymour commanding. The Spaniards were to be caught before they could re-form, and individual ships overwhelmed by mass attacks at close range. One English ship against one Spanish ship could not secure a quick decision; but four or more English against one Spaniard would be a very different matter. In short, the Armada was to be destroyed in detail, the obvious and orthodox method; and, because this coast, like that of Hayling-Bracklesham-Selsey, was also a drowned land, it may well have been their intention to scare the Spaniards pell-mell shorewards until they grounded on the treacherous banks. The wind now, still at around south-west, was on this coast slightly offshore, so that it favoured a Spanish escape; the Armada would have to be hard pressed at the critical moment, if it was to be run aground. It would have to be hard pressed anyway, to take full advantage of the few hours of confusion. And it was at this moment, at the vital onset of the battle, that Howard made for the English their one great mistake of the campaign. Medina Sidonia's faults were those of a gentle scholar, uncertain always of what was really best to be done, and doing nothing, or doing something too late. Howard's error was the opposite: the rashness of a fighting man with little experience, who had perhaps been prodded too often from Westminster to board and take some of the Spanish ships.

He had with him now newly joined volunteers from the court, aching for action, who must have brought with them stories of the Government's displeasure at his failure to board, for the clerk of the Council was to put these complaints officially, and on paper, within forty-eight hours. And the very first thing they saw, at daybreak that Monday, was the crippled flag galleass *San Lorenzo*, limping close inshore for the shelter of Calais harbour, her rudder gone, but steadied by a foresail and trying to steer with her oars. She was one of the most powerful units in the Armada and, as a flagship, must hold many noblemen of Spain as well as a rich treasure chest. True, she should not have been allowed to escape, but the swarms of English small craft could have settled the business. Already some of them were heading towards her. Howard then made a breathless mistake; he swung his whole squadron out of the line of advance, bore down on the crippled galleass, which he could not approach because she drew less water than the *Ark Royal*, and launched his longboat under the command of his lieutenant, Amyas Preston. Into her poured a crowd of gentlemen adventurers, including two courtiers, Thomas Gerard and William Harvey. In a moment, full of armed men, she was surging across the shallows towards de Moncada's flagship, while the big ships of Howard's squadron looked on out of range, unable to intervene; and also out of the battle at the moment when maximum weight was required.

Admiral Seymour's report seems dryly critical of his superior.

It being resolved the day before that my Lord Admiral should give the first charge, Sir Francis Drake the next, and myself the third, it fell out that the galleass distressed altered my Lord's former determination, as I suppose, by prosecuting the destruction of her, which was done within one hour after. Sixty precious minutes gone . . .

'In the meantime,' Seymour went on, 'Sir Francis Drake gave the first charge upon the Spanish Admiral, being accompanied with the *Triumph*, the *Victory*, and others.' Captain Vanegas, who was in the *San Martin*, confirmed it: 'The enemy's fleet seized the occasion by the forelock, and seeing the flagship alone and the rest of the Armada to leeward, charged upon her with three *capitanas* leading.' These were the flagships of Drake, Hawkyns and Frobisher. Medina Sidonia was soon in desperate trouble, so Seymour with his two squadrons swept past the gunsmoke of her brave defiance, and smashed into the rest of the Armada, still to leeward, and trying to come to the help of their flagship:

Myself, with the *Vanguard*, the *Antelope*, and others, charged upon the tail, it being somewhat broken, and distressed three of their great ships; my ship shot one of them through six times, being within less than musket shot.

The implication seems to be that some of the high-velocity culverin balls were penetrating the enemy from one side to the other, when fired from such close range.

In those Spanish ships now, mostly the best commanded

and strongest, men were falling in heaps, guns were dismounted, cagework shattered, sails rent to ribbons, and the dismal clanking of the pumps amid the roar of battle told of shot holes low down in their hulls. Soon, only the work of the damage control parties, which included divers, was keeping some of them afloat. Nevertheless, the moment of decision was passing, as part of the Armada started to re-form, with splendid discipline, into some sort of order. Howard, meanwhile, was three miles away, intent on preventing the escape of the galleass into Calais; in that, at least, he succeeded.

At the break of day [wrote Richard Thomson of the *Margaret and John*], we espied riding within shot of the town of Calais the greatest of the King's galleasses, the rest of the Spanish fleet being two leagues to leeward of her. My Lord Admiral began to go toward the galleass with his ship, the *Ark*, but finding the water to be shallow, other ships of less draught bare in with her and shot at her; whereupon she let slip and run the galleass aground hard before the town.

Some of these small ships were Seymour's, hoys and pinnaces by his account, which were of no great use in battle and could be spared for this operation. They were better suited to it than the 200-ton *Margaret and John*, which also ran aground in trying to get near enough to the galleass to bring her guns to bear. Howard's bigger ships had to remain further out still, or, as Wynter put it: 'My Lord Admiral did stay off and on, with some good ships with him, to give comfort and countenance to our men.'

The *Margaret and John*, however, had no choice but to remain where she was, aground on Calais Bar near the galleass, because the tide was going out, at half-ebb, and she could not be refloated until the flood, many hours later. As the tide fell, so the great galleass heeled over on the landward side, so that, to seaward, some of her bottom planks were showing, and her guns pointed helplessly at the sky. The crowd of hoys and pinnaces closed in to batter her with their light pieces. 'She was assailed by 15 or 20 English ships, small vessels of 30 or 40 tons,' wrote an anonymous Spanish witness who, judging by the detail he gives, was probably in or near the *San Lorenzo* at the time.

She was nearly surrounded by these small English ships, which fired off about 100 cannon shots at her upper parts. The guns on the galleass could not reply, as she had a list to landwards. But she was still very sound, as not one of the English cannon shots pierced the hull, but only her upper planks above the oars.

In the *Margaret and John*, Richard Thomson was arming himself to join her boarding party, of which he may have been the leader. Anyway, it was he who wrote the report on the storming of the *San Lorenzo*.

My Lord Admiral, seeing he could not approach the galleass with his ship, sent off his longboat unto her with 50 or 60 men, amongst whom were many gentlemen as valiant in courage as gentle in birth, as they well showed. The like did our ship send off her pinnace, with certain musketeers, amongst whom myself went. These two boats came hard under the galleass sides, being aground; where we continued a pretty skirmish with our small shot against theirs, they being ensconced within their ship and very high over us, we in our open pinnaces and far under them, having nothing to shroud and cover us; they being 300 soldiers, besides 450 slaves, and we not, at that instant, 100 persons.

So it appeared to Thomson. The anonymous Spanish witness did not agree, for he wrote:

The Italian sailors and artillerymen, with some others (presumably Spanish soldiers), were the first to escape and fly to shore; and so many went that not more than 50 men stood by the captain to defend the ship.

The popping and banging of musketry continued, mixed with the screams and cries of the galley slaves who manned the now useless oars, until a single lucky shot ended it by striking Don Hugo de Moncada. According to a gentleman from Salamanca, taken prisoner a few minutes later, 'a small shot of musket pierced both his eyes.' First into her was William Coxe, of the 50-ton pinnace *Delight*, who had already distinguished himself off Portland.

Within one half hour [wrote Thomson], it pleased God, by killing the captain with a musket shot, to give us victory above all hope or expectation; for the soldiers leaped overboard by heaps on the other side, and fled with the shore, swimming and wading. Some escaped with being wet; some, and that very many, were drowned.

'The loss amounted to about 50 English and a similar number of Spaniards and slaves, who made a terrible outcry,' wrote the anonymous Spanish witness. 'While the rest sought safety in flight, the English to the number of 200 entered, robbing what they could lay hands upon and carry.' Amyas Preston, Howard's lieutenant, was one of the casualties, severely wounded in the open pinnace.

The few soldiers remaining in the galleass [wrote Thomson], seeing our English boats under her sides and more of ours coming rowing towards her, some with 10 and some with 8 men in them, for all the smallest shipping were the nearest to the shore, put up two handkerchiefs upon two rapiers, signifying that they desired truce. Hereupon we entered, with much difficulty, by reason of her height over us, and possessed us of her, by the space of an hour and a half as I judge; each man seeking his benefit of pillage until the flood came, that we might haul her off the ground and bring her away.

According to Ubaldino, they

looted 22,000 golden écus which were there, belonging to the King, and 14 chests of very noble spoil, belonging to the Duke of Medina Sidonia, together with other monies and spoils and several prisoners, among them Don Roderigo de Mendoza and Don Giovanni Gonzalez de Solorzano, the true captain of the galleass.

The English had lost heavily in this encounter, their open boats being raked by Spanish fire, and they were in a savage temper. Many of their friends were lying huddled on the floorboards of the longboats, and the planks were wet with blood. They were in no mood for French courtesy from the good townsfolk of Calais, their hereditary enemies, who had been spectators at the battle and now sought to interfere, legitimately, for the galleass was in French waters commanded by the guns of the town.

During our fight to get her [sneered Thomson], the men of Calais stood in multitudes upon the shore hard by us and beholding all things, showing themselves at that instant indifferent lookers-on; but so soon as they saw us possessed of so princely a vessel, the very glory and stay of the Spanish army, a thing of very great value and strength, as was well known to them; then, I say, Monsieur Gourdan, seeing us thus possessed, sent aboard to us that were in her, in which boat came his kinsman and another captain, desiring to parle with us.

No other Englishman there either spoke or even understood French, except Thomson, so he stepped forward to question them.

I asked them from whom they came. They answered: From Monsieur Gourdan, the Governor of Calais. I demanded to know what his pleasure was.

Then came the politeness.

They answered that he had stood and beheld our fight and rejoiced of our victory, saying that for our prowess and manhood showed therein we had well deserved the spoil and pillage of the galleass, as a thing due unto us by our desert; and that he willingly consented that we should have the pillage of her.

Then came the catch.

He further required and commanded of us not to offer to carry away either the ship or ordnance, for that she was on ground under the commandment of his castles and town, and therefore did of right appertain to him.

Thomson was sarcastic.

I answered unto them that, for our parts, we thanked Monsieur Gourdan for granting the pillage to the mariners and soldiers that had fought for the same; acknowledging that without his leave and good will we could not carry away anything of that we had gotten, considering it lay on ground hard under his bulwarks.

And he added a hint of threat.

As concerning the ship and ordnance, we prayed it would please him to send a pinnace aboard my Lord Admiral, who was here in person hard by, from whom he should have an honourable and friendly answer which we all are to obey and give place unto.

Howard's presence had accomplished something, for the moment at any rate, for Thomson noted: 'With this answer, to my seeming they departed well satisfied.' But the English were not to get the great prize after all, which had already cost so much.

The high-born French envoys, one a relative of Gourdan, had hardly moved away out of Thomson's sight, before the blood-drunk, loot-mad English began to jostle them:

Some of our rude men, who make no account of friend or foe, fell to spoiling the Frenchmen, taking away their rings and jewels as from enemies. Whereupon, going ashore and complaining, they were the cause that all the bulwarks and ports were bent against us, and shot so vehemently that we received sundry shot very dangerously through us. They shot our ship twice through. And the like powder and shot did Monsieur Gourdan bestow upon sundry of our countrymen, and make us relinquish the galleass, which otherwise we had brought away, being masters of her above two hours, and gotten by hard assault, to the great credit of our country, if Monsieur Gourdan had not seemed by force to wrest from us that which we had gotten with bloody heads.

According to Ubaldino, the English now lost 'about 20 more in the sea, on account of the hurry in which they regained their boats.' About half the English losses in the entire Armada campaign seem to have occurred in this abortive and wasteful assault on the stranded *San Lorenzo*. No doubt those who came away safe from her, with écu-lined pockets, took a different view, although Thomson blandly reported 'very little or no treasure' in her, which was true enough after the English sailors and soldiers had finished with de Moncada's flagship.

The English were pleased with their high-ranking prisoners, who could be ransomed; but, all unaware, failed narrowly to put a Prince 'in the bag' also; but, they can hardly have expected to find the natural son of the King of Spain wandering about in a pinnace in the rear of the English fleet. As they were streaming away from Calais Bar, with the French guns thundering after them, they saw the lone enemy pinnace and chased it. 'I had decided to follow in the wake of the fleets,' wrote Ascoli, 'but I was so hotly pressed by the boats which had attacked and defeated the galleass flagship that not a sailor could be induced to stir.' The Prince was completely cut off, and never rejoined the Armada; later, he got into Dunkirk, where he found Parma supervising the loading of the invasion barges as a gesture to show that he had been ready all the time.

The Armada, however, was in no state then to think of invasion; Medina Sidonia's only concern was to save as many of the ships as he could from the rout.

15
'An Italian Ship All Full of Blood'

All that day we had with them a long and great fight, wherein there was great valour showed generally of our company. In this battle there was spent very much of our powder and shot; and there was some hurt done among the Spaniards.

John Hawkyns to Walsyngham

The businesslike Hawkyns was almost startled into eloquence by the events of that Monday off Dunkirk, but recollected himself in time, made one passing reference to 'a great ship of the galleons of Portugal, her rudder spoiled, so that the fleet left her in the sea', and hastily concluded: 'I doubt not but all these things are written more at large to your Lordship than I can do; but this is the substance and material matter that hath passed.' He was quite right. A score of witnesses on each side penned accounts which have survived; and there must have been many more not preserved. The ship casualties on the Spanish side were not known, even approximately, for days afterwards, as news came in of this ship seen to sink by so-and-so, of that one last seen out of control and drifting shorewards, now definitely reported taken by the Dutch. Even now, the full losses cannot accurately be stated. On the English side, however, there were no ship losses at all; not even any very severe damage to the Queen's ships, which were all minutely inspected by the dockyards afterwards. And two things were certain. Howard had thrown away the chance of a much greater victory; and God, by changing the wind at the critical moment, had saved the Spaniards.

The battle was, of course, confused; all battles are, from the point of view of the participants. So much going on, simultaneously, in every direction of the compass, that the brain of no one man could possibly take it all in, let alone remember the detail or record the exact sequence; and so much going on out of sight, hidden by the great clouds of powder smoke, lit by the lightning flashes of the artillery. But the purposes of the contestants were plain enough. 'Sir Francis Drake gave the first charge upon the Spanish Admiral,' wrote Seymour in unmistakable cavalry terms, while 'myself charged upon the tail.' The English object was to overwhelm the best and most powerful units among the scattered Spanish fleet; to defeat in detail the enemy's strongest ships, an application of orthodox military principles. The elements of sea and wind, however, having a powerful effect on sailing machines, must also have been considered. From the English side there is no hint of this; presumably, they were careful to preserve 'the secrets of the services intended'. But the Spaniards had no doubt about the English aims. Even the anonymous Spanish witness of the fight for the *San Lorenzo* saw it: 'The Spanish fleet is very powerful, but with bad weather it may be driven on to the banks, which is the English plan.'

Calderon tells us:

At seven o'clock in the morning the enemy opened a heavy artillery fire on the Duke's flagship, which continued for nine hours. So tremendous was the fire that over 200 balls struck the sails and hull on the starboard side, killing and wounding many men, disabling and dismounting three guns, and destroying much rigging. The holes made in the hull between wind and water caused so great a leakage that two divers had as much as they could do to stop them up with tow and lead plates, working all day. The crew were much exhausted by nightfall, with their heavy labours at the guns, without food.

While Medina Sidonia recorded:

The wind was blowing strong, from the north-west, nearly straight on to the coast. The enemy's fleet, wherein were 136 ships, came on suddenly with wind and tide in their favour, so as the Duke, who was in the rear, seeing that if he bare room with his fleet, it would be to their destruction, for that it was already very near the banks of Dunkirk, as he was assured by his Flemish pilots, chose rather to save it by abiding the enemy's fleet. And so he cast about to meet them, discharging his ordnance, and sending off pinnaces to order all the ships to keep a close luff, as otherwise they would drive on to the banks of Dunkirk. The enemy's flagship, with the greater part of their fleet, assaulted my flagship, with great shooting of ordnance, approaching within musket-shot, or even harquebus-shot; but my flagship did not bare room until the Armada was clear of the shoals.

Another Spanish witness wrote:

The Duke kept luffing up continually upon the enemy's fleet, transfigured and shrouded in the smoke of his guns, which he ordered to be fired with the greatest rapidity and diligence. In truth, if he had not held on upon that tack so long, it was not possible but that the greater part of our Armada must have run ashore and been the end of all.

'It was the greatest war and confusion that there has been in the world, in respect of the great amount of fire and smoke and of there being ships on the shores of Flanders,' wrote Fray Gongora in the *San Martin*. And he continued:

There were many ships which went on fighting in eight cubits of water. And all this day we had been holding ourselves with the bowlines hauled against the weather so as not to run aground on the banks, and thus our ships could not ply their artillery as they wished. Some of the people died in our ship, but none of quality, and it was a miracle that the Duke escaped.

It was touch and go whether or not the Armada could be run aground in a battle of total annihilation. Therefore Drake did not allow himself to be delayed by the *San Martin*, which was supported only by the *San Marcos* at that moment, although the Castilian galleon *San Juan* and the Portuguese galleon *San Mateo* were making their way back towards her. He fired his bow guns into the Armada flagship, altered course, poured in a broadside, and hurried on down after the bulk of the Armada, reloading as he did so; and after him, likewise, his squadron and that of Hawkyns, firing a hail of ball into the luckless flagship as they passed her ravaged sides. Only Frobisher stayed to fight, bitterly critical of Drake. 'He came bragging up at the first indeed, and gave them his prow and his broadside; and then kept his luff, and was gone again, like a cowardly knave or traitor,' snarled Frobisher afterwards.

The remainder of the Drake battle group struck the centre of the milling mass of Spaniards, who were beginning to shake themselves out into some sort of order again and in danger of grounding in the shallows meanwhile; trying to force the lumbering enemy vessels into fatally shoal water. Hawkyns and his squadron, which included Fenton's *Mary Rose*, old George Beeston's *Dreadnought*, and Richard Hawkyns in the *Swallow*, as well as John Hawkyns in the *Victory*, 'bare with the midst of the Spanish army, and there continued a hot assault all that forenoon,' according to Howard's report. The *Mary Rose*, going east, passed close alongside a galleon headed in the opposite direction, to help the Duke, and put such a broadside through her that Howard thought it worthy of remark. At such short range, it seems that some of the English high velocity guns were piercing the enemy hulls through and through. 'As soon as we that pursued the Spanish fleet were come within musket shot of them, the fight began very hotly,' wrote Henry Whyte, the evicted captain of the burnt *Bark Talbot*. 'Myself was now aboard the *Mary Rose*, of the Queen's with Captain Fenton, whose value for that day's service deserved praise.'

'That day,' reported a contemporary writer, 'Sir Francis Drake's ship was riddled with every kind of shot, and was letting fly everyway from both her broadsides, so that she seemed to repeat her fire as rapidly as any harquebusier.' That was the way the new-type galleons were meant to be fought; for it took many minutes to reload the guns in a battery, and it was foolish to stay in range while doing it. They bore down, fired one broadside, passed on, turned, came back and fired the other broadside. Consequently, they were in gunshot of the Spaniards only for a minute or so each time; and on the second run in there would probably be no reply from the empty Spanish guns. Or, as another contemporary writer expressed it:

The English ships using their prerogative of nimble steerage, whereby they could turn and wield themselves with the wind which way they listed, came often times very near upon the Spaniards, and charged them sore, that now and then they were but a pike's length asunder; so continually giving them one broadside on another.

It was method as much as courage which counted, stressed Ubaldino:

The judgement and military skill and naval seacraft of the English leaders, who made good use of the most reliable quality of their excellent and speedy ships, not crowded out with useless soldiers, but with decks clear for the use of artillery, so that they could safely play it at any hour to harm the enemy, at any moment which suited them best to do. [And he condemned] all the news spread by the press and by people who go about singing their praises and ineptly flattering them.[1]

There was nothing wrong with Spanish bravery; or Italian, for that matter, as they fought back desperately to prevent themselves being driven to ruin in the shallows. 'Since the ships were so scattered and could not help one another,' wrote a priest, Geronimo de la Torre, 'the enemy's galleons came together and charged us in such numbers that they gave us no time to draw breath.' Some Dutch mariners, who deserted from the Armada next day, reported: 'In the fleet we did see, through the port holes, an Italian ship all full of blood, which yet maintained the fight in her rank three hours after.' Spanish and Portuguese prisoners, taken later, spoke of: 'three great Venetian ships which were in danger of sinking, being sore beaten and shot through in many places, but were for the time being holpen by the carpenters.' According to Medina Sidonia, this battle in the centre was waged principally by three great Italian carracks, Don Alonso de Leyva's *Rata Encoronada*, Martin de Bertondona's *La Reganzona*, and the *San Juan de Sicilia* of Don Diego Tellez Enriquez; as well as by two strong galleons of Castile, the flagship *San Christobal* and the *San Juan*.

'Fighting in eight cubits of water', they gave ground eastwards, towards Dunkirk, and, hard as the English tried, they could not push them ashore; they were too tightly bunched together for the squadrons of Drake and Hawkyns alone to deal with. Sir Horatio Palavicino, the Genoese banker now serving as a volunteer with the English fleet, wrote:

There were made several very hot charges. A great quantity of ordnance was fired on one side and on the other. Our fleet had the wind throughout, and gave occasion to the enemy to open out to fight;

[1] This sounds like a first-hand comment from Drake, or Hawkyns. Nothing is more infuriating to the skilled technician than the thoughtless, sentimental insinuation that it was all done by brute force and ignorance.

but they chose rather to be followed and bear away, as well from Calais as from Dunkirk, than to open out and permit the fight to become general. So as it was not convenient to attack them thus together and in close order, for that our ships, being of smaller size, would have had much disadvantage; but in the continued assaults which they gave on them without entering, they made them to feel our ordnance; and if any ship was beaten out of their fleet, she was surrounded and suddenly separated from the rest.

Then, three hours late, long after the presence of his powerful squadron could have had maximum effect, Howard crashed into the fight with the *Ark Royal*, *White Bear*, *Golden Lion*, and the rest. 'This fight continued hotly,' he reported, 'and then came the Lord Admiral, the Lord Thomas Howard, the Lord Sheffield, near the place where the *Victory* had been before, where these noblemen did very valiantly.' The arrival of these fresh reinforcements, which had spent half the morning watching the fight for the *San Lorenzo*, hit the Spaniards hard; but the decisive moment was gone. 'We had not fought above three hours,' reported Whyte who, in the *Mary Rose*, was accompanying Hawkyns's *Victory*,

but my Lord Admiral with the rest of the fleet came up and gave a very fresh onset, which continued amongst us some six hours more; and truly, sir, if we had shot and powder sufficient to have given them two such heats more, we had utterly distressed them.

All these Spanish ships in the centre, as well as the group of galleons which had come to the support of his flagship to windward of them, reported Medina Sidonia,

sustained the assault of the enemy as stoutly as possible, so as all these ships were very much spoiled, and almost unable to make further resistance, and the greater part of them without shot for their ordnance.'

Meanwhile a third and quite separate battle had been going on downwind in the rear, where Seymour and Wynter, passing the struggling Spanish flagship, which was being hammered by Frobisher, and leaving the central group to Hawkyns, and possibly to Drake also, had charged what Wynter described as the 'starboard wing' of the Spaniards, which included some of the galleasses; that is, the most easterly of the groups which were re-forming, but still separated from each other. Wynter wrote:

My fortune was to make choice to charge their starboard wing without shooting of any ordnance until we came within six score paces of them, and some of our ships did follow me. The said wing found themselves as it did appear, to be so charged, as by making haste to run into the body of their fleet, four of them did entangle themselves one aboard the other. One of them recovered himself, and so shrouded himself among the fleet; the rest, how they were beaten, I will leave it to the report of some of the Spaniards that leapt into the seas and were taken up, and are now in the custody of some of our fleet.

Describing the same action, Howard wrote:

Astern of the Lord Admiral was a great galleon assailed by the Earl of Cumberland and Mr George Raymond in the *Bonaventure* most worthily, and being also beaten with the Lord Henry Seymour in the *Rainbow*, and Sir William Wynter in the *Vanguard*, yet she recovered into the fleet. Notwithstanding, that night she departed from the army and was sunk.

The 'great galleon which recovered into the fleet' after a battering from two English flagships and the ship of the pirate Admiral, the Earl of Cumberland, was the powerful war galleon of Portugal, the *San Felipe*, commanded by the Camp Master Don Francisco de Toledo, who put up a brave and desperate defence. Wrote Padre de la Torre:

He fought neither more nor less than most valiantly, placing himself in the hottest of the fight and fighting with twelve or fifteen galleons, without help except from God, and moreover close enough to use his muskets. My own vessel was received with such a hail of balls that it was cut to pieces alow and aloft. Yea, in the end I saw myself that day in such sore straits that it was a miracle of God we escaped.

While Calderon reported:

The *San Felipe* was surrounded by 17 of the enemy's ships. They directed against her a heavy fire on both sides and on her stern. They approached so close that the muskets and harquebuses of the galleon were brought into service, killing a large number of men on the enemy's ships. They did not dare, however, to come to close quarters, but kept up a hot artillery fire from a distance, disabling the rudder, breaking the foremast, and killing over 200 men on the galleon.

Two hundred dead meant many more wounded, cruelly torn by the whining wooden slivers that flew from the planks like hail under the thunderous impact of the cannon balls; the dead were down in heaps, the decks slippery underfoot with blood and the squirming remnants of men, their screams and moans a keening accompaniment to the roar of battle and the defiant popping of musketry all along the battered Spanish bulwarks, where the soldiers of the *tercio* of *Entre Douro y Minho* were trading musket balls for cannon shot. This was the spirit which had made the Spanish infantry invincible in Europe, which had enabled a few hundred men to carve out an empire in the New World. They died, jeering at the English, for their lack of courage in not coming to close quarters. The few dazed prisoners, weaker spirits who had leapt overboard, gasped out to their English captors that they had fought at Lepanto, that great battle of the galley fleets long ago, and that this unendurable cannonade was twenty times worse. And as the great galleon rolled idly in the swell, her foremast down and her sails and rigging trailing in the water, a consort came to her aid – another Portuguese warship, the *San Mateo*, commanded by another of the Camp Masters, Don Diego de Pimental.

The ships of Seymour and Wynter closed on her, too, firing into her on both sides simultaneously, the Spaniard towering above them. She fought, said Padre de la Torre, until

she was a thing of pity to see, riddled with shot like a sieve; and had it not been that the Duke afterwards sent his divers to her to get the water out of her, she must have gone to the bottom with all hands. All her sails and rigging were torn and sorely destroyed; of her sailors many perished, and of her soldiers few were left.

But the battle madness had infected the English also. As one of the English ships raced down her side, only a few feet of heaving sea between the cannon bellowing and shaking the timbers underfoot and the musketry banging away, an Englishman, crazy with excitement, leapt clean on to the *San Mateo* in a lone attempt to board. But no one followed his example, and, as Calderon wrote, 'our men cut him to bits instantly.'

Around her consort, the smashed *San Felipe*, the English were circling in the cold fury of victory, closing to within earshot before they fired their battery guns, and yells and jeers echoed across the water between them and the shattered Spaniard.

She had five of her starboard guns dismounted [said Calderon], and an Italian gunner, who was afterwards killed, spiked another of her great guns. In view of this, and that his upper deck was destroyed, both his pumps broken, his rigging in shreds, and his ship almost a wreck, Don Francisco de Toledo ordered the grappling hooks to be got out, and shouted to the enemy to come to close quarters. They replied, summoning him to surrender in fair fight. And one Englishman standing in the maintop with his sword and buckler, called out: 'Good soldiers that ye are, surrender to the fair terms we offer ye.' But the only answer he got was a gunshot, which brought him down in sight of everyone, and the Maestre de Campo then ordered the muskets and harquebuses to be brought into action. Thereupon the enemy retired, while our men shouted out to them that they were cowards, with foul words reproached them for their want of spirit, calling them Lutheran hens, and daring them to return to the fight.

The *San Martin* was now wallowing far astern, with the divers at work on her hull trying without success to stop the leaks. The English had left her, in order to bring their whole weight to bear in the centre and so smash the Spanish movement to re-form, because if even half the Armada could assume some sort of order, it would be almost impossible to break; they had not enough powder and shot left to do it. And because other ships were coming to the rescue of the two battered Portuguese galleons, the conflict began to revolve around them, as ships of both sides were sucked into the battle. In place of three separate battles – four, counting the fight for the *San Lorenzo*, which had occupied Howard for half the morning – there was now one great whirlpool of conflict. Even the battered Armada flagship came limping towards it eventually. According to Medina Sidonia, he actually climbed the mast to see what was happening over there.

Whenas the Duke heard the harquebus-fire and the musketry in the rear, but by reason of the smoke was unable to see from the top what it was, except that two of our ships were surrounded by the enemy, and that their whole fleet, having quitted my flagship were assailing them, he gave order to cast about to succour them, although the flagship was sorely distressed by great shot between wind and water, so as by no means could the leak be stopped, and her rigging was much spoiled.

Actually, there was nothing else he could do, unless he was prepared to face being cut off from the main body of his fleet. But before he got there, two other groups had come to the rescue of the *San Felipe* and the *San Mateo*.

The first consisted of Recalde's flagship, the *San Juan* of Oporto, and the ship Calderon was in, the *San Salvador*, vice-flagship of the hulks. They were shortly supported by Don Alonso de Luzon, Camp Master of the *tercio* of Naples, in *La Trinidad Valencera*, a 1,100-ton Italian carrack; another Italian ship, the *San Juan de Sicilia*, under Don Diego Tellez Enriquez; and Garibay's *Nuestra Senora de Begona*, of the Armada of Castile. The *San Martin* eventually broke through the battle smoke, followed by the *San Marcos*, which accompanied her all day, and in which Pedro Estrade was serving.

Then, said Calderon, his ship, the *San Salvador*,

with the Duke's flagship engaged an Admiral's and a commodore's flagships of the enemy, her bows, side and half her poop being exposed for four hours to the enemy's fire, during which time she received no aid.

If Calderon is correct, then he was probably helping to fight Seymour's 500-ton *Rainbow* and Wynter's 500-ton *Vanguard*, two warships of the latest type.

The *San Salvador* had a number of men killed and wounded, and her hull, sails, and rigging so much damaged that she was obliged to change her mainsail. She leaked greatly through the shot holes, and finally the *Rata* came to her assistance, distinguishing herself greatly. On board the *Rata* there fell, killed by a shot, Don Pedro de Mendoza, son of the Commander of Castelnuovo, Naples; and other persons. The Duke's flagship lost 40 soldiers; and others. The *San Juan de Sicilia*, which carried Diego Tellez Enriquez, suffered to such an extent that every one of her sails had to be replaced; Don Pedro Enriquez, who was also on board, had a hand shot away. The galleon *San Juan* also suffered very severely, as did the *San Marcos*; Don

Felipe de Cordoba, son of Don Diego, his Majesty's Master of the Horse, had his head shot off.

The casualty lists were almost a roll-call of the nobility of Spain. Estrade witnessed the death of Don Felipe.

This day was slain Don Felipe de Cordoba, with a bullet that struck off his head and splashed with his brains the greatest friend that he had there, and 24 men that were with us trimming our foresail. And where I was with four other men, there came a bullet that struck off the shoe of one of them, without doing any other harm, for they came and plied us so very well with shot. And, as I was below in the afternoon, discharging my artillery, there was a mariner that had his leg struck all in pieces and died presently. The *San Juan de Sicilia*, and the ship of Pedro de Ugarte (the *Maria Juan* of Biscay), and one hulk, remained this day among more than twenty galleons and ships; but they were not boarded but with bullets, and so they cleared themselves and cast about towards us, but very evil entreated.

Yet the English would not board our ships in any wise, although we did amain and tarried for them and suffered all their shot of good artillery. And the ship of Pedro de Ugarte remained much spoiled and we left her, for we had not time to take in all the people. So we bare out of the north and north-east with great disorder, some investing one with another, others separating; and the English in the wind of us discharging their cannons marvellously well, and fired not one piece but it was well employed, by reason we were so nigh one another and they a good space asunder one from the other.

From the opposite side, Captain Thomas Fenner of the *Nonpareil*, one of Drake's ships, made the same point, more brutally:

A thing greatly to be regarded, that the Almighty hath stricken them with a wonderful fear; in that I have hardly seen any of their companies succoured of their extremities which befell them after their fights, but left at utter ruin, without regard, bearing as much sail as possible they might, holding the rest of their army together.

Sir William Wynter, whose ships had been helping to pound Estrade, wrote:

The fight continued from 9 of the clock until six of the clock at night, in which time the Spanish army bare away NNE and N by E, as much as they could keeping company one with another, I assure your honour in very good order. Great was the spoil and harm that was done unto them, no doubt. I deliver it under your honour upon the credit of a poor gentleman, that out of my ship there was shot 500 shot of demi-cannon, culverin, and demi-culverin; and when I was furthest off in discharging any of the pieces, I was not out of the shot of their harquebus, and most times within speech one of another. And surely every man did well; and, as I have said, no doubt the slaughter and hurt they received was great, as time will discover it; and when every man was weary of labour, and our cartridges spent, and munitions wasted – I think in some of our ships altogether – we ceased and followed the enemy, he bearing hence still in the course as I have said before.

Wynter was bone-weary and bruised when he wrote that, for he had hurt his hip during the fight by the recoil of a demi-cannon.

The battle had indeed been more terrible than Lepanto, in the nerve shock of the gun-fight, the howling battle storm of missiles, to which the Spaniards were unaccustomed. But the casualties were nothing like as great, even in the worst-hurt Spanish ships, for the new and fearful weapons were actually merciful, hurling their rain of destruction at hulls and men alike. They could not rage with sword and dagger into every nook and cranny as a blood-maddened surge of boarders could. Their main effect was on the manoeuvrability of the ships, and upon morale; the Spaniards were 'appalled', wrote Drake.

When he sat down that night to write a report for Walsyngham, he made it brief, for the letter was to go by hand, and the bearer had been present at the battle.

God hath given us so good a day in forcing the enemy so far to leeward as I hope in God the Prince of Parma and the Duke of Sidonia shall not shake hands this few days; and whensoever they shall meet, I believe neither of them will greatly rejoice at this day's service. Business commands me to end. God bless her Majesty, our gracious Sovereign, and give us all grace to live in his fear. I assure your Honour this day's service hath much appalled the enemy.

After the signature 'Fra Drake,' he added a PS: 'There must be great care taken to send us munition and victual whithersoever the enemy goeth.' Walsyngham must have had this sort of postscript by heart, for no English Admiral, throughout the campaign, ever wrote him a letter without adding something to that effect.

Various grimly comic tales went round the fleet as to the colander appearance of the *Revenge* at that moment. The Dutch historian, Meteren, wrote:

Sir Frances Drake's ship was pierced with shot aboue forty times, and his very cabben was twice shot thorow, and about the conclusion of the fight, the bed of a certain gentleman lying weary thereupon, was taken quite from under him with the force of a bullet.

Ubaldino testified to the truth of that widely told story, and added:

Shortly afterwards the Earl of Northumberland and Sir Charles Blount were resting on the same bed in the same place when it was again hit by a ball of a demi-culverin which passed through without doing any harm other than scrape the foot, taking off the toes of one who was there with them.[2]

But Drake himself, unlike Howard, whose account is mainly personal experience narrative, would talk only of tactics, not of what he and his squadron had done. Except for Seymour's brief statement, we know little of his part in the victory; but it is enough. We know that he led the English fleet into action; and we know what the result of the battle was; and that the Spaniards, at any rate, were not laughing.

The news came into Calais that the two fleets had been seen, still cannonading each other, off Zealand; the fisherman who brought it reported:

He saw some ships broken into bits, others without masts or sails, from which they were throwing overboard artillery, trunks, and many other things, whilst men were striving to save themselves by escaping in boats, with such lamentation as may be imagined.

In Calais, they must have wondered: whose ships? What the fisherman had seen must in fact have been the end of Toledo's *San Felipe*, Pimental's *San Mateo*, Pedro Ugarte's *Maria Juan*,

----

[2] Compare with Estrade's narrative. Incidents such as these, not necessarily much exaggerated, are fairly typical 'battle stories'.

of Biscay, and possibly also the patache *San Antonio de Padua*, and an unknown ship which sank next day. For, including the flag galleass *San Lorenzo*, the Armada lost at least six ships as a result of the battle off Dunkirk. This was what Hawkyns meant, when he claimed, judiciously, 'there was some hurt done among the Spaniards.'

By sunset, the three big ships were drifting slowly, out of control, the water pouring in below; and the sea was getting up. Furthest away was the shattered *Maria Juan*, 665 tons, of Recalde's Armada of Biscay; her decks were almost awash and the remnants of her crew of ninety-two seamen and 183 soldiers were perched like black crows high up on the spars and rigging. The mizzenmast was over the side, with canvas and ropes trailing in the water; her rudder had been shot away. She was done for, and signalling desperately for assistance. 'The Duke sent the aid requested,' said Calderon, 'but it was possible to save only one boatload of men, for she sank, to the great sorrow of everyone.'

At about 7 o'clock, the *San Felipe*, 800 tons, had begun to fire slow cannon shots, as a signal for aid also. The galleass *Zuniga* and a Seville galleon circled her protectively, while the hulk *Doncella*, which had been battered off the Isle of Wight and had suffered more damage this day off Dunkirk, closed in to take off the men from the foundering Portuguese galleon. 'She found the galleon sinking,' wrote Calderon, 'and took on board 300 of her men.' They included the Camp Master, Francisco Toledo, and the captain of the *San Felipe*, Juan Posa de Santiso. 'Then', recorded Medina Sidonia, 'they heard a cry that the hulk *Doncella* was herself sinking.' Toledo's reaction to this news, according to Calderon, showed a wry spirit.

When Captain Juan Posa said that the hulk was going down, the Maestre de Campo replied that, if that were the case, they had better be drowned in a galleon than in a hulk; and they both went back to the *San Felipe*.

'This was a great misfortune,' wrote the Duke, 'for it was not true that the hulk was sinking, and Don Francisco was carried in the *San Felipe* towards Zealand.'

A similar determination to stay with his ship was shown by

the other Camp Master, Don Diego Pimental, of the 750-ton *San Mateo*, rolling in the swell nearby, her pumps hard at work, but unable to stem the inrush of water. 'The Duke ordered boats to go to bring away the people from the *San Mateo* also,' recorded Medina Sidonia:

But Don Diego Pimental would not leave the ship, and sent Don Rodrigo de Vivero and Don Luis Vanegas to me, to ask if it were not possible to save her; whereupon I sent a pilot and a diver from this galleon, though there was much peril in remaining without him, my flagship having suffered from great shot, whereby she was in danger of being lost. But because it was now late, and the sea grown very heavy, they could not reach the *San Mateo*, beyond seeing her afar off, going towards Zealand.

The determination of the youthful Pimental, who was twenty-nine, contrasted strongly with the indecision in the flagship; he and Toledo represented the best spirit of Spain. There were many in the Armada, at that moment, whose comments on the inoffensive Duke, and the real commander of the fleet, Diego Flores, who was with him all the time, were unprintable. Uncomfortably aware of this, Medina Sidonia tried to protect himself by concluding that day's entry in the War Diary:

This day the Duke wished to turn on the enemy with the whole Armada, so as he would not leave the Channel; but the pilots told him that it was impossible because with the sea and wind, setting straight on the coast, they must by force go into the North Sea, or else the whole Armada would be driven on to the banks. Thus in no way could they avoid leaving the Channel; nearly all the ships being spoiled and unable to resist longer, as well as from the damage they had received as from not having shot for their ordnance.

Whichever way one looked at it, it was defeat. The Armada was running away from Dunkirk, sailing further and further with every hour from the waiting invasion barges; and with stricken ships falling astern, to sink, or to drift helplessly ashore into the hands of the furious Dutch. Mixed emotions of sadness, rage, and terror filled the minds of the men who were part of that great, ruined enterprise. Sadness at the loss of friends, rage at the humbling of Spain, terror of the night and the spume-covered sandbanks to shoreward of them, and the deadly English ships riding easily somewhere in the darkness to seaward. 'Hardly a man slept that night,' wrote de la Torre. 'We went along all wondering when we should strike one of those banks.'

16

'Ask Diego Flores!'

Our ships, God be thanked, have received little hurt, and are of great force to accompany them, and of such advantage that with some continuance of the seas, and sufficiently provided of shot and powder, we shall be able, with God's favour, to weary them out of the sea and confound them.

John Hawkyns to Walsyngham

Next morning, the wreck of the enterprise was plain. The great *capitana* of the Armada, Medina Sidonia's *San Martin*, was driving helplessly on to the banks beyond Dunkirk, lagging behind, with one of her anchors down for sounding purposes. 'There appeared to be no hope for her; either she must fall into the hands of the enemy or run on the banks,' wrote Calderon. Oquendo's flagship came nosing up alongside, and the Duke cried out desperately to his Admiral: 'Senor Oquendo, what shall we do? We are lost!'

'Ask Diego Flores!' came the unfeeling reply.

Which, being translated, meant: 'Run aground, and be damned to the pair of you!' To rub it in, Oquendo shouted: 'As for me, I am going to fight, and die like a man. Send me a supply of shot.'

Astern, left to her fate, another great Spanish ship was wallowing out of control. One of Recalde's men, taken later, thought she was Castilian, but that is all we know of her identity, for her end was very sudden. The Queen's ship *Hope*, 600 tons, Captain Robert Crosse, had barely run alongside her, in view of both fleets, when she foundered. Howard reported briefly:

One of the enemy's great ships was espied to be in great distress by the captain of her Majesty's ship called the *Hope*; who being in speech of yielding unto the said captain, before they could agree on certain conditions, sank presently before their eyes . . . In all, we sank three of their ships, and made four to go room with the shore so leak as they were not able to live at sea.

Four certainly were ashore that morning, but we know nothing of the third ship which Howard claimed sunk. He, however, was sure of it; he referred to it in three separate documents, one of which included the delightful phrase: 'whereof there is three of them a-fishing on the bottom of the sea.'

In all, Howard claimed nine enemy ships sunk, stranded, or surrendered in the fighting since Plymouth: Don Pedro's *Rosario*, Oquendo's vice-flag *San Salvador*, de Moncada's *San Lorenzo*, Toledo's *San Felipe*, Pimental's *San Mateo*, the pinnace *San Antonio de Padua*, and three sent to the bottom, the *Maria Juan*, a possible Castile ship, and one unknown. Eight great ships and a pinnace. Both Seymour and Fenner made the same claim, independently, Seymour listing eight 'great ships' and Fenner eight 'of the best sorts of shipping'. And all this for no ships sunk, or even badly damaged, on the English side, and 'the least losses' of men, for the English decks were bare, except for mariners and gunners; there was no massed human target for the Spanish cannon to play on. Indeed, it was the necessary presence of such a target which made the Spanish losses so exceptionally heavy. History in future was to show such fights as surprisingly economical in life (the British losses at Trafalgar were only 1,158 killed), and the actual sinking of a ship as very much the exception to the rule (only one at Trafalgar, and she caught fire). But, by then, both sides had reverted to boarding, following bombardment, because there was no such tremendous disparity in numbers between one side and the other as that which had made the Armada campaign unique. The English had done well; but felt that, with a little luck and plentiful ammunition, they could have done very much better. The Armada, with its mixture of nationalities, began to fray at the edges; and first to go were the Dutch, who were being carried past and away from the shores of their own country in a defeated and probably doomed expedition.

They saw the ruined ships simply abandoned to their fate, and a group of Dutch mariners, fourteen in all, who were serving in one of the Armada vessels, read that as a lesson that there was no hope except for him who helped himself. That day, therefore, probably in the early hours of the morning, they had recourse to a desperate expedient, for their Dutch interrogator reported: 'Having made sails for their cockboat with their shirts, they are now fled away from the Spanish fleet.' They reported that three ships had been sunk in the recent battle, which is some confirmation of Howard's claim, and that 'one of her Majesty's ships valiantly passed through them to charge the Admiral, who fled away, and – as they say – doth seem to be wonderfully dismayed and discouraged.' A Spaniard taken later from Recalde's ship said much the same thing: 'The English fleet pursued the Spanish fleet in such sort as if they had offered to board the Spanish fleet, he saw their admiral so fearful, he thinketh they had all yielded.' Oquendo's jeered advice to his commander-in-chief was representative of much feeling in the Armada as a whole.

Meanwhile, in Dunkirk haven that morning, the Duke of Parma and Don Jorge Manrique almost came to blows. Juan Manrique wrote to Juan de Idiaquez, the King's Secretary: 'Don Jorge Manrique is here, and it is quite pitiable to see how he goes on.' Ships of the Armada were drifting ashore all along the coast, and the dull boom of cannon showed that the Dutch were furiously assailing them. Cruising off Dunkirk, where the waves seethed whitely over the banks, were forty Dutch ships under Count Justinus of Nassau, riding in plain view of the Spaniards; the Armada was gone from sight, harried by the English. The quays of Dunkirk and the other invasion ports were crowded with armed and armoured Spanish soldiery – 16,000 of them – and at last Don Jorge Manrique saw the pitiable craft in which they were supposed to cross the Channel, mostly flat-bottomed barges, mere empty scows. The King knew it, for Parma had told him often enough. The English knew it, for Seymour had reported to Walsyngham on 30 July: 'They be no boats to be hazarded to the seas, no more than wherries or cockboats.' But Don Jorge Manrique, the Inspector-General of the Armada, did not know it. No one in the Armada flagship apparently knew it, for the Duke had for days been showering Parma with begging letters, asking him to come out with his fleet to help the Armada. But, even when Don

Jorge Manrique saw what that fleet actually consisted of, he persisted in giving the Duke's message, and angrily tried to insist that Parma ought to comply.

At 10.30 that morning, he tracked Parma down on the quayside at Dunkirk, having missed him the previous day, for Parma had just left his main HQ at Bruges to visit the soldiers embarking at Nieuport; and there he presented to him Medina Sidonia's incredible demands. 'The Duke requests that we here should go and help him obtain a port, and especially to capture the Isle of Wight,' complained Parma to the King. 'This is the request brought to me by Don Jorge Manrique. Or else, that I should join him to engage the enemy . . .' Exasperated, Parma called in the Marquis de Renti and other experts, and questioned them in front of Don Jorge Manrique, so that the latter might be satisfied that he was not fabricating difficulties and that, in particular, these unseaworthy scows were not capable of a sea voyage of seven or eight days, which would be the time required to carry out the Duke's favourite plan, not yet abandoned, of capturing the Isle of Wight. Baffled by seamen's science, Don Jorge and some other officers from the Armada who had brought messages during the previous week, furiously pointed out that the scows had no guns, that they had seen no troops embarked in them, and that it appeared no real preparations had been made.

Parma patiently explained that his boats were troop transports, invasion barges; not fighting ships. The Armada was supposed to provide the fighting ships. 'The most we could hope from these boats,' he said, 'would be, in fine, settled weather, and with the Channel clear of enemies, to ferry our men across, as had been arranged.' As for the boats not being loaded, surely they did not expect the men to be herded into them like cattle for days at a time? They could all be loaded very quickly, when required, almost simultaneously, in the great network of rivers and canals behind Nieuport and Dunkirk. Three days was his estimate. Parma had detected long ago the flaw in the whole enterprise – the lack of a port in which the Armada could make a safe junction with the invasion craft and safely escort them out, granted that they had previously beaten the English fleet, and driven off the Dutch. That is, if the Armada seriously intended a full-scale landing in the Thames estuary, and was not just a gigantic bluff to influence the English peace commissioners (who were still at Ostend). One may suspect that Parma's ostentatious embarkation at Nieuport the previous day was a bluff, too, for only the most reckless commander would send out his soldiers in such craft across the Channel when it was obvious from the hysterical messages of Medina Sidonia that he was quite unable to cope with the English fleet at sea.

Into this heated discussion, however, strode Philip's bastard son, the Duke of Ascoli, whose pinnace had just got into Dunkirk after its narrow escape from the English; and also, in other small boats, two men with even more up-to-the-minute news, Captain Marolin de Juan, the Armada's navigator, and Major Gallinaro. Their news abruptly terminated the debate. Invasion had become an academic exercise. Parma summed up their reports: 'The Duke is running to the north, his full losses unknown, and the English continue to follow him with very swift vessels, manned by good and experienced sailors.' Ascoli begged to be allowed to rejoin the Armada, but Parma, taking pity on him, absolutely forbade it.

Meanwhile the Armada, or part of it, hemmed in on the banks by a north-west wind and the English fleet hovering with silent guns to seaward of them, was still in danger. Calderon's narrative implies that it was only the flagship which was in deadly peril, but Medina Sidonia wrote that it was the whole fleet.

The Duke shot off two pieces to collect his Armada, and sent a pinnace with a pilot to order them to keep a close luff, because they were very near to the banks of Zealand. For which cause the enemy remained aloof, seeing that our Armada must be lost; for the pilots on board the flagship – men of experience of that coast – told the Duke at this time that it was not possible to save a single ship of the Armada; for that with the wind as it was, in the NW, they must all needs go on the banks of Zealand; that God alone could prevent it. Being in this peril, without any sort of remedy, God was pleased to change the wind to WSW, whereby the fleet stood towards the North without hurt to any ship, the Duke sending order to every ship to follow the flagship, for that otherwise they would go on the banks of Zealand.

Possibly there is some exaggeration here, for the Duke also wrote that he was in this plight because he and some other ships had remained in the rear and defied the English, 'in the hope of returning to the Channel'; which was very far from being their intention. This was the crushing moment of defeat, the season for excuses; and the War Diary was duly written up to this effect, Medina Sidonia inserting a paragraph at this point to show where the blame really lay.

In regard to the fighting, and the turning to relieve and assist his ships, and the abiding of the coming of the enemy, the Duke took counsel with the Camp Master Don Francisco de Bobadilla; but in regard to the conduct of the fleet, and such matters as related to the sea, the Duke had the council of the general Diego Flores, whom he also ordered to move into the flagship, because he was one of the oldest and most experienced in sea affairs.

Quite clearly, the Armada's calculated policy of desertion of all its damaged ships, from Don Pedro's *Rosario* off Plymouth to the last unfortunate ship which went down that day, her survivors being picked up by the English, not the Spanish, had aroused outspoken resentment; as it was bound to do. It was just about the worst possible blow that any leader could deliver to morale and to his own authority; in effect, an abdication of leadership. Hence the well-calculated stress, written into the War Diary, of the brave part played in the actual fighting by the *San Martin*, the ship of the headquarters trio – Medina Sidonia, Bobadilla, and Diego Flores de Valdes.

There is no word, from the English side, of any attempt to put the Armada ashore, off the Isle of Wight, off Dunkirk, or on this day. But then, except for an occasional hint from Howard, the English leaders are resolutely silent about their battle aims, even in official correspondence. In the public accounts of the campaign, written shortly afterwards, there was naturally no highlighting of the dreadful fact that the whole Spanish fleet was running away from empty guns, for that reflected just as badly on the efficiency of the English Government as it did on the nerve and resolution of the Armada leadership. But we do know that there were outbursts of rage among the English; for, clearly, this was the moment to tear into them, hammer the defeated, damaged, demoralized enemy, and sink, cripple or ground many more of his ships. We know, from the statement of Fray Bernado de Gongora, that the previous day 'many of the ships went on fighting in eight cubits of water, and as the enemy knew the danger we were in, they harried us so much that we were almost lost.' And we know, from Estrade's narrative, that at that time the Armada was in 'great disorder'. To drive their worst-beaten opponents on to the banks was an obvious gambit which the English would not have overlooked; but the victory could be made final and crushing neither on the Monday nor on the Tuesday because there was not enough powder and shot left in the English ships with which to do it. That they knew what opportunity was missed is very clear. Howard was to tell Walsyngham so, on 17 August; and Henry Whyte was to write in the same terms on the day following: 'By this simple relation, your Honour may see how our parsimony at home hath bereaved us of the famousest victory that ever our navy might have had at sea.'

As it was, on this day, Tuesday, 9 August, the shot-torn Armada presented to the English an unhappy spectacle, as Thomson wrote:

At this instant, we are as far to the eastward as the Isle of Walcheren, wherein Flushing doth stand, and about 12 leagues off the shore; and the wind hanging westerly, we drive our enemies apace to the eastward, much marvelling, if the wind continue, in what port they will direct themselves. There is want of powder, shot and victual amongst us, which causeth that we cannot so daily assail them as we would, but I trust her majesty may, by God's help, little fear any invasion by these ships; their power being, by battle, mortality, and other accidents, so decayed, and those that are left alive so weak and hurtless, and they could be well content to lose all charges to be at home, both rich and poor.

It was imperative, in both fleets, that urgent decisions be made; and both Howard and Medina Sidonia called to council in their flagships. We know that the Spaniards asked for ammunition states, damage reports, and casualty returns, or, as Gongora put it in the more dramatic language of the day:

Finally it was decided that a count should be taken, with all the ships, of how it had gone with them, and how many people were dead; and it was found that the ships which were from the fight, all no longer had any cannon balls, and they came to the flagship to ask for them.

That is, the strongest and most important ships, which had borne the brunt of battle, were reduced to musket and harquebus fire in future, unless the weaker ships could be milked of some of their ammunition. The English must have reported, informally, under similar headings; and we know from a dozen or more witnesses that they were almost out of shot, like the Spaniards, and lacked in addition powder and victual. But damage and casualties had been relatively light. 'Received little hurt' was the phrase used by Hawkyns; 'the least losses that ever hath been heard of; I verily believe there is not three score men lost of her Majesty's forces,' reported Fenner. The position in the Armada was very different, according to the Duke: 'The ships were spoiled and unable, that hitherto had resisted the enemy,' another reference to the decimation of the most powerful units.

Ironically, neither side knew that the other was out of ammunition. Armada ships had been cannonading until late the previous day, and although the guns of some ships had fallen silent, so that the only reply from them was musketry, these few were in a shot-torn and sinking condition, with masts gone by the board and guns dismounted, blood running from the gun-ports in their holed and splintered sides; that firing aboard them virtually ceased was only to be expected. All the English estimates of Spanish weakness after the battle speak of the shot-damage, the inevitably terrible battle casualties among the close-packed men aboard, the equally inevitable sickness casualties, the loss of sailing power, anchors, and boats. Similarly, and throughout the whole series of Channel battles, no one in the Armada guessed at the continual English ammunition shortages; when the English broke off each action, the Spaniards flattered themselves that they had 'beaten off' the enemy.

The simultaneous shortage of ammunition in both fleets, however, did not leave them equal. Far from it. The offensive power of the English fleet lay solely in its guns; when its artillery fell silent, it was impotent. The Armada, on the other hand, still had teeth – the remnants of the 19,000 fighting soldiers originally embarked. According to the Dutch deserters, 10,000 of these were highly trained fighting men, virtually without equal in Europe, the rest being 'vine-growers, shepherds, and the like'. Except for the unfavourable wind, and the ruined condition of some of the ships, there was now nothing whatever to stop Medina Sidonia returning to the Channel, or even landing this still formidable force of troops on the shores of the Thames estuary. The Duke had a real card left to play; Howard had nothing up his sleeve. Consequently it was with some trepidation, and the thought of a kingdom at stake, that he regarded the great hulls of the retreating Spanish ships that afternoon. If they decided to beat back to the Channel, as some of the Spanish leaders were even then urging, there was nothing he could do to prevent it.

Howard must have been excessively conscious of the empty threat his guns now presented, for his assessment of the Armada at this point is strikingly different from that of every other English seaman who put his views on paper. 'Their force is wonderful great and strong,' he wrote on the evening of the battle, 'and yet we pluck their feathers by little and little.' 'Some made little account of the Spanish force by sea,' he wrote a week later, 'but I do warrant you, all the world never saw such a force as theirs was.' And the day after, he told Walsyngham, 'It is very likely they will return; for, in my thinking, they dare not go back with this dishonour and shame; for we have marvellously plucked them.' Of course, the Spanish force *was* 'wonderful great and strong' compared to a fleet without an army aboard, and with no powder and shot for its guns. Possibly he was overpainting the picture a little, in his reports to the authorities in London, in the belief that only a dramatically presented threat would stir them into further action. Hawkyns, cold, accurate, businesslike as usual, ended his own favourable assessment of the situation with the sharp reminder, 'Yet I gather certainly, there are amongst them 50 forcible and invincible ships . . .' These he listed, as a pertinent hint that his demand for powder and shot was no idle request.

Fenner thought the Armada was done for; Wynter was confident, too. 'And in my conscience, I speak it to your Honour, I think the Duke would give his dukedom to be in Spain again. But the worst is to be reckoned of . . .' and he at once went on to demand 'victual, powder, shot, match, lead, and canvas to make cartridges.' Drake was worried only about Parma's force, for, unlike Wynter and Seymour, who had been watching it for months, he did not know how weak it was, and perhaps feared a sudden descent on the English coast on a calm day. On 10 August he wrote:

We have the army of Spain before us, and mind, with the grace of God, to wrestle a pull with him. There was never anything pleased me better than to see the enemy flying with a southerly wind to the northwards. God grant you have a good eye to the Duke of Parma; for with the grace of God, if we live, I doubt it not ere it be long so to handle the matter with the Duke of Sidonia as he shall wish himself at St Mary Port among his orange trees.[1]

Whatever Howard wrote, his actions belied his words; for the decision of the council, held on the afternoon of 9 August, off Walcheren, was to detach two squadrons from his force that night to guard the approaches to London. In short, he intended to weaken his force by nearly a third, and with the remainder to 'set on a brag countenance, and give them chase, as though we wanted for nothing, until we had cleared our own coast and some part of Scotland of them.' Wynter did not receive the bad news in person, and so was unable to argue.

I was not able to go aboard, by the reason of a hurt that I had received in my hip, by the reversing of one of our demi-cannons in the fight.

[1] On 2 September, Drake put his expert finger on the fatal flaws in the Spanish plan, which was Philip's. It demanded, he pointed out, an impossible combination of a high spring tide, a flat calm sea, a wind favourable for England, a lightning embarkation within twenty-four hours, and an unimpeded assembly. 'My judgement is that the Duke of Sidonia, his fleet, needs jump with fair weather, the highest of a spring, with good wind, and the Duke of Parma embarking all in one day. This were very meet for them; for if any one of these fail them, they shall never perform as much as they have promised to the King, their master. Now, for the Duke of Sidonia, his fleet, there is no harbour for them upon that coast, so that to stir it requireth fair weather; which, when it happen that we should find them there, he is like, God willing, to have unquiet rest.'

But after the Council was ended, my Lord Admiral sent aboard me a gentleman of his, both to see how I did, and also to tell me that my Lord Seymour had order to repair back again, to guard the Thames mouth from any attempt that might be made by the Duke of Parma; and that I was to attend upon him, and so were all the rest that were of his former charge; and that we should bear away in the twilight, as the enemy might not see our departing. And so, obeying the commandment, I did about 8 of the clock in the night, bear back again through our fleet.

But Seymour was present, and Seymour was furious. He complained about it officially, not only to Walsyngham, but to the Queen. Although

his Lordship was altogether desirous at the first to have me strengthen him, so having done the uttermost of my good will (to the venture of my life) in prosecuting the distressing of the Spaniards, I find my Lord jealous and loth to have me take part of the honour of the rest that is to win, using his authority to command me to look to our English coasts, that have been long threatened by the Duke of Parma. I therein have obeyed his Lordship much against my will, expecting your Majesty's further pleasure. I pray God my Lord Admiral do not find the lack of the *Rainbow* and that company; for I protest before God, and have witness for the same, I vowed I would be as near or nearer with my little ship to encounter our enemies, as any of the greatest ships in both armies; which I have performed to the distress of one of their greatest ships sunk, if I have my due.

But this was mere eagerness for battle, for he told Walsyngham: 'I presume the Spaniards are much distressed for victuals, which I hope will be the cause to make them yield to her Majesty's mercy.' And so, in the darkness off Lowestoft that night, the Narrows fleet set course for Harwich.

The council held the same day in the *San Martin* confirmed exactly the assessments of the majority of the English leaders. There were 3,000 sick already, and victuals left for less than a month, the way home round Scotland and out into the Atlantic being long and arduous. For the record – and for the record only – an undefeated note was inserted in the War Diary. 'The Council was wholly of the opinion that they should go back to the Channel if the weather would permit it; but if not, that then, constrained by the weather, they should return by the North Sea to Spain . . .' But in a letter to the King, written at sea nearly two weeks later, when all pretence had gone, Medina Sidonia confessed:

This Armada was so completely crippled and scattered that my first duty to your Majesty seemed to save it, even at the risk which we are running in undertaking this voyage, which is so long and in such high latitudes. Ammunition and the best of our vessels were lacking, and experience had shown how little we could depend upon the ships that remained, the Queen's fleet being so superior to ours in this sort of fighting, in consequence of the strength of their artillery and the fast sailing of their ships.

Fray Bernado de Gongora, also in the flagship, was slightly more explicit.

The enemy did not dare to come alongside because he knew the advantage we had. The Duke offered him battle many times and he never wanted it, but only to fire on us, like a man who had better artillery with longer range.

The King's own prediction of the English tactics, made so many months before, echoed in defeat. And Medina Sidonia's warning, too. 'If you send me, depend upon it, I shall have a bad account to render of my trust.'

But for Howard, there was no exultant sense of triumph. He had been promised that powder and shot would be sent after him, but it had not arrived. It never did arrive. On 19 August, Sir Thomas Heneage, Vice-Chamberlain of the Household, was told by the Earl of Cumberland that 'Her Majesty's navy has not received a corn of all that was set down in paper by my Lord Treasurer, which I take to be above 30 last, and sent by us . . .' The Armada flew from an enemy not capable of fighting even half a battle, and the pursuing English were unable to complete their hard-fought victory of Dunkirk. Howard summed up: 'If we had had that which had been sent, England and her Majesty had had the most honour that ever any nation had. But God be thanked; it is well.'

And Seymour echoed him: 'I can say no more, but God doth show his mighty hand for protecting this little island, for His glory and to the honour of our country.'

17

'It Will be to Their Great Ruin'

The Armada was abreast of Lowestoft, when Seymour and Wynter turned back for Harwich on the evening of 9 August; next day, it was well on its way to Newcastle. But astern of the Armada, more than a hundred miles astern on Wednesday, 10 August, Don Diego Pimental's abandoned galleon *San Mateo* was still resisting, fighting on into the afternoon against an encircling ring of Dutch ships. She had fought against heavy odds all day on the 8th, 'until she was a thing of pity to see, riddled with shot like a sieve'; she had been hopelessly aground on the banks to seaward of Blankenberg all day on the 9th, moving sluggishly in the waves, a stranded wreck, with 350 shot holes in her hull; and on Wednesday, 10 August, the Dutch had come down to get her. Sir Pieter van der Does, Vice-Admiral of Holland, led the attack, and in one of his ships went an English liaison official, William Borlas. He expected a swift surrender from the riddled thing, but from her ruined sides Pimental's seasoned infantry sent out volley after defiant volley at the savagely determined Dutch. 'They fought it out until they saw no remedy,' was the report that reached the Earl of Leicester at Tilbury camp a few days later. But the actual battle had little chivalry; it was grim and, with the fall of the first Dutchman, waged without quarter.

William Borlas penned a brief description to Walsyngham, from Flushing.

The last July [10 August] my Lord Governor was advertised by a small boat that came from the sea that there was one great ship of the Spaniards lying between Ostend and the Sluys. Whereupon my Lord sent out presently three men-of-war that lie here before the town, and I myself went out in them; so that the same day about one of the clock we came where he was, having been beaten and dispersed from the fleet by her Majesty's ships; yet he fought with us two hours, and hurt divers of our men; but at the last yielded himself. The commander in her was Don de Pimental, the son and heir of the Marquis de Tavara. There was another marquis's son in her, and divers particular gentlemen of good account. I was the means that the best sort were saved; and the rest were cast overboard and slain at the entry. There was slain in her two Englishmen; the one was a brother of my Lord Montagu's as your Honour shall see by a letter that I found in the ship.

When the States of Zealand reported on this to Queen Elizabeth, they wrote:

The Spanish prisoners do hold it for a miracle that amongst the slain, as well by the English ordnance as our own, for the little it did, hath always struck down the principal traitors, and amongst others hath slain the banished English lords.

The same day, another group of Dutch ships closed in on the equally battered galleon *San Felipe*, aground between Nieuport and Ostend, in full view of Parma's forces. As most of her crew had transferred to the hulk *Doncella* on the evening of the battle, she put up small resistance, and Don Francisco de Toledo, who had gone back into her, remarking that if he had to die, he had rather do it in a galleon than in a hulk, escaped to Nieuport with some of his companions in boats sent out by the Duke of Parma. Pimental of the *San Mateo* was also alive, but a prisoner at Flushing. The Dutch had also spared the lives of two youths, Frantz Muelenpeert, of Herenthals, seventeen years old, who had been for the last nine years in Spain and forgotten almost all his Flemish; and William Olychers, of Luxembourg, twenty years old, who had been in Spain a similar time. Truly, the Armada was an international force, whereas the English fleet was manned entirely by Englishmen – if we exclude one Genoese banker known to be aboard. In fact, so distrustful of foreigners were they, that they chose, at this turn of the crisis, not to rely in any way even on their allies, the Dutch.

Howard had contemptuously reported, after the battle off Dunkirk, 'There is not one Flushinger or Hollander at the seas,' which was probably a contributory factor – their lack of victuals was the other – for sending Seymour and Wynter back to guard the Straits. But the Dutch fleet, as it had just shown, was ready to pounce on any Spaniard; and if Parma's unarmed barges came wallowing out, they were in favour of letting them get out, right out into the middle of the Channel first. It would be a long way to swim, in breastplate and helmet. But the English Government was worried. Indeed, they wrote, on the day the *San Mateo* was taken, a warning letter to Howard, to inform him

that some Englishmen, and Spaniards also that are taken, do say that the intent of the Spanish navy is to draw along the English navy from the coast of Flanders, that the sea being clear, the Duke of Parma might come out with his forces to invade the realm.

Only the Dutch knew what complete mastery they had in their own waters and, although the States of Zealand wrote to the English Queen to assure her of it, the English continued to believe in the possibility of a sudden descent on their coasts by Parma, and the arrival of the Spanish army even in the Thames.

In the end, the Dutch lost both their Spanish prizes, for the *San Felipe* and the *San Mateo* had been so shattered that they sank, reported the States: 'One in the haven of Flushing, and the other athwart of Rammekens. The third sank between Ostend and Blankenberg, without anything being saved.' The third ship was presumably the seventy-five-ton pinnace *San Antonio de Padua*, whose loss off Ostend was reported by Parma. News of the captures, however, embittered some of the English. Seymour wrote: 'These Hollanders have lighted upon these argosies which *we* did distress; and they have received great spoil thereof.' Rights of pillage were then highly regarded; and legitimate.

Together with their well-meant warning about Parma, the Council sent that day to Howard a lengthy questionnaire calculated to delight the heart of any accountant with a few weeks to spare. 'What number of ships are in service, and of what burden? How many are the Queen's own ships? How many of them are ships of good bulk? How many are pinnaces, and how many of the country's charge?' Three questions simply begged for a NIL Return: 'How are the Queen's ships victualled?' 'How are the other ships victualled?' 'What powder and shot every ship hath?' Then, understandably, 'How much powder and shot doth the navy use to spend in the fights with the enemies upon one day?' And so on endlessly:

What losses of men and ships hath been on the Spanish side? and where were the losses? and where are the prisoners? And what powder, munition and any treasure hath been taken upon them? What losses hath happened to the Queen's army of ships and men? What causes are there why the Spanish navy hath not been boarded by the Queen's ships? And though some of the ships of Spain may be thought too huge to be boarded by the English, yet some of the Queen's ships are thought very able to have boarded divers of the meaner ships of the Spanish navy.

That was the sting in the tail, from the bureaucrats in their offices in St James's.

Oddly enough, only the previous day, Calderon had reported a contrary rumour current in the Armada: 'We learnt that the enemy had orders from the Queen, that, on pain of death, no ship of theirs was to come to close quarters with any of ours.' And on Thursday, 11 August, he drew an equally fallacious conclusion from observed facts. 'The enemy's fleet now numbered only 90 vessels, which continued to follow us. It is to be concluded from this that their ships had suffered much, and had been obliged to put into port to refit.' Then came a startling observation.

On this day the Duke ordered Don Christobal de Avila, captain of the hulk *Santa Barbara*, to be hanged; and condemned to the galleys other ship captains, as well as reducing some army officers. It is said that this was because on the day of the battle they allowed themselves to drift out of the fight.

One of the captains condemned to death was Francisco Cuellar of the Castilian galleon *San Pedro*. His narrative is rather different, and probably more accurate, giving a plausible reason for this outburst of savagery on the part of the Duke, whose neighbour in Spain Don Christobal de Avila was.

The order now enforced was that promulgated by the Duke on 1 August, after the rout of his rear wings off Plymouth, that 'the sergeant majors should range the fleet, giving to each ship captain in writing his place in the fleet, and that if any ship left her appointed place, they should without further stay hang the captain of the said ship.' With them had gone the hangmen, ready to carry out the order. This erratic vengeance, not invoked at any time during the fighting, now fell when the entire Armada, led by the Duke, was hot-footing it homeward, hustled on towards Spain by an English fleet with empty guns. And, moreover, leaving behind them, still fighting, better men than they in the two stranded galleons of Portugal. If the craven leadership of the Armada had had one-half the spirit shown by Pimental and Toledo, the English Government might have rued their administrative shortcomings. Nothing, certainly not the weather, 'constrained' the Armada from returning to the Channel, except the anxiety of Medina Sidonia, Diego Flores, and Bobadilla not again to face the English. And the immediate cause of their fury was that Don Christobal and Cuellar had gone ahead of the fleeing flagship, in order to lie-to for a while and repair damage sustained in action. It was the reaction of a man who, after a bad day at the office, expends his temper on his own family.

Don Christobal must have been overwhelmed by the sudden irrationality of the order, for in a short time he was writhing by the neck from the yard-arm of a pinnace, which displayed his kicking body throughout the fleet. Cuellar was made of sterner stuff. First, he shouted at the executioners, quoting the casualty list of his ship. Then he asked for a copy of their orders. Then he insisted that his crew should be questioned, to prove that this ship at least had never shirked her duty. 'If any of them should blame me, you can cut me into four quarters!' he roared. But afterwards he wrote:

They would not listen to me, nor to many gentlemen who interceded for me, answering that the Duke at that time kept his cabin and was very unhappy and did not want anybody to speak to him. For besides the ill-success he always had with the enemy, on the day of my tribulation he had been told that the two galleons, San Mateo and San Felipe, had been destroyed and sunk, and almost all hands drowned. For this reason the Duke kept himself in his cabin, and his Councillors did acts of injustice right and left in order to correct his neglect, disregarding the lives and honours of those that were not to blame, and that is so public that everybody knows it.

The news must have been brought by a pinnace, so that it was obvious to everyone that Don Diego de Pimental had gone down fighting, alone, forty-eight hours after the Great Armada had given up the fight and fled north for Spain. No one, not even the premier nobleman of Spain, could ever outlive that disgrace.

Medina Sidonia was a thing that no one cared to look upon at that moment; and forever afterwards. As for Diego Flores, no fighting man in the Armada would ever take another order from him. Oquendo had not even bothered to attend the Council held after the battle; or had not been invited, because his insults would be unendurable. The man now in charge of the retreat was Don Francisco de Bobadilla, the Camp Master; and that was fitting, for according to Medina Sidonia, it had been at his promptings that the Armada had always abandoned its cripples. Cuellar, who 'had thought to burst into a passion' when he first heard his sentence, was carried to the flagship and brought before Bobadilla. He must have argued equally forcefully there, for Bobadilla washed his hands of the matter and ordered Cuellar to be given into the custody of the Judge Advocate, Martin de Aranda, whose ship was one of the Levant squadron. Aranda made brief enquiries, and reported to the flagship that there were no grounds for an execution and that he refused to carry out the sentence unless he received a written order from the Duke in person.

And the Duke sent answer to the Judge Advocate that he should not execute the sentence upon me, but upon Don Christobal, whom they hanged with great cruelty and insult, considering that he was a gentleman and known to many.

But Cuellar was not given back his command; he remained under open arrest in the Levanter in the custody of the Judge Advocate, as the Armada continued its homeward voyage. And at noon on Friday, 12 August, the Spaniards saw the English fleet, those familiar ships which had dogged them at the heels since Plymouth, wear round and dwindle rapidly to the south. They were alone.

Howard had expected the Spaniards to put into the Firth of Forth, and had based his plans on that. 'Verily thinking that they would put into the Firth, his Lordship had devised stratagems to make an end of them,' he wrote. But the Armada had had enough, and it was Howard who set course for the Firth of Forth. A Queen's pinnace, the *Advice*, and a caravel of Drake's, were left to shadow the Spanish fleet 'from afar off, until they were shot beyond the Isles of Orkney and Shetland,' wrote Fenner. If for any reason the Spaniards turned back, the pinnaces were to report it.

Therefore the 2nd [12th] of August, about 12 of the clock at noon, we hauled west, the better to recover our coast to attain the Firth, the enemy going away North-West and by North, as they did before. The third [13th] of August in the morning, about ten of the clock, the wind came up at North-West. Counsel therefore taken – it was thought meet to take the benefit thereof for our reliefs of powder, shot, and victual, so as to bear with all possible speed to the North Foreland; and as if the enemy should return, we might be beforehand furnished of some of our wants, the readier thereby to offend them.

In this report, written on 14 August from the *Nonpareil*, Captain Fenner made his prophetic estimate.

I verily believe great extremity shall force them if they see England again. By all that I can gather they are weakened of eight of their best sorts of shipping, which contained many men; also many wasted in sickness and slaughter. Their masts and sails much spoiled; their pinnaces and boats many cast off and wasted; wherein they shall find great wants when they come to land and water, which they must shortly do or die; and where or how, my knowledge cannot imagine. As the wind serveth, no place but between the Foreland and Hull. If the wind by change suffer them, I verily believe they will pass about Scotland and Ireland to draw themselves home; wherein, the season of the year considered, with the long course they have to run and their sundry distresses, and – of necessity – the spending of time by watering, winter will so come on as it will be to their great ruin.

Barely had Fenner finished the letter, when the wind, favourable for the return of the Armada, if to return was their intention, changed once again.

Within two hours after the writing of this letter the wind came up at South-West, so as thereby the enemy was able neither to seize England, Ireland, Scotland, Flanders, and hardly the out isles of

Scotland. This 4th day and 5th [14th and 15th], especially at night, continued very great storm at South-West, we being forced to ride out in the sea in the extremity thereof. Which storm hath, in mine opinion, touched the enemy very near. Mine opinion is they are by this time so distressed, being so far thrust of, as many of them will never see Spain again.

Scattered by the storm, the English fleet put into this port and that in small groups. Howard wrote:

My Lord of Cumberland bare with a pinnace into Harwich; I bare with some of the ships into Margate road; where the rest are gone I do not know, for we had a most violent storm as ever was seen at this time of the year, that put us asunder athwart of Norfolk, amongst many ill-favoured sands. I know not what you think at Court, but I do think, and so doth all here, that there cannot be too great forces maintained yet for five or six weeks, on the seas.

The chickens of ill-preparation, which had prevented crushing victory, were coming home to roost.

By 18 August, most of the ships were safely in, and the English Admirals had time to write to Walsyngham. 'Whether the Duke mind to return or not, I know not,' said Drake, 'but my opinion to your Honour is that I think he neither mindeth nor is in case to do so.' But he added, in a letter to the Queen: 'My poor opinion is that I dare not advise her Majesty to hazard a Kingdom with the saving of a little charge.' And, again to Walsyngham: 'The Prince of Parma I take him to be as a bear robbed of her whelps; and no doubt but, being so great a soldier as he is, that he will presently, if he may, undertake some great matter.' And Howard conjectured that the Armada might after all go to the Orkneys, or to Norway, or to Denmark, to rest, repair damage, and revictual, before coming south again, 'for I think they dare not return to Spain with this dishonour and shame to their king, and overthrow of their Pope's credit.'

With a sheaf of doubtful letters on his desk, Walsyngham complained to the Lord Treasurer: 'It is hard now to resolve what advice to give her Majesty for disarming, until it shall be known what is become of the Spanish fleet.' And to the Lord Chancellor, he wrote: 'I am sorry the Lord Admiral was forced to leave the prosecution of the enemy through the wants he sustained. Our half-doings breed dishonour and leaveth the disease uncured.'

Disease was present in the most literal sense, for the wooden ships were insanitary and the food, stored and prepared under appalling conditions, probably semi-poisonous. On 20 August, Howard wrote to Burghley from Margate:

My good Lord – Sickness and mortality begins wonderfully to grow amongst us; and it is a most pitiful sight to see, here at Margate, how the men, having no place to receive them into here, die in the streets. I am driven myself, of force, to come a-land, to see them bestowed in some lodging; and the best I can get is barns and such outhouses; and the relief is small that I can provide for them here. It would grieve any man's heart to see them that have served so valiantly to die so miserably.

An infinitely terrible epitaph.

Not only were the men dying, but they were dying unpaid, wretchedly, in poverty, begging for a place to lie, for a bite of food. Howard was so furious at the Lord Treasurer's neglect, that he raided Don Pedro's golden hoard, kept safe aboard Drake's *Revenge* until now, and pawned his own plate. He explained to Walsyngham exactly what he had done.

Sir, I send you here enclosed a note of the money Sir Francis Drake had aboard Don Pedro. I did take now, at my coming down, 3,000 pistolets, as I told you I would; for, by Jesus, I had not £3 besides in the world, and had not anything could get money in London; and I do assure you my plate was gone before. But I will repay it within 10 days after my coming home. And by the Lord God of Heaven, I had not one crown more; and had it not been mere necessity, I would not have touched one; but if I had not some to have bestowed upon some poor and miserable men, I should have wished myself out of this world.

All Howard kept for himself were the banners from the captured *Rosario*; anticipating a later commander-in-chief who, having obtained an enemy's written surrender at Luneburg Heath, retained the document for his own personal files. On 4 September, however, Howard was prepared to loan the standards to the Government for a victory celebration, telling Walsyngham: 'I have sent a good many ancients (ensigns) and banners by this bearer, Thomas Cely; but Sir, they must be returned when they have been used; they may be kept till I do come home.' Cely, who seems to have been present at the capture of the *Rosario*, had a job after his own heart now. After so many years spent 'in the King of Spain's most filthy galleys', he was to convey the fallen standards to London for the great thanksgiving service to be held at St Paul's Cross on 8 September. Nor did he waste his time in London; there is a note of jewellery and valuables he took off Spanish prisoners incarcerated in the Bridewell. For him, history had come full circle.

The reason for planning a victory celebration was the arrival of two confirmatory reports, one from a merchant ship coming into Southampton on 1 September, the other from one of the pinnaces which reached Dover on 3 September. Sir George Carey, the Isle of Wight Garrison commander, wrote on the 1st:

This morning there arrived here divers mariners of this island, which came in a bark of Hampton from Shetland; who upon oath affirm that on this day fortnight, being the 8th of this present [18 August], they being 12 leagues from Shetland, where they had been fishing, they descried a very great fleet of monstrous great ships, to their seeming about 100 in number, lying just west, with both sheets aftward, whereby their course was to run betwixt Orkneys and Fair Isle.

Edward Wynter reported from Dover two days later: 'Young Norreys, that was sent after the enemy's fleet to discover which way they meant to take their course, brings certain news that he left them to the westwards of the Islands of Orkney, which is their course directly for Spain.' That same day, he reported that he had spoken aboard the *Ark Royal*, in Howard's cabin, to a spy who had been in Dunkirk a few hours earlier. Parma had gone to Brussels, the victuals had been unshipped from the landing barges, and the sails stripped from their yards. The Armada campaign – and the invasion crisis – were over. Let the bells ring.

But the Spaniards did not know it. No one in Europe knew it. Only one authentic report reached Philip and, although its source was England, security precautions had rendered it vague. Dated Calais, 21 August (31 August), it ran:

The messenger I sent to England has returned hither. He brings no letters, as no one dares to write letters nor he to carry them. He reports that the Lord Admiral has arrived with part of the fleet, and to Court on 8th [18th] instant. Drake arrived with the rest on the 14th [24th]. Both of them were compelled to return in consequence of shortness of victuals, leaving the Spanish Armada beyond Newcastle in Scotland. They say, however, that the principal reason for their return was lack of powder, as they had not enough for one day's fighting. They do not say much about the losses of the Spanish Armada, except of the six ships that were lost on these coasts (i.e., Calais-Ostend), nor do they boast much of their victory. They do not dwell yet upon their own losses. Their ships have arrived in very bad case. They report that the horses had to be thrown overboard from the Spanish Armada near Newcastle, in consequence of lack of water. They are speaking rather ill of the Lord Admiral, who they say did not do his duty. All the credit is given to Drake. They still have an army of 8,000 men between Sandwich and Dover, under the command of a brother of Norris, the Camp-Master being Thomas Scott. Neither of them knows much. There is another army in Essex under Leicester. The Queen was at Dartford and crossed the river to visit that army. They have seven armies under arms but they have no money, and if the affair lasts many of the men will desert.

Apart from a few minor inaccuracies (Newcastle is in England, not Scotland) and a naturally too optimistic tone, it was a reasonable enough summary of affairs in England during the last two weeks of August. But the unfortunate spy was not believed, for news of great Spanish victories in the Channel and in the North Sea had been echoing through Europe for weeks.

On 13 August, an otherwise accurate report from Rouen was followed by a hurriedly scribbled postscript, describing a full fleet engagement in which 'the Spaniards captured Drake with many ships, sinking others, and disabling 15 which took refuge at Harwich; the Lord Admiral was in as bad case as Drake.' The cautious Philip was wary, writing to his ambassador in Paris, Bernadino de Mendoza:

As you consider the news to be true, I am hopeful that it will prove to be so; particularly as the author claims to have been an eye witness. I am looking anxiously for the confirmation, this report having been the first intelligence I have had of the event.

The King also wrote, ironically, to Medina Sidonia, requesting confirmation. 'This news is asserted in France to be true, and witnesses of the engagements are said to be in Havre de Grace and Dieppe. I hope to God it may be so, and that you have known how to follow up the victory . . .'

On 20 August, Mendoza had confirmation of a previous rumour about a Spanish victory in the Channel.

You will see that, in their description of the engagement between the Armada and the English off the Isle of Wight, the Breton sailors did not lie, for the English lost seven ships, and amongst them three of the largest the Queen possessed. As the London people were so alarmed, Don Pedro de Valdez and the rest of those who were captured, owing to their ship being disabled, had been taken in carts to London, so that the people might see that some prisoners had been captured; the rumour being spread that the whole Armada had been dispersed.

This part of Mendoza's report was perfectly accurate, but he concluded with a vague statement:

Letters from Rouen, dated 9th, say that there is a man there who left London on the 2nd, who asserts that the English lost heavily in the engagement, and they were very sad, as it was said that Drake had been wounded in the legs by a cannon ball.

On 21 August a Spanish spy in London, Antonio de Vega, sent a long and fairly authentic account of the whole series of Channel battles, including a description of how the 'bonfires were lit all over the city, and the bells rung' when the news of the taking of the *Rosario* and the *San Salvador* reached London. He was obviously an eye-witness, and well informed otherwise, reporting accurately that forty prisoners had been lodged in the Bridewell prison for examination and that Don Pedro and his friends 'were afterwards carried to the house of Richard Drake, 16 miles from here, where they are well treated.' Of the Calais-Dunkirk battle, he reported that some Portuguese deserters had swum to the English ships one night, telling their captors that 'the Armada would be ruined in a very short time'; and that the English Admirals had, at one point, 'looked upon the Armada as lost, as it was surrounded by sand banks.' All this seems to be authentic, adding detail to our knowledge. He reported the Armada as last seen heading for Norway, and added that the English were claiming three ships sunk, in addition to those lost in other ways, 6,000 Spaniards killed or captured, and their own loss as less than 300. But, he wrote, 'it is really over 1,500, and it is secretly stated that they have lost 12 ships, although they deny it.'

Thus it was still possible to believe the stream of rumours which continued to come in, describing a Spanish victory in the North Sea. On 24 August, an Advice from Antwerp had news of this engagement and the capture of 'about 30 English ships'. Four shiploads of killed and wounded had arrived at Dover. On the same day, an Advice from Bruges confirmed it, with the crews of two of Parma's pinnaces quoted for authority, and giving Newcastle as the site of the Spanish victory.

The 'Battle of Newcastle' was again referred to in Advices from Dunkirk via Lille on 30 August.

It was asserted in England as a positive fact that the English have lost 40 ships of their fleet, the flagship, the vice-flagship, the *Elizabeth*, and the *Virgin* having been sunk. The great sailor, John Hawkyns, has also gone to the bottom, not a soul having been saved from his ship. Drake escaped in a boat, wounded in the cheek.

As late as 4 September, these rumours were still being forwarded to Spain. On that day, on the authority of some fishermen, it was reported that:

M de Gourdan advises that Drake's death is confirmed from Holland. The Lord Admiral has returned to England with 36 ships in very bad case, no person being allowed to land. The Catholics were disturbed.

And on the same day, not uninfluenced by the news that Drake had been wounded in the legs/cheek and was now dead/ captured/escaped, the King thought it would be well to remind his Captain General of the Ocean of his main task:

It occurs to me to instruct you that if the Duke of Parma should consider that the presence of the Armada would be of use to him . . .

and the Armada be strong enough . . . you will endeavour to follow his instructions.

It might be thought that poor communications were responsible for the spread of these rumours, but that is not so. On the first day of World War Two, the British press had the Polish army advancing victoriously into Germany, as a glance at the files will show; indeed, for many years, the start of every victorious German offensive was reported as an Allied victory by the Ministry of Information. Modern communications meant that their untruths were exposed more rapidly, that was all. Not that Mendoza and his spies were lying; they merely desired victory too much. Perhaps they really thought the Armada invincible and could expect nothing less. There was plenty of cold fact mentioned in the agents' reports, pointing to an English victory, but if the spies themselves chose to disregard it, one can hardly blame Mendoza too much. Any authentic news from England was instantly and furiously suppressed, as Mendoza reported:

The English ambassador here has had some fancy news printed, stating that the English had been victorious; but the people of Paris would not allow it to be sold, as they say it is all lies. One of the ambassador's secretaries began to read in the palace a relation which he said had been sent from England, but the people were so enraged that he was obliged to fly for his life.

But, whether in victory or defeat, men die; and, for the relatives, waiting anxiously in Spain for news of the great enterprise in which sons, fathers, and husbands were engaged, this was a time of long trial. For nearly two months they heard nothing, except rumours of great battles, with no word as to the dead and wounded, except for the names of a few senior officers in the great ships taken between Plymouth and Ostend. Then reports began to come in from a different quarter. Ireland.

18

The Grave of the Son of the King of Spain

The course that shall be held in the return of this army into Spain. The course that is first to be held is to the NNE until you be found under 61½ degrees; and then to take great heed lest you fall upon the island of Ireland, for fear of the harm that may happen unto you upon the coast . . .

(*Captured Spanish document in State Papers, Ireland*)

'Friday the 12th of August the English left us and went towards the shore, and we followed our voyage with evil and contrary winds until we came to 61 degrees, leaving every day behind us ships that were spoiled,' wrote Estrade in the *San Marcos*. 'On the 13th, and until the 18th, we experienced squalls, rain, and fogs, with heavy sea, and it was impossible to distinguish one ship from another,' noted Calderon in the *San Salvador*. 'We climbed to 62 degrees, where it is not warm,' recorded Fray Gongora in the *San Martin*:

I am cold, because I left my cloak behind when, by a miracle, I came out of Don Pedro de Valdes' ship. But now the Duke himself has given me a cloak of his which for me is cape and bed for the preaching of the Gospel. The Lord may He receive it as a penance for our great sins.

The fair weather sailors of Spain, Portugal, and the Levant were going north to the endless, icy seas, with Norway on their right hand and Orkney and Shetland on their left. Even Seymour, 700 miles to the South, was then complaining about his 'summer ship,' the *Rainbow*. 'Our men fall sick,' he wrote, 'by reason of the cold nights and cold mornings we find; and I fear me they will drop away far faster than they did last year, which was thick enough.'

It is possible to be cold at sea in the middle of an August

heatwave; the wind, blowing across hundreds of miles of water, picks up some of the chill of the ocean depths, so that men shiver under a blazing sun. But this was a wild and bitter August, and as the Armada turned west on to the second leg of its course for home and ran between Orkney and Shetland, for the safety of the open Atlantic, it entered on to a desolate and tossing waste of water, inhabited by the mammals of the northern seas, the whale and the seal. The great waves, riding free for 3,000 miles, came punching down on the shot-battered hulls of the salt-caked ships; icy water swept across their decks and streamed below through the cracks in the planking; hissing sheets of rain stormed at and blinded them, carried by a howling wind that roared in the rigging and bellied the torn canvas of their sails. There was no way to get warm, no way to stay dry; and, just when they needed hot food, their ration of rotting victuals had to be reduced, for their way home was long and tortuous, straight out into the Atlantic for the high latitudes, well clear of Ireland, before turning southward for the last, long run to the Groyne or Ferrol in sunny Galicia. There was, too, very little water; in some of the ships, hardly any was left. Therefore the horses and the mules had to be abandoned, forced over the side, to stream away astern, a strange and dreadful trail of flotsam in the wake of the defeated fleet. A German ship captain, who saw horses' heads rearing out of the waves, miles out at sea, out of sight of land, carried his weird tale to England.

On the damp and heaving decks, shivering and cold, the wounded and the sick lay wrapped in sodden blankets in their own private and personal hells. For them, the fate of the Armada no longer had any meaning, pain and weakness engulfed them; helpless, they were carried on into an eternity of suffering. On his own initiative, Calderon had the hospital stores carried in his ship distributed among the vessels nearest to the *San Salvador*: rice for the sick, and the delicacies to supplement the ordinary rations. Originally, these had been earmarked for the use of the artillerymen in a land campaign, but there was no use husbanding them any more, if they could save lives now.

On 19 August, the Armada again collected, and we found ourselves near the galleon *San Marcos*, the Duke's flagship, and thirteen other vessels. I supplied Juan Martinez de Recalde with a quantity of delicacies, and tried to do the same for the *San Marcos*, but was prevented by the rough sea.

The mainsails and topsails of the *San Marcos* were torn to ribbons, according to Estrade, but otherwise she was better off than most, having had only twenty killed in battle and no other fatal casualties. Recalde's *San Juan* of Oporto, however, the vice-flagship of the whole Armada, was losing four or five men dead every day, from thirst, hunger, and sickness combined, according to the statement of one of her crew, Emanuel Fremoso, a Portuguese. And she, he said, was by no means the worst off. Five Scottish fishing vessels had been captured off the Shetlands, but their catch, such as it was, would not suffice to feed the whole Armada. Some of the ships would have to put into an Irish port, or risk the death of their crews by thirst and starvation.

By late August, the Armada was visibly no longer a fleet; it consisted of scattered groups of refugee ships. The largest group, those following the flagship, continued to steer out into the Atlantic, to avoid the danger of turning south while still too near the coast of Ireland. Others, badly damaged, were no longer able to keep on course as long as the wind stayed at south-west, and drifted slowly towards Iceland. Others again, began to work back for the west of Ireland. If the wind changed to north-west, they would be in deadly peril. Calderon's diary depicts best what happened. On 19 October, when a break in the weather brought better visibility, many ships were missing.

We looked anxiously for the *San Juan de Sicilia*, on board which was Don Diego Tellez Enriquez, son of the Grand Commander of Alcantara, who had fought so bravely. She had been so much damaged that not a span of her sails was serviceable; and as we could not find her, it is feared she may be lost.

We know from Cuellar's narrative that three large vessels of the Levant squadron, one of which was the *Lavia*, the vice-flagship, and another probably the *Juliana*, were unable to hold the course set and drifted into Sligo Bay, where they took shelter. They were quite unable to work out, against the wind, round the great westward projecting bulge of County Mayo, and they had lost their heaviest anchors off Calais, under fireship attack. If any great storm blew up, they were doomed.

The weather being very heavy on the night of 19 August [wrote Calderon], we lost sight of Juan Martinez de Recalde and all the ships that followed him; so we continued our voyage alone, through squalls and fogs. On the 24th the Duke asked me whether I had heard anything of Don Alonso de Luzon [in *La Trinidad Valencera*], as he had not seen him for 13 days, although he had sent the despatch boats to seek him. I replied that I had not, nor of the galleon *San Marcos* and the other 13 vessels from which I had parted company two days before, under the command of Juan Martinez de Recalde, who was dreadfully in need of everything, and his ship in a very injured state. From the 24th August to the 5th September, we sailed without knowing whither, through constant storms, fogs, and squalls, but on the 5th discovered the main body of the Armada again. 13 ships with Recalde were still missing, and on this day, as we ourselves were drifting to leeward of the Armada, we saw the ship *Villafranca* of Oquendo and another ship fall away towards the Faroes and Iceland.

The former was Martin Villafranca's command, the *Santa Maria de la Rosa*, also known as the *Nuestra Senora de la Rosa*, vice-flagship of Oquendo's Armada of Guipuzcoa.

From then until mid-September, Calderon's ship was alone, 'always working to windward, breaking our tackle and making a great deal of water.' On 11 September, they saw, across the tossing wave-crests, the distant sails of a group of unknown ships, but could not close them. Then they saw land, a large and unknown island, obviously part of Ireland,

the sea running strongly towards the land, to the great danger of the hulk. I ordered her to tack to the north-west, which took her 30 leagues distant, and it is believed that the rest of the Armada will have done the same. If not, they will certainly have lost some of the ships, as the coast is rough, the sea heavy, and the wind strong from seaward.

The *San Salvador* did not sight Ireland again, but ran out to safety on an SSW course.

By then, the galleass *Zuniga* was also alone. On 3 September she broke her rudder in the heavy seas – the rudder was a weak point of the design – and was told by the Duke that he could do nothing for her. On 8 September she sighted Recalde's group of thirteen ships, and spoke to them. For a full week after that, she was struggling southwards along the Irish coast, using her twin banks of twenty-eight oars in lieu of a rudder when necessary, but was trapped on 15 September.

We saw we were in great danger, and in order not to be driven ashore in the strong wind we followed the creek and, by God's grace, found shelter in an uninhabited place. Here we cast anchor, not far from a tower held by the enemy, where we remained for eight days, until the 23rd, when we went out with a wind astern.

The tower was Liscannor Castle. The *Zuniga* then passed out of the Irish story, but her troubles were not yet over; far from it. A trail of Armada wrecks was soon to be reported, from as far north as Fair Isle, between Shetland and Orkney, right down the Irish coast, inside the Hebrides, in the west of England, and on the north coast of France. Already, the guns were thundering again in the Channel, as the English went in to violate neutral waters in an attempt to finish off an Armada cripple at Le Havre.

From the third week of September onwards, the commanders of the English garrisons in Ireland were receiving reports of Spanish ships sighted off the coast – there were no fewer than fifty-nine sightings, many of them naturally of the same ships; and of unknown ships ashore and splintered in the shallows, and of unknown men drowned or slaughtered as they staggered up out of the sea. 'A ship lost off Cape Clear, from which 60 men were drowned or killed,' read one of the early, laconic reports. 'In the Bay of Tralee 25 men surrendered, amongst them some servants of the Duke.' No one knows to this day what ships these were. There were no survivors. Lady Denny, wife of the local English commander, parleyed with the men, who said they were 'all of Castile and Biscay', and then hanged them, because 'there was no safe keeping for them'. When this news reached the Spanish spy group in London, on 11 October, they speculated on 'the special hatred which Captain Denny bore against the Spaniards,' because he had once had an important Spanish prisoner who had escaped through the intriguings of Bernadino de Mendoza, then Spanish ambassador in London. They heard that 'The

Council has sent order for everyone to be hanged, as they do not want to feed them, and Spain will not ransom them. I cannot believe they will do it.' But they did.

Occasionally, they held their prisoners for a short time, for interrogation, so that some of the reports are detailed and accurate.

Admiral Juan Martinez de Recalde has entered an Irish port with another ship of 900 tons and a bark, and is still there. His ship is in a very bad state, having had 14 or 15 cannon-shot through her, and her mainmast damaged so much that she could not carry sail. He has but few sailors, mostly very ill. They are dying daily in great numbers and being thrown into the sea.

Recalde had sent watering parties ashore, and some of the men had been captured, including the Portuguese, Emanuel Fremoso, and three others whose interrogations survive. One, a Fleming, reported: 'They have bread sufficient; their beef is corrupt; water they want; many of them are sick.' Fremoso testified:

There is left but 25 pipes of wine, and very little bread; and no water, but what they brought out of Spain, which stinketh marvellously; and their flesh meat they cannot eat, their drouth is so great. It is a common bruit among the soldiers, that if they may once get home again, they will not meddle again with the English.

Of Recalde's thirteen ships, only these three were still together, he said, although, as they neared the Blaskets, he had seen 'one great hulk of 400 ton, which was so spoiled as she cast towards the shore about 20 leagues from Dingle-i-couch.' It may have been the great ship *Trinidad* of the Castilian squadron. It was in any case distinct from the wreck for which Lady Denny organized her hanging party, for it was separately reported by the English as:

Another large ship was lost off Tralee, in which there were 30 gentlemen, with a bishop, a friar, and 69 men who surrendered to William Bourke of Ardnerie; the rest of them were drowned or killed. Of those who got ashore, a single Irish gallowglass killed 80.

According to a later account, the gallowglass who knocked eighty bedraggled Spaniards on the head was McLaughlan MacCabe, a Scottish mercenary soldier, of whom there were many in Ireland. In due course, this English report was laid on the desk of Philip of Spain, who annotated it: 'Perhaps they called Don Martin de Carrion a bishop. No bishop went.' He knew all the details, for the Armada was peculiarly his enterprise; but from now on, he had news only of its sorrowful end. Including the supposed death of his own son, and the reported capture of the Duke of Medina Sidonia.

The Fleming taken from Recalde's longboat had told the English, accurately enough, 'There is a bastard son of King Philip, called the Prince of Ascoli, in ship with the Duke. This Prince passed from them in a pinnace about Calais.' But before the saga of Blasket Sound was over, the English had another prisoner from another ship – the sole survivor – who told them that the Prince of Ascoli had been aboard her. His name was Antonio Meneses and his ship was the *Nuestra Senora de la Rosa*.

Recalde was a dying man when he brought the great *San Juan* of Oporto through the difficult entrance into Blasket Sound, not far from Dingle. But he knew that coast well. With him came a forty-ton pinnace, and a galleon of Castile, the 750-ton *San Juan Bautista*, a vice-flagship, aboard which was Marcos de Aramburu, paymaster of the Castilian squadron. They had already seen the *Trinidad* drifting away out of control towards Tralee, and they had a few breathless moments as they followed the 1,050-ton *San Juan* of Oporto through a rocky channel about as wide as their ship was long. But, said Aramburu, one of the Scotsmen taken from the fishing boats off Shetland was in Recalde's ship, and he conned her through safely some time on 15 September. A longboat with eight men was sent away on reconnaissance at once, and never returned; this was the boat containing Emanuel Fremoso and the other men taken prisoners and interrogated at Dingle. On the 17th, wrote Aramburu,

Juan Martinez sent a large boat with fifty harquebusiers to look for a landing place, to collect information, and to treat with the Irish for a supply of water and meat. They found nothing but steep cliffs on which the sea broke; and on the land, some 100 harquebusiers were seen, waving a white flag with a red cross on it. It is supposed that they were English, and that the eight men sent in the long boat had been taken prisoners by them, or perished in the sea.

Notwithstanding this, the Spaniards spent the next three days taking in water; though much reduced from their paper strength of about 800 men, they still considerably outnumbered the English troops, and their ships could of course beat off any attack. On the morning of 21 September, a great westerly gale began to blow, sending tremendous seas surging through the anchorage. Recalde's *San Juan* began to drift down on Aramburu's *San Juan*, and bumped against her stern, smashing the lantern and the tackle of the mizzenmast. At midday, two more Spanish ships were seen approaching the anchorage. From the nearest, which was the vice-flagship of Oquendo's squadron, Martin Villafranca's 945-ton *Nuestra Senora de la Rosa*, came a puff of smoke and the dull boom of a gun, a signal for help. 'She had all her sails torn to ribbons, except the foresail,' noted Aramburu.

She anchored with a single anchor, as she had no more. And as the tide, which was coming in from the south-east, beat against her stern, she held on until 2 o'clock, when it began to ebb. And at the turn, she started drifting, about two splices of cable from us, and we with her; and in an instant we saw she was going to the bottom, with not a soul escaping – a most extraordinary and terrible occurrence. And we were drifting down on her to our perdition.

As they came down with the tide on to the wreck, a spare anchor, which Aramburu had borrowed from Recalde and repaired, was dropped; and the *San Juan Bautista* brought to. When they raised the anchor which had failed to hold them, they found that it was broken and the cable itself nearly cut through by chafing on the rocks. The ship which had come in with the *Nuestra Senora de la Rosa* was still afloat; she was commanded by Miguel de Aranivar. Then, at four in the afternoon, yet another derelict came drifting into the anchorage; and she was yet another *San Juan*, the vessel commanded by Fernando Horra. With one mast gone, she presented a strangely gaptoothed appearance; and to complete the picture of distress, as she swung round to anchor, rolling and pitching on the gale-lashed water, her foresail blew to shreds, dissolving before their eyes as if someone had worked a conjuring trick. Nothing could be done that day, as the seas were too wild for any boat to be lowered, but on the 12th, her longboat put over to Recalde to inform him that she would not float much longer. His decision was to distribute her men among the remaining ships, get the guns out of her, and burn her. Removing the guns proved to be quite impossible, in that sea, and with so many weakened by sickness; in Recalde's ship alone, 200 men had died. So the *San Juan* went to the bottom of the Sound, with all her artillery on board, to join the silent guns and drowned men of the *Nuestra Senora de la Rosa*, black fathoms down in the swirling tide.

Then first, the *San Juan* of Aramburu, and later, the other ships and pinnaces, put out to sea for the stormy voyage home to Spain. As Recalde's flagship at last left that anchorage of dread, she carried sail only on the mainmast and mizzen; the foremast was bare, weakened by Drake's guns off Plymouth and only hastily repaired. The English ashore were glad to see them go. Mr James Trant, their agent for the Dingle district, responsible to Sir Edward Denny in Tralee, had found them too much of a handful to attempt anything, and was unable to prevent them watering. He could only nibble at the edges, and one of the prisoners he took was the sole survivor from the *Nuestra Senora de la Rosa*. Unseen in the confusion of impending disaster, this youth had drifted ashore on some wreckage. He was, he said, the pilot's son; Don Antonio Meneses was his name, according to the English report which eventually reached Philip of Spain, but the Irish papers give it as Antonio de Monana.

This frightened boy, pressed by his interrogators for the names of the great nobles in the ship, stammered out a great many, including the Prince of Ascoli, went on to describe the rich treasure in her, including 50,000 ducats in gold, 50,000 ducats in silver, and masses of gold and silver plate off which the grandees were served. Her armament, he said, included '50 great pieces, all cannons of the field' (i.e., stored for use of the army); '25 pieces of brass and cast-iron belonging to the ship; and 50 tuns of sack.' The 25 brass and iron guns seem reasonable for a vice-flagship; at that moment Burghley was snarling over a report that, after the people of Dorset had whipped the best pieces out of the blown-up *San Salvador*, there was left, 'to wit, eight pieces of brass, four old iron minions, and two old fowlers'. In short, a collection of old junk, an apt commentary on the artillery deficiencies of the Armada. The treasure seems inflated, and, of course, the Prince of Ascoli was not dead. But these stories were believed, and when the grotesquely swollen corpses rose from the bottom of the Sound and bobbed horribly to shore, their place of burial was named *Uaig Mhic Ri Na Spáinne*, the Grave of the Son of the King of Spain.

One other group of ships, seven in all, put into an Irish port, and mostly got out again; this was Scattery Roads, in the Shannon, to the north of Tralee. Here, too, one of them was so shattered that she had to be burnt, the men being distributed among the remaining ships. She is sometimes supposed to be the *San Marcos*, but Estrade, who was in that ship, makes no mention of changing house. Off County Clare, north of the Shannon, near where the *Zuniga* lay at anchor in Liscannor Bay, two unknown ships were driven helplessly on shore, with their few fit men, their wounded, their sick, their dying. At Doonbeg, from a wreck which may have been the *San Esteban*, sixty men struggled ashore through the surf, leaving 200 dead behind them in the sea. From another great ship, which went down on a reef inside Mutton Island, four men only escaped, giving to that bare rock a new name – Spanish Point. All along the coast where they struck, headlands and reefs acquired these names – *Port na Spáinneach, Carraig na Spáinneach*. Their graveyards and burial grounds similarly – *Reilg na Spáinneach, Tuama na Spáinneach*. And another, even more sinister, as in the case of the survivors from the wreck at Doonbeg, who were marched to the castle of Boetius Clancy, the Queen's Sheriff of County Clare, and taken to a place, still called after what happened to them there, *Cnoc na Crochaire*, Gallows Hill.

19

'Those Rags Which Yet Remain'

After the Spanish fleet had doubled Scotland, and were in their course homewards, they were by contrary weather driven upon the several parts of this province and wrecked, as it were by even portions, three ships in every of the four counties bordering upon the sea coasts – namely, in Sligo, Mayo, Galway, and Thomond – on the rocks and sands by the shore side, and some three or four besides to seaboard of the out isles, which presently sunk, both men and ships, in the night time. And so can I say, by good estimation, that 6,000 or 7,000 men have been cast away on these coasts, save some 1,000 which escaped to land in several places where their ships fell, which since were all put to the sword.

Sir Richard Bingham, Governor of Connaught
to the Queen's Secretary, 1 October, 1588

Bingham was speaking for Connaught only, the area for which he held responsibility under the Lord Deputy of Ireland, Sir William Fytzwylliam; for Sligo, Mayo, Galway and Clare (which was known then as Thomond); not for Cork or Kerry in the south, nor for Donegal, Derry and Antrim in the north. But he knew of them, for he added: 'Other great wrecks they had both in Munster (the south) and Ulster (the north), which being out of my charge I have not so good notice of, but the same (I doubt not) is fully made known unto your Honour.' These include five known wrecks in Munster – the unknown vessel at Cape Clear, the two known ships in Blasket Sound, the two unknown ships near Tralee. In Ulster there were seven more, three with names, four unknown. Some twenty-five ships in all, in the three provinces of Munster, Connaught and Ulster. But from the north, Ulster, the English reports were as yet vague. Munster and Connaught they held, with a force of 2,000 men; but the north was a focus of resistance, which they could penetrate but not firmly control. With their comparatively tiny force of occupation troops – for the experienced soldiers were at the front, in the Netherlands – they could not line the coasts with men; they had to move outward from central points when Spaniards were reported ashore; and the foul weather of that summer had brought floods which made movement difficult and slow. Moreover, it was faulty news which made Bingham pass on a rumour that soon reached Spain. 'The Duke himself was upon the coast of Erris in Mayo,' he wrote, 'and there received into his ship Don Alonso de Leyva, with a 600 men that had been cast ashore out of the *Rata*, Horatio Palavicino his ship, which ship lies there all split to pieces.'

The wreck he had seen was certainly all that remained of the proud *Rata Encoronada*, headquarters ship of the Land Forces commander, Don Alonso de Leyva, who had indeed been taken off by another ship. But the captain of the *Rata* was Horatio Donago, not Palavicino (who was serving with Howard), and the Duke was far away. Nevertheless, the story, embellished, was in London by 5 October, where it was picked up by the Spanish spy ring, of which Marco Antonio Messia (a friend of Palavicino's) was a leading figure. It was duly transmitted to Spain, together with a new rumour from the continent, which chimed exactly with all the previous tales from that source, of a crushing Spanish victory.

Reports come from Rouen that the Spanish Armada has arrived at Lisbon with various prizes, but here (in London) quite the opposite is asserted; namely, that after it had almost reached Spanish waters it was caught in a great storm and driven back to Ireland. Trustworthy news has been received from there, saying that 15 ships have been wrecked on the coast, amongst them the galleon *San Martin* with the Duke of Medina Sidonia on board, the Duke himself having been taken. It has since been asserted, however, that he had left the galleon and gone on board the *Rata*, of which ship nothing has been heard.

In effect, Bingham's story, the other way round, a week before Bingham penned his report on Connaught. The Spanish spy caught up with it, before it had even arrived, for he wrote a postscript to his own report a few days later:

Since I wrote the above I was told on Change this morning, by a person who was with the Secretary for an hour last night, that two

THE IRISH WRECKS

Identification of wrecks varies from fairly certain to vague or doubtful. Recent research places the *San Juan de Sicilia* at Tobermory and the *Santa Maria de Vision* at Streedagh Strand instead.

squadrons were seen off the Irish coast, one being that of the Duke of Medina, who sailed away again. The other squadron was caught in a storm, and 18 ships were lost. They say that what with these drowned, killed by steel, and taken prisoners, 6,000 men have been lost.

The fate of the Armada was the topic of the town, right up until December, for Spanish wrecks were occurring even at the beginning of November; and the English were afraid of what might happen if large numbers of Spanish soldiers got ashore from them and established themselves. 'The news spread hourly here keeps one in suspense,' complained a Spanish agent, to whom Palavicino reported in confidence (possibly with tongue in cheek) that the Spanish losses now totalled more than thirty. Which in fact they did, although not all occurred in Ireland.

In Thomond (present-day Clare), the most southerly county for which Bingham was responsible, his three reported wrecks have documentation but no names. In Galway, immediately to the north, there are only two known wrecks within the present borders of the county; one, almost certainly the *Falcon Blanco Mediano*, in Galway Bay, possibly at Barna, and the other, perhaps the *Concepcion*, near Ards Castle, at a place now called *Duirling na Spáinneach*. The 'common sort' among the prisoners were put to death, to the number of about 300, and the 'better sort', to the number of about fifty, were held by Bingham in the hope of ransom. But when Fytzwylliam heard the news, he was not pleased by this clemency. Off the borders of Galway and Mayo is Clare Island, and here a third wreck occurred, which Bingham may have included in his list of three for Galway. If so, it would make his arithmetic – three in each county – absolutely exact. This last ship was the 1,160-ton *Gran Grin*, vice-flagship of Recalde's Armada of Biscay. She made Clew Bay in a sinking condition, and about a hundred men out of her, under Pedro de Mendoza, landed on Clare Island; they were attacked by the local Irish, under Dubhdara Rua O'Malley, and slaughtered for their valuables, 'saving one poor Spaniard and an Irishman of the County of Wexford'. The *Gran Grin* then drifted away, to sink finally at a place not properly identified but known as 'Fynglase'. Sixteen survivors 'wearing chains of gold' got ashore, and were handed over by the Irish to the English.

In Mayo proper, there were two certain wrecks. Bingham himself saw the *Rata*, 'all split to pieces', in Blacksod Bay. A second vessel came ashore at Inver, in Broadhaven, with not a single stick left; she is remembered as 'an long maol', the bare ship. There is tradition, but no documentation, for a third ship supposed to have sunk off the savage cliffs near Kid Island. Perhaps she was one of those reported 'sunk to seaboard of the out isles, in the night time', of which, naturally, there would be little trace. To complicate matters, the wreck identified by the gallowglass McLaughlan MacCabe who killed eighty sick, starving, half-drowned Spaniards for his master, William Bourke (or Burke), which was placed by the English report at Tralee, far to the south, is connected with Mayo by a recent Irish author, who maintains that the place meant must be 'Tyrawley', between Killala and Belderg. On the other hand, he says that 'the exact place is not given, nor is it remembered in tradition,' as one would expect it to be, had it occurred there.

Bingham's three reported wrecks in Sligo, however, are not in dispute; for they came ashore, side-by-side, on Streedagh Strand, and one of them was the *Lavia*, vice-flagship of the Levanters, in which Cuellar was being held under open arrest by the Judge Advocate, Martin de Aranda. For Bingham and Fytzwylliam, however, there was plenty of confusion, for these events were occurring nearly simultaneously, tending to interlock, and tending to move north into Ulster, their most sensitive point. Don Alonso de Leyva was their first worry, for he was a fine general and he brought his force ashore from the wrecked *Rata* virtually intact, with arms, armour, money, and plate. Then he fortified himself in the castles of Ballycroy and Doolough. Shortly afterwards, he marched his men over to Tiraum Castle, near Elly Bay, and was joined there by the survivors from the Broadhaven wreck, 'an long maol', the bare ship which had lost her masts. When two Spanish ships appeared off the coast, he embarked himself and most of his men in one of them, the 900-ton hulk *Duquesa Santa Ana* of the Andalusian squadron; was promptly blown to the north by a gale, and wrecked again, this time in Ulster, at Loughros Bay, County Donegal, just across the water from Streedagh Strand in Sligo. There were four other wrecks in Ulster, from which some survivors came to shore, and one very large wreck from which a large, armed force landed and established itself under Don Alonso de Luzon. If the two main forces of Don Alonso de Leyva and Don Alonso de Luzon could join together, and rally also the scattered survivors from the other ships in Ulster, and perhaps also some of the men saved at Streedagh Strand, on the borders of Ulster, the Spaniards would have an armed force in Ireland of a strength at least equal to that of the total English garrison of only 2,000 men. And it would be concentrated in the north, the potential centre for Irish revolt, which was in a ferment anyway. Fytzwylliam and Bingham moved out savagely against them, to try to mop them up at once, before the Spaniards could establish themselves.

Streedagh Strand was the first place they reached, and there they saw a sight to gladden any English commander's heart. The beach was strewn with wreckage, described by Fytzwylliam as: 'timber enough to build five of the greatest ships that ever I saw, besides mighty great boats, cables, and other cordage, and some such masts for bigness and length, as I never saw any two could make the like.' Five miles of wreckage and more than a thousand corpses, drowned or slain, estimated Secretary Fenton. The first English horseman had reached the scene soon after the disaster. From hiding, Cuellar had watched them go thundering down on to the sand, where his friend, Martin de Aranda, and Don Diego Enriquez, the hunchback Camp Master, lay dead at the edge of the tide.

They were the victims of the English guns, partly, which crippled their ships, and partly of the great bay formed by the counties of Mayo, Sligo, and Donegal. Once in, with the prevailing winds, such unwieldy ships could never get out, as Cuellar reported:

The ship I sailed in was from the Levant, to which were attached two others, very large. On account of the severe storm which rose upon the bow, we were forced to make for land and anchor, where we remained four days.

Apart from the *Lavia*, the other two Levanters were probably the *Juliana* and the *Santa Maria de Vision*; all were between 666 and 860 tons. Then, on the fifth day there sprang up so great a storm on our beam, with sea up to the heavens, so that the cables could not hold nor the sails serve us, and we were driven ashore with all three ships upon a beach, covered with fine sand, shut in on one side and the other by great rocks. Such a thing was never seen: for within an hour all three ships were broken in pieces, so that there did not escape 300 men, and more than one thousand were drowned.

The scene was the more terrible for Cuellar, for he could not swim. Nor could many other Spaniards. Standing there in the howling, screaming wind, with the great breakers building up from seawards, and racing down to beat upon the stranded, shifting hulls of the ships, many took to desperate expedients. On the deck of their ship was a large, decked boat. Don Diego Enriquez, the Camp Master, two Portuguese gentlemen, and the son of the Count of Villafranca, got into it, with 16,000 ducats' worth of jewels and crowns, and had the hatchway fastened down over them and caulked. Immediately it had been launched, wrote Cuellar,

seventy men who were still alive threw themselves from the ship on to the tender, and while that was struggling to make its way to shore, a great wave came over it, which sunk it and washed off all who were on it. The tender went tossing with the waves hither and thither, until it reached the beach, where it stuck fast upside down, and the gentlemen who had got under the little deck perished inside. After it had been aground a day and a half, some savages came and rolled it over, and breaking the deck took out the dead men. Don Diego Enriquez breathed his last in their hands. They stripped him and took the jewels and money, letting the bodies lie there without burial.

If foaming sea was of awe-inspiring strength, the prospect which visibly awaited them on that desolate beach was equally horrifying.

I placed myself on the poop, and gazed at the terrible spectacle. Many were drowning inside the ships, others were throwing themselves into the water, vanishing from sight; others were clinging to rafts and barrels, and gentlemen on pieces of timber; others cried aloud from the decks, calling upon God; captains cast their chains and crown pieces into the sea; and the waves swept others overboard. The waves and storm were very great, on the one hand; but, on the other, the land and shore were full of enemies, who went about jumping and dancing with delight at our misfortunes; and when any one of our people reached the beach, two hundred savages and other enemies fell upon him and stripped him of what he had on until he was left in his naked skin. Such they maltreated and wounded without pity, all of which was clearly visible from the battered ships. So I went up to the Judge Advocate – may God have mercy on him – he was very sad and downcast, and I bade him try to do something that might help save his life before the ship should break up completely, as it could not last more than ten minutes; and in fact it did not.

Don Martin de Aranda had sewed gold coins in his doublet and hose, which was bound to destroy his buoyancy, so they looked around for some rough life raft, and eventually found 'a scuttle-board as large as a table'. Over the side it went, and they jumped after it. 'I sank six fathoms under water and swallowed so much of it that I was almost drowned,' wrote Cuellar feelingly. Of course, he went nothing like as deep as that, but, to a non-swimmer, it was a terrifying experience to be deep down in the choking depths of the sand-stained sea. Both of them reached the scuttle-board and hung on, until an enormous breaker reared up under them, the board rolled over with the crest, and Martin de Aranda was plucked away instantly. Hampered by the heavy weight of the coins, he struggled convulsively, the waves going completely over his head, his mouth open, breathing water in his last agony for life. His head came up once, and Cuellar heard him scream, 'calling upon God.' Then he was gone.

Four waves came, one after the other, and without my knowing how to nor being able to swim, they carried me ashore, where I landed; but I could not stand up, for I was all bruised and bleeding, from a log of wood which almost broke my legs when I was in the water. The enemy and the savages who were on the beach stripping all those who had succeeded in swimming ashore, seeing my plight, legs, hands, and linen all covered in blood, did not touch me, nor did they come near me; so I crawled along, little by little, as best I could.

The survivors, from their immersion in the water, the cutting wind on the beach, and the fact that many were now completely naked, were shaking uncontrollably with cold. Cuellar crawled off the beach into a field, where a boy, who had been stripped naked, joined him; the youth was so chilled and terrified that he could not utter a word, even to say his name. It was then about nine o'clock in the evening, the light dim, the wind dying away, and the sea calmer, although the waves still roared all along the curve of the bay. In this ghostly light, Cuellar saw two black shapes approaching from inland, coming towards the beach: two men, both armed, one with a great iron axe. The strangers walked up to the two shivering Spaniards, and looked down on them silently; then without a word, they began to cut rushes and grasses, which they piled over Cuellar and the youth, before they went down to the beach, still without saying anything.

In pain, but now better protected from the cold, Cuellar drifted off to sleep. He was awakened at about one o'clock in the morning by the thunder of hooves, as a great troop of horsemen, about two hundred in number, went galloping down to the beach. Turning to see how his companion was, Cuellar found that the youth was lifeless.

I learned afterward that he was a gentleman of quality. But there he lay, with more than six hundred other dead bodies which the sea had cast up. The crows and the wolves fed upon them, and there was nobody to bury any of them, not even poor Don Diego Enriquez.

It was clear that he ought to get away from the beach, so Cuellar set off for a little monastery which, when daylight came, he could see inland, hoping to receive food and help from the monks. But the English had been there before him. The place was a wreck, smoke-blackened, with the holy images destroyed; and in the window apertures, black against the sun, their heads turned at a dreadful slant, their toes sweeping the floor, were the suspended bodies of twelve hanged men; survivors from the wrecks. 'As I found nobody in that monastery except the Spaniards dangling from the iron grates in the church windows, I went out very quick and took a path that led through a wood,' said Cuellar, with considerable understatement.

Limping along as quickly as he could, he came on an old crone, driving before her a herd of cows, to hide them from the English. 'Thou Spain? Thou Spain?' she mouthed at him, telling him by signs not to go on, as the English were there, and beginning to sob at his wretched state. She gestured for him to go in the direction of the beach, and he did so, keeping in cover as far as he was able, and avoiding the obvious danger spots, where people with carts were milling around among the wreckage, loading up the spoils that had come from the sea. Seeing, but not being seen, he stepped out of hiding when two moaning, naked men appeared, staggering inland, their wounds still bloody. 'They told me of the cruel deaths and tortures that the English had inflicted upon more than a hundred Spaniards whom they had captured.' But death from starvation awaited them if they did not get food soon, so the three distressed men went down again to the scene of the disaster.

We saw dead bodies – for the sea was still throwing them up. We recognized some of them, among others, poor Don Diego Enriquez, and in spite of my forlorn condition, I could not bear to pass him by without burying him, and so we dug a hole in the sand by the water's edge, and there we laid him, with another much honoured captain, a dear friend of mine.

Then their luck changed. They found food on the beach, mainly biscuits, and when four Irish rushed up to tear the blood-stained linen from Cuellar's back, a man who was obviously a chief stopped this, then showed the Spaniards to a road leading inland. They were to go along that road, he said, and would find a village, where they would get help. Limping, the tattered trio set out on a stony path, knowing nothing of the land to which they had come, nor what to expect from its people. They were 'on the run', with death for penalty if the English caught them.

Where the Spaniards landed in force, there was no plundering by the poverty-stricken inhabitants of the country. In the extreme north of Ulster, near Lough Foyle, Don Alonso de Luzon's great Levanter, the 1,100-ton *Trinidad Valencera* of Venice, limped to land in a sinking condition on 14 September. Her pumps had been working continuously for two days and she had crammed into her half the 200-man crew of the 600-ton *Barca de Amburg* (the bark of Hamburg), which had gone down out at sea, north of Ireland. The other 100 men had been taken off by the *Gran Grifon*, flagship of the hulks, shortly to be wrecked in her turn on Fair Isle. One of her crew, Juan de Nova, a Galician, testified that: 'All the soldiers [except forty who remained in the ship and were drowned when she afterwards foundered] were put on shore, with their arms, in a little boat.' Their commander, Don Alonzo de Luzon, stated:

We landed by shipwreck as many of us as could in a broken boat of our own, some swam to the shore, and the rest were landed in a boat of O'Doherty's country, for the use of which we gave in money and apparel 200 ducats. I and five more of the best of my company landed first, only with rapiers in our hands, where we found four or five savage people, who bade us welcome. We were about two days landing our men, and had very ill entertainment finding no other relief of victual in the country than of certain horses, which we bought of poor men for money, which we killed and did eat.

This large armed force worried the English, but they had so many wrecks to deal with – there were four more within fifty miles of the *Valencera* – that they could only spare 400 men to head them off, but having some advantage as half these were cavalry and the Spaniards facing them had many sick and weak. They marched up, banners flying, horsemen, harquebusiers, and bowmen, and the Spanish column came to a halt, both sides facing each other, and beating the drums for a parley. 'Who are you?' was the first question. 'Spanish soldiers wrecked on this island, who wish to hire a ship in which to return home.' 'That cannot be,' was the reply, 'you must surrender as prisoners of war.' 'If that is the alternative, we would rather die fighting, as befits Spaniards,' was the retort.

The two bodies of armed men remained camped opposite each other, in a rising tension, for thirty-six hours; then the English launched a night attack. Next morning, they again beat their drums for parley and, as food was short, de Luzon went down to talk to them in a chastened mood.

I and my whole company yielded ourselves, within six or seven days after our landing, to the captains that carried the Queen's ensigns, O'Donnell and his wife being present, upon condition that our lives should be saved until we came to the Viceroy; whereupon we laid down 350 muskets and calivers and some few pikes to her Majesty's use, all which were seized on by John Kelly, whom they term sergeant-major, and Captain Richard Hovenden's lieutenant; after which one promise was not kept with us, for the soldiers and savage people were allowed to spoil us of all we had.

Then began the march into captivity, by a line of nearly naked men, hemmed in by the armed English soldiers. They had been promised that they would be housed and reclothed in a castle that night, but the English commander rode up later to say that, as the road was bad, they would bivouac in the open instead. Silently, they were marched off the road into a field; then, with shouted orders, the men were separated from the officers, who were forced inside a square of armed men, together with the Spanish chaplain-general, the vicar of the shoeless Carmelites of Lisbon, and two other friars.

Next morning, seeing that some of the Spanish officers were still with their men, the English came to get them, leaving only the soldiers and seamen. These were then driven into a field, wondering helplessly what was about to happen. They saw the English forming up their soldiers, a troop of cavalry on one side, a line of harquebusiers on the other. There was a harsh command. The muzzles of the fire-arms came down to cover them, the horsemen broke into a trot, then a gallop; then, with a flash of steel and the crackling of musketry, the massacre was on. 'The harquebusiers came at us from one side, the cavalry from the other,' wrote Juan de Nova. 'With lance and bullet, they killed over 300 of us.' The men fell in heaps, groaning and screaming, as the English fired into them, then rode them down, lances thrust viciously at the fleeing, naked men. It was not a tidy affair. One hundred and fifty Spaniards escaped, among them de Nova, running desperately through a bog and turning and twisting like snipe to avoid their assailants.

But, unlike Cuellar, they had been ashore long enough to know that there was a strong resistance movement among the Irish in Ulster, although the motions of 'collaboration' were gone through; and they knew where to contact it, at the castle of bishop Cornelius. He passed them on to a chief named O'Cahan, who kept them for a few days, then passed them on in turn to his brother twelve miles distant. The plan was to get them to Sorleyboy McDonnell, lord of Dunluce, who would get them out of the country and into Scotland. An underground escape route came suddenly into being; Cuellar was drawn into it later, after fantastic adventures, was hidden by O'Cahan, and passed north to Dunluce the following year. But the master of the *Valencera* was in London by 13 December, reporting to the Spanish spy ring.

Meanwhile, Don Alonso de Luzon and the other officers were marched along the stony roads to Drogheda for questioning. It was the road to the Lord Deputy of Ireland, Sir William Fytzwylliam, and for most of them it was the last road they would ever take. When Don Alonso was brought in for interrogation, he was faced, had he but known it, by an old shipmate of the Armada, who had sailed with the great enterprise from Lisbon but had never seen England from a Spanish ship. It was David Gywnn, galley slave in the *Diana*, who had escaped the wreck, got to La Rochelle, and crossed over to England with the aid of some English merchants there and a tale of the important information that had come into his possession. If contemporary Dutch historians are to be believed, he was also claiming to have freed the slaves and captured the galley on the high seas, instead of being a fugitive from its wreck. There is no mention of that in the English records, merely a brief heading to the list of set questions to be put. 'Instructions for the Lord Primate, and Sir Henry Wallop, knight, and David Gywnn, gent., or any two of them, to be dealt in with the Spanish prisoners at Drogheda.'

But David Gywnn, gent., did not last. On 26 October, a Mr Eustace Harte deposed to the Lord Deputy that he had met Gywnn at Rochelle and that the wretched man,

being in necessity and want, did make a report that a Spanish secretary had showed him a letter which had come from Mr Secretary Walsyngham, that he was wholly for them, and would deliver her Majesty's person into their hands. Moreover, he did take forth a paper out of his pocket, wherein were written certain verses by him of her Majesty, concerning the estate of England, and did name her Majesty by the name of Bess.

There had been a demand 'to get that lewd, prating fellow punished', but he had said nothing upon it at the time, because he thought the English authorities would deal with him. Shortly after Mr Harte's deposition before the Lord Deputy, David Gywnn, gent., became David Gywnn, captive, once again.

By 13 December, the number of Spaniards 'put to the sword' in Ireland by the English totalled 1,100, according to Bingham. Amongst them were 'divers gentlemen of quality and service, as captains, masters of ships, lieutenants, ensign-bearers, other inferior officers and young gentlemen, to the number of some fifty, whose names I have for the most part set down in a list.' They included that Ensign Juan Gil, who, under the Duke's orders, had gone off to capture the English fishing boat near Plymouth. Bingham had hoped to receive ransom money for them, but 'I had special direction from the Lord Deputy to see them executed, reserving alive only Don Luis de Cordova, and a young gentleman, his nephew, until your Highness's pleasure be known,' he wrote to the Queen.

My brother George had two Spanish gentlemen, and some five or six boys, who coming after the fury and heat of justice was past, by entreaty I spared them, in respect they were pressed into the fleet against their wills. But the Lord Deputy caused both these two Spaniards to be executed, and the Dutchmen and boys that were spared before, reserving none but Don Luis and his nephew.

Bingham summed up his news:

I, your poor and faithful soldier, present your highness with these humble and few lines, as a thanksgiving to Almighty God for these his daily preservations of your sacred person, and the continual deliverance of us, your Majesty's subjects, from the cruel and bloody hands of your Majesty's enemies . . .

Bingham was an old soldier; he had fought at Lepanto, long ago, on the side of the men he had been slaughtering that month. He knew Spaniards; and he had given them as much mercy as they would have given him: none at all. The unfortunate Dutch boys had been a different matter; but in none of the English reports is there a sign of regret; on the contrary, they were extremely satisfied. Sir John Popham, another of the commanders in Ireland, wrote: 'The people in these parts are for the most part dangerously affected towards the Spaniards, but thanks be to God that their power, by her Majesty's good means, is shorter than it hath been.' The tone was set by Fytzwylliam who, after looking at the shambles on Streedagh Strand, wrote religiously to the Queen: 'Since it hath pleased God by His hand upon the rocks to drown the greater and the better sort of them, I will, with His favour, be His soldier for the despatching of those rags which yet remain.' And the gentlewoman, Lady Denny, marching out to hang up by the neck twenty-five shipwrecked men, is clear sign that he was not alone in this attitude.

Of course, it was very embarrassing for Ubaldino when he came to write the history of the campaign for contemporaries; he was an Italian, and could not share these sentiments. Indeed, he had to find excuses for them. Admitting that the Lord Deputy had been 'sour and severe', he felt in duty bound to point out that 'in every nation there are to be found men of every kind'; not all the English were like that. Against these acts, 'leaving a lasting record of their shame for all those who read,' he quoted an opposite case, that of Christopher Carleill. Carleill was Governor in Ulster. He had taken fourteen wretched men who had stumbled ashore from some unknown wreck, and was told by Fytzwylliam 'to put them to death in any manner'; which meant on the gallows, slow death by strangulation, kicking and struggling, tongues protruding, eyes sticking out of their heads. Instead, he paid a Scottish boatman to get them overseas before the Lord Deputy could 'make a progress' into Ulster. And it was in Ulster, too, that the final act of the tragedy took place; which ensured that Don Alonso de Leyva and the young nobleman cadets who were with him should never fall into the hands of the English, to die in such a fashion. This was the man the English were really worried about, the man who might, with force enough, shake their hold upon the whole of Ireland.

Having been wrecked in the *Rata* at Blacksod Bay, but ferried all his men ashore with their weapons, he had embarked them in the *Duquesa Santa Ana* and been wrecked in her, further north, at Loughros Bay in Donegal, shortly after. In this wreck he was seriously injured. According to one of the crew, James Machary of the Cross, captured later, there fell a great storm which broke in sunder all our cables, and struck us upon the ground; and Don Alonso was hurt in the leg by the capstan of the ship in such sort as he was able neither to go nor ride.

But de Leyva was not finished yet. He heard of yet another Spanish ship, at anchor further up the coast, which was not damaged beyond repair. Four men carried him in a chair the nineteen miles to Killibegs, where they found that the report was true. The galleass *Girona* lay at anchor with a broken rudder, as her compatriot the *Zuniga* had off Liscannor. Cuellar had heard of her, too – and he set off with twenty companions from O'Rourke's country, where the Irish had been hiding them, but they were too late. The *Girona* had gone, with Don Alonso de Leyva and the crews of the *Rata* and the *Duquesa Santa Ana* packed into her – 1,300 men in all. She was dreadfully overcrowded, and with not enough food even to consider making Spain; and so she sailed to the northwards, round Ulster, to bring the wheel full circle, and perished not far from Dunluce Castle, the fortress of Sorleyboy McDonnell, the most influential man in the whole hurriedly improvised escape organization.

When Juan de Nova was passed on to Dunluce by the Irish underground, with his friend Francisco de Borja, he found the survivors of the *Girona* already there, and talked to one of them, a sailor. He gave them the story in detail, explaining that de Leyva had intended to make for Scotland originally, but that the wind had come up fair for a quick passage to the south, and their pilot had promised them that they would make Spain in five days. But the wind had swung round and blown a full gale off the north coast of Ulster. 'We ran upon a submerged rock and the galleass went to pieces, more than 1,300 being drowned,' the sailor told them. 'There were only nine men saved.' The flower of Spanish chivalry perished with the splintered galleass, rolled under by the tides that washed at the foot of Dunluce, a grim castle on a great cliff overhanging the never-ending thunder of the sea.

Captain Merriman reported to Fytzwylliam on 7 November:

With regard of my most humble duty, I thought good to acquaint your Honour with the occurrents here, that the Spanish ship which arrived in Tyrconnel with the McSweeny was on Friday the 18th of this present [28 October] descried over against Dunluce, and by rough weather was perished, so that there was driven to the land, being drowned, the number of 260 persons, with certain butts of wine, which Sorley Boy hath taken up for his use.

It was not until the following year, 1589, that Cuellar came at last to Dunluce.

I went travelling by the mountains and desolate places, enduring much hardship, and at the end of my journey, I got to the place where Alonso de Leyva was lost, with many others. I went to the huts of some savages who were there, who told me of the great misfortunes of our people who were drowned, and who showed me many jewels and valuables of theirs, which distressed me greatly.

He was still not out of danger, and it was only in October, 1589, that the man who had been condemned to death by the Duke of Medina Sidonia, and survived not only that but many perils much greater, could sit down in the city of Antwerp to explain why it was that he was no longer under open arrest for cowardice; and, incidentally, to give a vivid picture, probably the most detailed in existence, of conditions in Ireland at that time.

He had certainly shown more initiative than eight other Spanish soldiers, survivors from the *Valencera*, from the *Lavia*, and from the *Juliana*, two of the three ships destroyed at Streedagh Strand. For when Captain Cobos, a Spanish liaison officer to the Irish underground, came over to Ulster in November, 1596, eight years after the defeat of the Armada, they were still there, serving the Irish chiefs as soldiers. They asked to see Spain once more, and if Cobos would not allow it, because of their value to any Spanish invading force, then at least, please, could they have their back pay?

20

'Take, Burn or Sink'

During September and October, 1588, Armada ships were coming to grief in the most surprising places; the most northerly wreck was separated from the most southerly by a distance of over 1,200 miles and there was just under a thousand miles' distance between the most westerly and the most easterly, which we know about. Some ships may have sunk, unreported, out in the Atlantic, which would place the wrecks within a box 1,200 miles square. There could be no better illustration for the complete defeat and scattering of the great Enterprise of England. The last ship of all to sink was one of the vessels taken off Plymouth, which went to the bottom with some of her prize crew while en route to Portsmouth on 25 November. The English were cock-a-hoop, now, at the humbling of so mighty a force, a combination of the power of half Europe, which the tiny island had first defied, and then defeated, entirely alone (for they never counted on their allies, the Dutch, but made their dispositions without regard for any help from that quarter).

For the Spaniards, the news of their defeat, and the first hint of their terrible roll of casualties, came in slowly and haphazardly; in reports from their spies in London, which were not believed, and, more surely, from the French port of Le Havre, at the mouth of the Seine, which eventually became a funnel for the escape route from Ireland. By the end of the year, ragged survivors of the wrecks in Ireland brought testimony that could not be disbelieved. One ship, which actually got back to Spain in the end, came direct to Le Havre from the west coast of Ireland, and was holed up in that French port, in continual danger of English attack, for a whole year. In so doing, she had made a more than complete circumnavigation of the British Isles.

This was the galleass *Zuniga*, which had anchored off Liscannor Castle, to repair a broken rudder pivot, her crew and galley slaves half dead of hunger. 'The inhabitants were rustic savages devoted to England, with a few officials amongst them,' recorded Juan de Saavedra, a captain in the Neapolitan Regiment.

We were in such dire need of food that nearly 80 of our soldiers and convicts died of hunger and thirst, the inhabitants refusing to allow us to obtain water, nor would they sell us food. By necessity, we took up arms and obtained supplies by force.

According to the collated diaries of several of her crew, the galleass went out of Liscannor Bay with a wind astern on 23 September.

On the 28th we were driven by a furious gale into the English Channel. Next day, two guns were thrown overboard, we were in great trouble for want of food, and the ship was leaking very badly, both fore and aft. On the 2nd, with the same wind, we entered the roadstead of Havre de Gráce.

And there, under Havre Castle, they saw the stranded wreck of another Armada ship, with splintered sides and shot-torn masts.

The wreck was the 768-ton *Santa Ana*, flagship of Recalde's Armada of Biscay. Her purser, Pedro de Igueldo, watched the disordered galleass limp in.

I found that the galleass *Zuniga*, storm beaten with the rudder and spars broken and the ship in a sinking state, had brought up at the anchorage before the town. As she was in great danger, we got her into the port, not without much trouble and risk, as she grounded at the entrance of the harbour and was within an ace of being lost. She arrived without a bit of food, or drop of water; a day later, and they would all have perished of famine. I have brought bread, cider, and other necessities, and am distributing the ordinary rations. They need it badly enough, so emaciated are they; pitiably broken and miserable.

The galley slaves, a motley collection of condemned men, including Spaniards and Frenchmen, had had enough. No sooner was she in, than they took the first opportunity to make an attempt at freedom. 'The convicts tried to escape at the entrance to the town, and those who were Frenchmen succeeded, with some others. The rest were detained with great trouble, and are under strong guard,' reported the harassed Igueldo. The poor purser had been forced to take charge of the men from the *Santa Ana*, as her commander, Camp Master Nicholas de Isla, had been mortally wounded at the battle of Le Havre, three weeks before, when Captain George Raymond had led in an English force to get her. Now he had the helpless survivors of the *Zuniga* on his hands as well, and the galleass little better than a wreck.

His own ship, the *Santa Ana*, although the former flagship of Recalde's squadron, was not Recalde's own ship. She proved unseaworthy, being dispersed from the Armada in that same storm which had sent the galleys running for port, on 27 July. Nevertheless, the old soldier, Nicholas de Isla, did not want to be out of the fight; and so the *Santa Ana* crept from French port to French port on her way to the rendezvous with Parma. First, she put into Conquet, in Brittany, then to La Hogue. Parma advised: 'The Channel being so full of enemies, it will be highly imprudent for them to go in search of his Majesty's Armada.' But Nicholas de Isla would not turn back, and when he got her into Le Havre, Mendoza remarked with relief: 'They are now, thank God, out of peril.' He had heard, however, that the Governor of Le Havre was pro-English, and reported: 'M de Montpensier has sent word to the coast of England for them to come and capture the galleon.'

Le Havre was almost directly opposite the English naval base of Portsmouth, and from there the Earl of Sussex reported on 9 September that the *Elizabeth Bonaventure*, Captain George Raymond, the *Aid*, Captain William Fenner, the *Foresight*, Captain Christopher Baker, and the *Charles*, Captain John Roberts, had ammunitioned. 'So as, upon Tuesday, about two of the clock after midnight, they set sail for the coast of France. Hoping very shortly to hear some good news of their happy success in this their enterprise.' In the 70-ton pinnace *Charles* sailed William Monson, then a young officer volunteer.

On the afternoon of 9 September [reported Igueldo], we were informed that three great English ships, one of 500 tons, the others of 200 tons each, with a patache, had appeared in sight, and it was feared they were coming to attack us. The Maistre de Campo and I went on board at once, and at dawn yesterday morning the three ships and the patache bore down on us, and the patache opened fire. We replied, and meanwhile the Governor of the port sent off a boat to them, requesting that they would not break the peace in neutral waters, as he would resent it with all the means in his power. They replied that they came at the command of their Queen, and would not retire for anybody until they had taken, sunk, or burnt the *Santa Ana*.

It was Mers-el-Kebir – the Battle of Oran – in miniature, 352 years earlier. The English intended to let no Armada ship escape, if they could help it; and any Frenchman, friend, foe or neutral, who stood in the way, was going to be unlucky.

Le Havre echoed and re-echoed to the thunder of their gunfire; the main yard-arm of the *Santa Ana* came down almost at once, crushing and pinning underneath it the gallant Nicholas de Isla but leaving unscathed Purser Igueldo, who was standing by his side. Another shot severed the mooring cables, and the Spanish flagship went drifting away with the tide, bumping on the ground two or three times, and heeling over under the press of water almost to the point of capsize. But the rising flood lifted her free each time, carrying her nearer and nearer to the town and fortifications of Le Havre.

The townspeople helped us all they could, firing at the English from the fort, and dragging out two guns on to the shore, which inflicted much damage on the enemy. The English then fired on the people ashore, as well as us. I had the ship moved by the port pilots, and taken to another place; and that was the salvation of all. I had the Maestre de Campo put on shore, where he now is in grave danger, unable to speak, his head and chest badly crushed. The enemy was in sight, cruising near us, all that night, but they did not attack us.

Isla died of his injuries a few days later, and the *Santa Ana* broke free from her moorings in a gale, going aground near the castle, where she was looted by the French and finally lost.

The *Zuniga* was repaired during the winter and, in April, 1589, made one of several unsuccessful attempts to get home, under the command of Captain Marolin de Juan, nearly going ashore on the English coast. Masts, booms and yards were carried away, the decks opened; twelve guns, their ammunition, the anchors, cables and barrels of provisions were jettisoned to save her, and in the last extremity, more than half her oars as well, thirty of them, 'which the convicts were ready enough to throw overboard'. And back she went to Le Havre, with all to do again, and promptly ran aground once more. In the end, she made Spain; but the galleass design was abandoned, as too weak for ocean work.

On 26 December, a number of Scottish vessels put into Le Havre, bringing thirty-two soldier survivors from Don Alonso de Luzon's *La Trinidad Valencera* of Venice and a number of sailors, including some from the *Girona*. They brought certain news of the extermination of most of de Luzon's men and of the death of de Leyva. During their stay in Scotland, which had become the mid-point staging post for the return of shipwrecked men from Ireland to the Spanish Netherlands and neutral France, they had heard of the fate of other ships also. After questioning them, Captain Marolin de Juan, former Pilot-General of the Armada, reported:

The ship *San Juan Bautista*, of Ragusa, of 800 tons, was burnt in a Scottish port, with Don Diego Manrique on board. They say that the only persons who escaped were 15 who were on shore at the time.

The story of the 'Tobermory Galleon' had begun. Even then, there were conflicting stories concerning her identity, for on the same day that Marolin de Juan made his report, on 27 December, Bernadino de Mendoza, the Spanish ambassador in Paris, separately reported to the King what he had been told by a 'person who has just come from Scotland'.

A Spaniard of rank was in the Scottish islands; he frequently went from one island to another, and he carried with him 400 or 500 harquebusiers, who guarded him well day and night. These islands must be the Hebrides because, according to another advice, there is a Spanish galleass amongst these islands, and the Queen of England had sent three ships to try to capture it.

Mendoza's unlikely story was in fact more or less correct but he was confused because he thought there was only one Spanish ship in the area, whereas there were two. Both ships had been unable to get round Ireland at all, presumably because their sailing gear was so badly damaged that they could only go with the wind; consequently, they drifted backwards and forwards between Ireland and Scotland. The 'Spaniard of rank' was Admiral Juan Gomez de Medina in the *Gran Grifon*, flagship of the squadron of hulks, which piled up on the Fair Isle, between Orkney and Shetland, but got ashore with most of his men, and was taken off eventually by a fishing vessel bound for Scotland. The *San Juan Bautista* 'burnt in a Scottish port' while some of the men were ashore, was the other ship, but not a galleass, for which the English were hunting. She put into Mull, in the Hebrides, and was destroyed by internal explosion, just as the *San Salvador* had been off Plymouth; this, too, was sabotage, this time by one of Walsyngham's agents.

Thus began one of the most extraordinary mysteries of the sea ever to be recorded, still unsolved, and probably never now to be solved. There were so many *San Juan*s and *San Juan Bautista*s that she could be several different ships – but not a 'Treasure Ship'. But it is precisely a treasure ship that she has become, and not just a treasure ship, but the only one in the Armada – the 'Greate Treasure Shippe of Spaine'. Of course, everyone who looks at the records, both Spanish and English, knows where the treasure was, and how much it was; and what happened to it. Indeed, it is not even necessary to consult a single contemporary document to tell where it was; ordinary military and naval practice gives the answer. The money was with the paymasters, and the paymasters were in the headquarters ships, the flagships and vice-flagships. And they are all accounted for. The 'Tobermory Galleon' was not a treasure ship in any sense of the word; or if she was, then so is any old packet boat to the Isle of Wight. There is small point now in diving to the Tobermory Galleon, except out of archaeological interest; and that will be of little value, for the rabid treasure seekers have smashed her up. Whatever she had – the purser's official chest, the captain's personal plate, and above all, the immensely valuable guns, is likely to have been lifted long ago, by diving bell.

For several centuries she was the *Florida*, according to local tradition; then the scholars got to work, and found no ship of that name in any Armada list. So they decided she must be the *Florencia*, actually Gaspar de Sosa's *San Francisco*, the galleon of the Duke of Florence, which figures several times, quite prominently, in Medina Sidonia's accounts of the fighting. She ended her career, smashed to matchwood by the English guns, and was scrapped immediately after the Armada campaign. In due course, some other scholars caught up with the previous results of scholarship, and decided she was the *San Juan de Sicilia* of Don Diego Tellez Enriquez, easily confused with the Don Diego Enriquez buried by Cuellar on Streedagh Strand.

The Tobermory Galleon has been dived on certainly since 1607, twenty years after the sinking, but these first divers kept very quiet. The standard method of dealing with a ship from a diving bell was to raise the items from the upper deck first, then tear the deck clear off in order to get at the deck below. The diver was equipped with a number of fearsome instruments, in the rough shape of tongs, bills, baskets, and hooks for recovering guns and 'goodies'; and there was apparently some method of coaxing guns out of gunports, which may have required the diver to leave the bell.

The Government of Elizabeth had a great many Spanish wrecks on its hands, and it was particularly interested in the guns, a practical and valuable salvage proposition. To put the matter of the treasure in perspective, the average amount carried in an Armada flagship was about 50,000 ducats; and the cost of the anchors and cables lost at Calais, according to what Friar Gongora heard, was 100,000 ducats. The value of the guns in a single ship was immensely greater. Consequently, when Sir George Carew, Master of the Ordnance, went over to Ireland during the summer following the Armada, he found himself in the undersea salvage business. Indeed, he was away so frequently, that in some light-hearted official correspondence it was suggested that his wife might become a 'diving widow'. 'Repair to that part of Thomond upon the sea,' Fytzwylliam directed him, 'where some of the Spanish fleet perished, and where there are certain pieces of ordnance meet to be recovered, carrying with you artificers and setting forth boats and other necessaries.' Soon afterwards, Carew was able to report:

Already we have weighed three pieces of artillery of brass, and yesterday we fastened our haullsers to a cannon of battery or Basalyke, as we suppose by the length, for they lie in four fathoms and a half of water, which was so huge that it brake our cables. Our diver was nearly drowned, but Irish aqua vitae hath such virtue as I hope of his recovery. If the diver of Dublin with his instruments were here, I would not doubt to bring good store of artillery from thence, for if I be not deceived, out of our boats we did plainly see four pieces more. As yet I cannot find any small pieces of brass or iron. I think the inhabitants of this country have gotten them.

After that, he was sent to Ulster, 'her Majesty's gallyon, called *The Popingay*', being ordered to assist him; and there, too, someone had been before him. He was told by Mr Auncyent Dallawaye that 'there are two Spaniards and a Scottish captain come over to weigh the ordnance in the Routt; and it is reported that there is great store of gold and silver there . . .' Sir Henry Bagnall wrote:

I long to hear of the safe arrival of your last comfort (i.e. Carew's wife). If she be come, let her know that there is no artillery left at Dunluce to draw you from her. The king of Scots, as I hear say, sent for the same, and at first they did weigh two great pieces. I am sure they have all, and are gone . . .

The Government of Elizabeth was eventually presented with an Armada wreck right on its own doorstep, not far from Plymouth; but the loot was depressingly poor. Two *San Pedro*s re-entered the Channel, going round and round the British Isles in a great circle. The first, the hulk *San Pedro el Menor* (Saint Peter the Lesser), anchored off Morvien, on the Brittany coast. This was the vessel which had reached the Lizard in June, with the other storeships, and had been in action then; her master and pilot had subsequently deserted off Calais, just before the fireship attack. On 20 October, her captain, Don Juan de Monsalve, reported:

Our persistent evil fortune has just decreed that the cruel weather we have experienced should break our cables and drift the hulk ashore this morning. She is now half full of water, and I am taking out the powder and other things I can rescue.

Meanwhile, the *San Pedro el Mayor* (Saint Peter the Greater) was not far behind; she was one of the two hospital ships attached to the Armada, and serving in her was Rodrigo de Calderon, comptroller of the hospital, brother of Pedro Coco Calderon, Auditor-General of the Armada, who was in the *San Salvador*, vice-flagship of the same squadron. On 7 November she ran out of sea in Hope Cove, near Salcombe, Devon, and well and truly piled herself up on rocks owned by Sir William Courteney of Ilton, to the great annoyance of the English.

Late again, George Cary of Cockington galloped down to the shore side, to find that, as in the case of the *Rosario* at Torbay, the locals had been there before him.

Having understanding of the great pilfering and spoils that the country people made, I rode thither. She is a hulk, in burden, as they say, 550 tons, but I think not so much. The ship is not to be recovered; she lieth on a rock, and full of water to her upper decks. She will prove of no great value; the ordnance is all iron, and no brass, their ground tackle all spent. There hath been some plate and certain ducats rifled and spoiled at their first landing, and such drugs and pothecary stuff as came to 6,000 ducats.

The report which reached Spain, that the Council had ordered the execution of her whole crew, was apparently correct; for Anthony Ashley learned on 22 November of 'your Lordships' pleasure for the deferring of the execution of the Spaniards'. He also reported on the international nature of her crew, which included Spanish soldiers and mariners; Portuguese soldiers; and French, Italian and Dutch mariners. But murdering the crew of a hospital ship, on home ground, was apparently just a little too much for the Council, and they relented. One of the prisoners, Gonzalo Gonzales de Castilla, of Granada, did not get out of England until 1592, by which time the Armada was distant history, a golden tale of the past. The puzzle of why she piled up there at all is answered by the statement of her crew: 'We were pursued by continual tempests; the ship was unseaworthy; and we were in want of food.' They were, quite literally, dying of starvation.[1]

The last report on the sinking of an Armada ship was made by John Thoms, an official of Portsmouth Dockyard, on 25 November:

And may it please your Lordship to be advertised of the great Spaniard; she was lost at Studland, but, God be praised, there is saved 34 of our best men. By good hap there came out of Studland a small man-of-war and saved these men. And there was lost 23 men, whereof 6 of them was Flemings and Frenchmen that came in the same ship out of Spain.

She was the gutted *San Salvador* of Oquendo, being sailed to Portsmouth Harbour for final disposal. The man who sank her, alleged John Thoms, was Mr Nicholas Jones of Portland Castle, recommended to him by George Trenchard as a sailmaker who would supply him with the canvas necessary to move her that short distance. 'Pray send for it, you shall have it, and a dozen of oars,' Jones had promised him.

But it was the least part of his meaning, for the next day the said Jones rode away to London, and left no order to deliver the same sail; neither none could be had. And please your Lordship, I charged him before Mr Trenchard, that the ship or men should miscarry, that he should answer for it. There be of his neighbours that are saved, and others of the company, that will venture their lives whenever they meet with him; for all those that are saved will depose that he was the casting away of the ship and the death of the men.

The 'one Almain woman' found aboard the *San Salvador* was not among the drowned, but six of the crew who had sailed the ship from Spain went down with her.

A garland of ropes and shrouds, trailed from bobbing masts and yards, drifted slowly on the cold winter sea, marking only

[1] All that remains of the wreck was fleetingly seen in 1960 by George Tessyman of Dartmouth, who, finding himself under-weighted while aqualung-ing in Hope Cove, stuck his knife into a wooden post to keep himself on the bottom. Only as he was returning to the surface did he notice that there were many similar posts sticking out of the sand – the ribs of a big wooden ship. He never saw them again, for the tides had exposed them only momentarily, but Spanish coins of the Armada period are sometimes picked up on the beach after a gale.

for a brief space that very silent grave where English mariners and the last men of the Armada lay at peace together. Seventeen Englishmen, four Germans, two Frenchmen. They lie there still, with no treasure seekers to tear apart their tomb. And the unknown woman, whose husband – or was it father? – lay deep in the English sea; where was she then, and how much did she grieve? No one knows.

21
'The Year of the Eights'

I pray that God in His mercy will grant us fine weather, so that the Armada may soon enter port; for we are so short of provisions that if for our sins we are long delayed, all will be irretrievably lost. There are now a great number of sick, and many die. Pray consider the distress of this Armada after so terrible a voyage, and the urgent need for prompt measures of relief.

Medina Sidonia to the King, 25 August

On 21 August, when still far north in the Atlantic, Medina Sidonia had sent Don Baltasar de Zuniga in a fast pinnace for Spain, carrying the War Diary of the Armada and a desperate plea for help to be available on the quayside when the surviving ships came home. 'Crippled . . . scattered . . . no ammunition . . . provisions scanty . . . rations reduced . . . half a pound of biscuit a day . . . 3,000 sick . . . without counting the wounded . . . who are numerous . . .' On 4 September, he sent another letter on ahead, reporting that he was with some of the ships in the Bay of Biscay, again stressing 'the urgent need for prompt measures of relief'. Philip had been warned what to expect, but what he had not anticipated was that the plight of the ships would be so terrible that they would attempt to struggle into the first Spanish port they saw, instead of putting into the naval dockyards in the north-west, where an organization existed which could take care of them. Even so, the first sight of the leading ships of the Armada must have horrified the watchers on the shore.

The waves were still thundering on the rocks of Santander, in the aftermath of gale, when the weather-stained, shot-battered hulk of a great galleon was seen, drifting with limp sails towards the rocks in the shore-setting current; and along-side her, a little caravel, equally weather-beaten. Puffs of

smoke leaped out from the galleon's sides, hazing her outline
in the still air. Again and again, she fired; distress gun after
distress gun. The fishermen put out hurriedly to take her in
tow; and found that she was a reeking charnel house inside.
Hardly a man on board could keep his feet, so many were sick.
Of her crew, 180 had been thrown overboard, dead of typhus
and other diseases; and many more corpses from those killed
in action. The wounded and ill lay feverish and untended on
filthy decks. There was only one pilot left alive among four.
Out of the retinue of the great admiral aboard, sixty were dead
or incapable, and only two of his staff remained on their feet.
The admiral himself, his eyes deep sunken in his face, gave the
impression of being, not merely a sick, but a broken man. He
did not wait to see his flagship brought safely into Santander,
but scrambled into a boat and, head bowed, hurried ashore, as
if he could not too quickly put a great distance behind him that
abode of evil memories. The galleon rolling helplessly off the
rocks was the great, gilt-adorned *San Martin*, flagship of the
Great Armada and of Spain's Captain General of the Ocean.
The Duke of Medina Sidonia had come home.

In a short while, many more of these floating wrecks came
drifting in. Eight into Santander, but not the *San Martin*, for a
fresh wind made her uncontrollable and she was blown down
the coast to Laredo. Soon, twenty-one great-ships were
anchored there, in Laredo, with their cargoes of agony,
together with the three galleys which had never seen England,
and the *Patrona*, the only surviving galleass of those which had.
The Levant squadron was gone, almost wiped out; but
Oquendo was off shore with five or six ships, running for the
Biscay ports, a dying man. Still far out at sea was Recalde,
staggering home on two masts in the great *San Juan* of Oporto,
never leaving his bunk, and like Oquendo, dying. Calderon, on
21 September, the day the Duke came home, was still out to
sea, but within sight of land; not a drop of fresh water was left
in the *San Salvador*, and the pumps had been groaning day and
night, for days, to keep the water in the holds from gaining.
Nothing they could do could force it out; it was a question of
whether they would get to the shore before the sea pulled them
down. They saw four ships steering confidently for Brittany;

white canvas, painted hulls, healthy, purposeful ships, which had never been to England. But the water-logged hulk did not signal for help; on the contrary, 'we wished to avoid them,' said Calderon. They needed to be alone with the dishonour and shame of their defeat.

Only another Armada ship would know what they had gone through, and understand; and you could easily tell an Armada ship, just by looking at her. 'On the 22nd, in the afternoon, we sighted a dismasted ship, which fired a gun,' he wrote. The *San Salvador* made no reply; she was beyond giving help to anyone.

At nightfall she came to reconnoitre us. It was the *Nuestra Senora de Juncal* of Don Pedro de Valdes's squadron; one of the best ships in the Armada, with three captains of infantry on board. She reported that she was much damaged, with many sick, and entirely without food; and did not know her position. On the morning of 23 September, we sighted another hulk, which followed in our wake with the other ship. We entered Santander that night, and there I found the Duke had already arrived, but was very ill, though delighted at my arrival, as he had quite given me up for lost.

On the following day, Bernadino de Mendoza, Spanish ambassador in Paris, wrote his usual letter to the King. Philip had grown slightly impatient with the stream of rumours about the total ruin of the English fleet, the death of Drake, and the downfall of the Lord Admiral. Mendoza had just received a stiff letter from him, in which he had said, in effect: 'I am not satisfied with your spies. Get some better ones.' Mendoza was hurt, explaining that he was only passing on reports received from the crews of fishing vessels. And he promptly passed on the two latest. From Hamburg, that a vessel 'had met your Majesty's Armada, 115 to 120 sail, in the Northern Sea, sailing in good order and fine weather.' And, from 'a man who left Edinburgh on 24 September', that the Armada had captured the entire Scottish and English fishing fleets and 'had nearly 300 sail, and the weather was so fine that it would very soon arrive in Spain.' Even on 29 September, he was still at it, confirming the news; and, just to stress its authenticity, he passed on a revealing story from 'a trustworthy source'.

[When] a Flemish heretic (i.e., a Protestant) complained at court of the little courage displayed by the Queen of England, the Queen said that your Majesty had undertaken an enterprise which she and others believed you never would undertake. She had been much injured by your Majesty's Armada, even under the shelter of England. She had lost 4,000 men, and over 12 ships, two of them the finest she possessed, and she hoped to God she should now have peace with the King of Spain, with whom she was sorry she had gone to war.

But, by now, the King had had enough of Armadas sailing victoriously home with captured fishing fleets, and he scrawled on Mendoza's letter the words: 'Nothing of the sort, and it will be well to tell him so.'

The English were, in fact, counting their losses. A complete inspection of the fleet was undertaken at this time, towards the end of September. It makes tedious reading; there is very little battle damage, mostly hard wear, although the *Revenge* 'is to have a new mainmast, being decayed and punished with shot as otherwise.' There had been a serious loss of boats. *Triumph* – 'The long boat lost at sea.' *Elizabeth Jonas* – 'The grete botte lost at sea.' *White Bear* – 'The great boate with all her furniture lost, with the saile.' *Victory* – 'Item, the longe boate, with a shever of iron in the hed & one other in the daffid.' *Golden Lion* – 'The longe boate not serviceable, with a shyver of iron in the hedd and one in the davith. Flags of St George, two, old.' *Elizabeth Bonaventure* – 'Flags of St George, two, and "a bluddeye flagge". Ensigns of silk, one, spoiled with shot and given to the captain.' (A little souvenir of the campaign for George Raymond.) Boats were vulnerable items in battle, particularly when towed astern, which presumably explains these losses.

They were much less particular about the human element. But the figure of around 100 killed in action is frequently mentioned; and too many witnesses exclaimed with delight on 'the least losses that ever hath been heard of' to doubt that battle casualties were remarkably light. Equally, it is impossible to doubt that sickness casualties were very heavy; although no exact figure is given.

The English were also trying to work out the Spanish losses. Eight great-ships lost in the Channel battles, plus the pinnace; about 4,000 men. Eighteen to their knowledge already lost in Ireland, probably not less than 10,000 men. Cuellar, who was only in the north, had heard of twenty, and the real figure was higher. Indeed, the full toll of Spanish losses, being so widespread, was never accurately determined. But ships were still being destroyed, even as they reached home. The hulk *Doncella* went down off Santander, and the flagship of the Armada of Guipuzcoa, another *Santa Ana*, was accidentally burnt inside San Sebastian. And there was the *San Juan Bautista* (of Tobermory), the *Gran Grifon*, the two *San Pedros*, *mayor* and *menor*; and the shambles at Le Havre. Including David Gywnn's late ship, the galley *Diana*, and the *Barca de Amburg*, which foundered out at sea, the total could not have been less than forty-five, and may well have been more. And most of them were great-ships. It was a staggering loss. But the toll in human life and suffering was far worse. Probably half the men in the expedition perished: by battle, shipwreck, murder, or typhus.

The unfortunate man who had to sort it out, almost single-handed, with no organization behind him, was Garcia de Villejo, who took over from the Duke at Santander. He reported, on the last day of September, to Andres de Prada, Secretary of the Council of War: 'The Duke left today, saying that he had no instructions to give me. He leaves affairs in such a condition that I feel it my duty to say what I think about it.' And he did. At this port alone there were over 1,000 sick already, and the list must lengthen if they continued to 'sleep in ships full of stench and wretchedness'. So many ships were missing, presumed lost, and those which had returned were so shattered, that the Armada could be considered no longer in existence. 'If you cannot come here at once, yourself, I shall look upon the Armada as in abeyance until the year '90,' he wrote bitterly. 'I am bound to think that the year of the eights, so ardently looked forward to, will turn out to be 1800.'

What Europe thought of it was made gallingly clear to Bernadino de Mendoza, ambassador in Paris, at the court of a captive king, a satellite of Spanish power. The news had produced a change in this wretched man, and Mendoza was forced to report on 13 October:

This King in conversation with some of his favourites, greatly praised the valour, spirit, and prudence of the Queen of England, aided, as she was, by marvellous good fortune. He said that what she had done lately would compare with the greatest feats of the most illustrious men of past times, for she had ventured, alone and unaided, to await the attack of so puissant a force as Spain, and to fight it whilst preventing the passage of the Duke of Parma's fleet, which was as powerful as the Spanish. He said that it had taken your Majesty four years to gather these great fleets, which had been the wonder of the world, and yet it might be said that the Queen of England had triumphed over them all.

And Mendoza had to listen. There was nothing a Spaniard could say.

22

Secrets From the Sea

In summer seas, deep-laden, the great armadas came,
Biscay and Castile, the might and power of Spain;
With painted sails and banners, and castles peak and stern;
With brazen ordinance, and ordinance of iron;
With galleons great-masted, and heeling in the breeze –
The golden fleets of Spain ploughed up the northern seas.

North, by the land of the Norsemen, by the isles of Orcady,
North, by the crags and fiords, and the thunder of the sea;
The surge of the grey Atlantic, under the gull and fulmar's cry;
By the sobbing of the sea-birds, under the driving, drenching sky,
Screaming out forever, the wave-tops bared like teeth;
And yesterday's sick under hatches, laid now on the deck in death.

Night, on the storm-blown water, bleak on the Irish coast,
Black rocks of Clare and Antrim, where even hope is lost;
The screaming wind from seaward, where the howling horses ride,
The great ships driven shoreward, on the thunder-breaking tide;
Stark cliffs stand up above them, the breakers burst ahead . . .
And dawn finds timbers only, and the white faces of the dead.

                                                                      A.M.

Searching for evidence under the sea is a very different matter
from researching among documents, although nowadays the
same people may be doing it. You do not walk into a library
and ask for a book or a bundle of papers. You have to organize
an expedition, or join an expedition which someone else has
organized, and then get into the sea that drowned the nobility
of Spain. Only rarely can you do anything on your own.

It was the mistaken hope of treasure that drew divers to the
'Tobermory Galleon' as recently as 1982, but twenty years
before that, in 1962, I wrote in *Triton*, the magazine of the
British Sub-Aqua Club:

Any large Armada wreck would be worth investigating for a different reason, however – to discover the armament. Nothing reliable is known about the guns of Armada ships and, consequently, historians spend years of their lives beating each other over the head with dusty copies of bound documents on behalf of some theory or other. Divers could possibly prevent this waste of talented time.

This idea had been germinating for some years in my mind; nor was I the only amateur diver to think of finding and examining an Armada wreck. In 1961 I was corresponding with Roger Jefferis of the London Branch of the British Sub-Aqua Club regarding various Armada wrecks, particularly the *Santa Maria de la Rosa* in Blasket Sound, Ireland; and in 1963, following up a report by Jefferis, I tried to find the remains of the *San Pedro el Mayor* in Hope Cove, Devon.

I went there with a crowd of Southsea divers much more interested in modern wrecks than a problematical search for a really important one. Nevertheless, without aqualungs but with my fourteen-year-old son, I managed a long swim over the area where the buried ribs of a wooden ship had been seen during a seabed scouring period. We went three hundred yards to sea-ward, found ourselves being carried by a rip current out into the Channel, and then, finning fast, cut across it towards the Shippen rock. The depth was around twenty–twenty-five feet and the visibility thirty-five feet, so we could see the bottom from the surface. Just off the Shippen, on the bright sunlit sand below, I noticed a tiny, rimmed semi-circle of a very odd colour. With a deep breath I went down the twenty feet or so, and grabbed a large lump of sand with something hard in it. Back on the surface, I looked at my find. A coin! And not just a coin, but an Elizabethan coin, with a date. 1961. Wrong Queen.

Roger Jefferis, however, did get treasure from this wreck – a cheque for five guineas for a newspaper article!

The ship which became a target for a number of different expeditions at this time, the *Santa Maria de la Rosa*, was supposed to contain much treasure, according to the testimony given by the sole survivor to the English before they killed him. As she was only a vice-flagship, this was doubtful. More likely that the terrified Italian boy told his captors a jolly good story, just to prolong the hours of his life, and perhaps tempt them to mercy.

For historically minded divers, the attraction of the *Santa Maria* was that she had actually sunk, and in deep water, too; whereas most of the Armada's doomed ships had either been stranded on sandy beaches or arrived on rocky coasts. Inexperienced though we all were at that time, we knew that such hulls must be broken and their contents scattered and probably plundered long centuries ago. As evidence, they could not match a ship which had gone down suddenly out at sea with almost everyone on board.

Sydney Wignall went out to Ireland in 1963 to search for the *Santa Maria* in Blasket Sound, and failed. Roger Jefferis had the same experience the following year. I had originally planned to go out with Jefferis in 1964, but had to cancel because I could spare neither the time nor the money. I appreciated that the search area was not merely distant, expensive and inhospitable but also formidably large. In December, 1964, I decided that I would pursue the alternative line of research into ships and guns of the Tudor period by actively searching for the *Mary Rose*, sunk almost on my door-step, with few survivors. Logistically, this should have been easier. In fact, it was not. Precisely because she was not a 'treasure ship', merely a critical piece of historical research, it was for many years virtually impossible to get backing. Fortunately, however, unlike Sydney Wignall, I did not reach the verge of bankruptcy.

Wignall's risky decision was to prepare an elaborate and expensive April-to-September expedition for 1968, enlisting the help of Lieutenant-Commander Grattan, RN, an expert on searching large areas underwater. Their plan was to be influenced by an associated group of divers who believed they had sighted some guns which they were unable to buoy. So this was where they began their search-pattern, rather than the vicinity of Stromboli Rock initially favoured both by Wignall and Jefferis, based on the research of Spotswood Green at the turn of the century.

Sometimes in horrendous conditions of huge, breaking seas and furious tide races, they searched the entire area. The 'cannons' reported by the other team were thought to be found, when some iron pipes were seen sticking out of the seabed. However, a trail of Spanish anchors, some broken, were found leading towards Stromboli Rock. A picture of the disaster, with the ships driven down upon each other by wind and tide, began to form in their minds – history recreating itself. Two mounds of stones were found near Stromboli, but were dismissed as possible ballast from Armada shipwrecks – for where were the twenty-six guns of the *Santa Maria*? Then they realized that part of the area had not been properly searched – two of the more inexperienced divers had often 'flown' too high and might have missed seeing a perhaps largely buried wreck. Back they went to re-do the entire search once more. The result was negative. The anchors were seen again, but no wreck.

They very nearly gave up and went to look for Captain Cuellar's ship and its two wrecked companions on Streedagh Strand. But Stromboli Rock was pulling at them, where the line of lost anchors pointed. One more try, they decided. The two mounds of stones were relocated on the same dive, by two men on opposite ends of the searchline, when they were almost due to come up. One mound was composed of large boulders, the other of smaller, more regular stones – and one of these had a lava-like concretion attached. The diver hacked at the concretion with his knife and the blackened crust fell away to reveal a round, metallic object. Then he had to go for the surface.

It was next day before they could dive again. At the end of it, Colin Martin was to write:

We had found, amongst the stones, great piles of iron roundshot, lead musket bullets, a small piece of glazed pottery, a cluster of six boat-shaped lead ingots and one rectangular one. We had seen, protruding from the shingle at the edge of the mound, the blackened ends of oak beams and planks. The mound rose three feet from the seabed and ran 100 feet in a north-south direction and was 40 feet across at its widest part. It was clearly the stone ballast from an ancient shipwreck. The deepest point was 115 feet below the surface.

There was little time left that season. They mapped the visible remains on the site, in order to understand it; and raised samples of the iron and stone roundshot. There were seven different sizes, to fit guns from two-inch bore to seven-and-a-quarter-inch; and two sizes of leadshot to fit the harquebus and the musket. On reaching air, the iron shot began to disintegrate at once, sometimes uncontrollably so. But where were the guns?

In 1969 they came back for six months with a small, highly experienced team, and began with a methodical metal-detector survey of the whole area. There were few contacts and none of them large. A limited dig to two feet down in shingle alongside the ballast mound produced concretions; one of those contained part of a harquebus and a small pewter plate. While Martin chipped away the concretion round the harquebus, Wignall cleaned the encrustation off the plate. Beneath the rim were six incised letters: MATUTE. During the second interrogation of the sole survivor, Giovanni from Genoa, the lad had testified: 'The Captain of this ship was Villafranca of San Sebastian, and Matuta was Captain of the Infanterie . . .'

Certainly, they had found the *Santa Maria de la Rosa*.

Only one member of her crew was found, and not all of him – the lower part of a skeleton lying trapped under ballast – with two coins in his pockets, one gold, one silver, the one struck in Seville, the other in Mexico City.

Trenching was begun to reveal the structural details of the ship, which turned out to be more slightly built than they had expected (but then the *Mary Rose* turned out to be more slightly built than we expected). Too much could be made of this; the strongest shipwreck ever raised, the Swedish galleon *Vasa*, proved to be more stoutly built than normal, and this was a major factor in her capsize, recalling the legendary perfect battleship which had everything – armour, gunpower, speed – but, alas, would not float.

The guns of the *Santa Maria* were never inspected, because never found. Probably the entire upper part of the hull broke away and lies somewhere out to sea in deep water. The meagre nature of the finds on the site suggests this.

Another diver originally interested in the *Santa Maria* was a Belgian professional, Robert Sténuit. But it was the galleass *Girona* which was four-starred in his list. In 1967, he went to Northern Ireland with one companion and, having already spent 600 hours working on the documents, found her within the hour on his first dive. I visited this coast when I was about ten years old, and had the impression that the wreck lay somewhere between Dunluce Castle and the Giant's Causeway. Sténuit found a better clue in the names of places just beyond the Giant's Causeway – Spanish Rock and Port na Spaniagh. And when he got there, he purchased a little local guidebook which exactly and correctly identified the cove where the bodies had come ashore. It was an awful spot, with great swells rolling shoreward and leaping high in the air as they burst over the barely submerged reefs; and bitterly cold in the water.

No ship's hull could survive in twenty–thirty feet of water on such a coast; much of the seabed would move and roll around, in times of great storm; there would be movement of the lighter artefacts even by ordinary wave action. The first unnatural object which Sténuit saw among the lashing weed fronds was a lead ingot, triangular in shape. The next find was 'a large verdigris-coloured cylinder'. A bronze cannon. Then another bronze gun of curious design – a breech-loader – and beside it the gunpowder chambers. More lead ingots, at least a dozen. And iron roundshot everywhere, rust stains, and a single copper coin.

That was the beginning of two-and-a-half years' work, ending in 1969, the fruits of which may be seen in the Ulster Museum. Some 12,000 artefacts were plotted in position and then raised. Many of them were items in common use aboard, others exquisite treasures belonging to the noblemen from all the three ships' crews who sailed in her to their dreadful end: 405 gold coins, 756 silver, 115 copper, and a number of gold chains, whose links could be broken off, if required, as the sixteenth-century equivalent of a twentieth-century piece of banker's plastic. Most of the guns, however, had vanished in the sixteenth century, raised by either the Irish or the English.

It was Wignall who suggested that the team which had found the *Santa Maria de la Rosa*, 945 tons and 26 guns, vice-flagship of the Guipuzcoan squadron, should now try for *El Gran Grifon*, 650 tons and 38 guns, a Rostock merchantman and flagship of the hulks, the transport squadron of the Armada. In their search for the *Santa Maria*, using John Grattan's swimline search system, they had covered fifteen million square yards of seabed off the Blaskets, before finding the wreck in the last area to be searched. *El Gran Grifon* should be simpler. She had been wrecked on Fair Isle, between Orkney and Shetland, and the locals claimed to be able to pick out the exact spot. She was in a cove under high cliffs, known as Stroms Hellier – Norse for 'Cave of the Tide Race'. An ominous name. A certain rock there was said to be the solidified remains of her hull.

In May, 1970, Colin Martin went out to make a solo recce, diving alone in the aftermath of a gale. His own description is altogether too modest; there is nothing between the west coast of Fair Isle and the east coast of the USA but water – immense, interminable driven wastes of water. Even in summer, that water is deathly chill, for Norway and the Arctic Circle are not too far away. And the scenery is like Norway, except that the fiords are called *geos*. I spent time on nearby Orkney as a wartime infantryman; a group of us even went for a short – very short! – swim in a *geo* on one occasion. But never again. Martin chose to go for a dive in a place like that, with no underwater backup, in seas so stirred up by the gale that he could hardly see a hand in front of him.

He found it hard to believe that the exact site of the wreck (as distinct from the general area) could have been remembered, in spite of the fact that divers had been there before him – Captain Jacob Rowe's team in 1732. He could see the half-submerged rock which the locals said was the petrified remains of *El Gran Grifon* – a preposterous story which could not be true. He kept to the north side of the *geo*, and was swimming over shingle at fifty feet, when the light faded and the seabed went dark. He was inside a cave, exactly the place into which wreckage might be swept and become buried. Martin dug with his hands for twenty minutes and found nothing.

In spite of this disappointment, they decided to mount a small expedition that year, and began diving in June, concentrating on the deeper water ouside Stroms Hellier rather than in the south-eastern corner of the *geo* where some local men had said the wreck lay. They quartered the area down to the twenty-fathom line, and found nothing. The last area to be searched was the south-eastern corner and the vicinity of the 'petrified' rock.

It was Martin's turn to dive when the time came to search the southern gulley. In the top layer of fifty feet of water he had trouble clearing his ears. While he was pinching his nose and blowing hard to get his tubes to 'click', he noticed a drainpipe sticking out of the shingle at the bottom of the gulley. Swimming slowly down because of his recalcitrant ears, he saw the drainpipe take on shape and the bright green colour of bronze underwater, quite distinctive. The bore was a trifle under three inches – a Spanish *media sacre*, similar to a gun Sténuit had raised from the *Girona* three years before. And close in to the cliff were three more guns, iron pieces, this time. Martin surfaced at once with the news. And now, as they looked around from the inflatable boat, they could see it. There was the overhanging cliff where the masts of *El Gran Grifon* had lodged, so providing an escape route up the rock face for the shipwrecked Spaniards; and there in the sea a few feet away was the rock reef which tradition said was the ship's hull, turned to stone. Of course, there was no hull, but this was the wreck, all right.

During excavation a further bronze gun was found, slightly larger than the first, with a four-and-a-half-inch bore – but very badly made, undoubtedly dangerous in use. There were five small-calibre cast-iron guns of two-inch, three-inch and four-inch bore; and two wrought-iron breech-loaders about six feet long with bores of three inches and three-and-a-half inches respectively. The ammunition was for guns no larger than these. There were no heavy guns at all, and the built-up breech-loaders were of obsolete type as well as being small.

For a comparison, the second gun I raised from the *Mary Rose* in 1971 was also a built-up breech-loader, but the bore was eight inches, twice the size of the largest iron gun found in *El Gran Grifon*. Some of the bronze guns from the *Mary Rose* are of comparable size – with a bore of more than eight inches – and of much greater weight and power.

The most interesting pieces of ammunition were a dozen lead shot for harquebus or musket – they were splayed on one side. Clearly, these had been fired from English small arms at very close range into the timber of the flagship of the hulks, and had fallen out on to the seabed as the wood disintegrated.

Of the treasure she had undoubtedly carried there was no sign. The team knew, before they started work, that the Spaniards had removed it all; and taken it to Scotland with them during their escape run for home.

The guns of the *Santa Maria de la Rosa* were missing and have never been found. Most of the guns of the Italian *Girona* were salvaged soon after her destruction. The German *El Gran Grifon* proved to be poorly armed; but one would expect that of a Hanseatic hulk from the transport squadron.

The fourth Armada discovery, made in 1971, was of a large armed merchantman converted to a warship. She was a Venetian ship called by the Venetians *La Balanzara* and by the Spaniards *La Venetiana Valencera* or, more popularly, *La Trinidad Valencera*, of 1,100 tons and forty-two guns since the Spaniards had added ten more to her original thirty-two. Everyone knew she was in Kinnagoe Bay on the Donegal coast of Ireland, probably somewhere at the eastern end of that two-mile stretch of sand. Many divers had been looking for her since 1969. In February, 1971, they found her, at the west end of the bay, where she should not have been, and during an ordinary training dive by thirteen members of the City of Derry Sub-Aqua Club, some of whom were inexperienced.

'Keep your eyes peeled for the *Valencera*!' That was the usual exhortation before a dive in Kinnagoe Bay, but few took it seriously any more. One pair, Archie Jack and Paddy Stewart, went out along the line of a low kelp-covered reef at around thirty feet for 300 yards and were about to turn back when they saw an isolated rock. Closing in, they saw an object on top of the rock, long, regularly shaped and pastel green. A ten-feet-long bronze gun. But how to mark it? Neither man was towing a surface buoy.

One diver stayed down with the gun, his exhaust bubbles rising to the surface above, while the other went up and began to shout for help. A marker buoy was brought over to the bubbles and the line swum down to the gun. A rapidly improvised search, during the short winter's day, located two more bronze guns, one of them large and marked with the arms of Spain plus the date,

1556. The latter had a bore of seven-and-a-quarter inches – a large siege gun. Not far away was a large spoked wooden wheel – a field carriage wheel for just such a gun.

Such a find was tremendously exciting, but also daunting because unexpected; the divers were not prepared to deal with it and had to organize themselves in a hurry. What was the legal position? Unclear. If the news got out, would pirates move in? Probably. Would anything raised fall to pieces once it had been lifted? In some cases, certainly. There was going to be a good deal of unfamiliar work for everyone. And it was going to cost money. And they had better get the guns before anyone else did.

Colin Martin's long involvement with the *Valencera* began soon afterwards, at the symposium on Marine Archaeology held at Bristol University in April, where he and Wignall were speaking on their Armada work and I on my search for the *Mary Rose*. The two BBC men involved in this field, Paul Johnson and Ray Sutcliffe, were there, of course, and at the end of the proceedings learned that the *Valencera*'s guns were to be raised next day by the Derry Sub-Aqua Club. So next day Martin, who had never handled an underwater movie camera before, found himself under Kinnagoe Bay, in an ill-fitting borrowed wet-suit, filming for BBC 'Chronicle' the raising of one brass gun and, while doing so, finding another which, but for a few inches of a dolphin-shaped lifting handle, lay buried and invisible.

Over the years, the site was mapped and a great many Armada artefacts raised and restored. Not merely ship's fittings and stores – down to barrels of gunpowder and tar – but the soldiers' boots, helmets and arms. Perhaps the most moving is part of a banner, which may have flown bravely above them as they went to war.

For the great debate on Armada guns there was now solid evidence in the shape of the two largest bronze cannon. Both had seven-and-a-quarter-inch bores, were about ten feet long and weighed some 5,400 lbs. They had been cast by Remigy de Halut at Malines/Mechlin in what is now Belgium but was then the Spanish Netherlands. By a pleasing coincidence, on leaving Corunna the 1,100-ton *Valencera*'s crew had been increased by

53 to 415 men – precisely the number of the 700-ton *Mary Rose*'s complement in 1545. Probably the two ships were of approximately the same size, for the Spanish measurements seem to be some one-third greater than the English for exactly the same ship.

And for the *Mary Rose* we have most of the guns to compare with her inventory of 1545 and to compare also with the actual pieces from an almost equivalent Armada ship. The Tudor salvors recovered £100 worth, probably mostly the light guns from the castles. The brothers Deane, in 1836 and 1840, recovered four brass guns and about a dozen wrought-iron pieces, which I managed to document and discover during my research in the 1960s. But the bulk of the ordnance from the starboard side of the hull lay some twenty feet below the mud and clay at Spithead; the guns pointing silently through the open ports, and their gun crews lying dead alongside them. A few planks only remained of the broken-up *Valencera*, nothing at all of the *Girona* and *Gran Grifon*; but in the *Mary Rose* we had most of one side of a carrack in excellent condition, complete with virtually all its contents.

As I write, plans of the *Mary Rose* have yet to be published; however, I have the results of a survey I directed in 1973 of frames and planking near the waterline at the stern. Anything less like a modern structure with standardized parts cannot be imagined. The frames (ribs) varied from around 13″ × 9″ to about 9″ × 9″, and their spacings from each other varied from two to six inches. Clearly, Henry VIII had never heard of Henry Ford.

What he did do was to employ the best designers, workmen and gunfounders from abroad, so the *Mary Rose* herself and some of her bronze guns also were Italian – that is, Mediterranean. A Royal Commission of 1618 reported:

. . . but since the change of weapons and fight, Henry the Eighth, making use of Italian shipwrights, and encouraging his own people to build strong ships of war to carry great ordnance, by that means established a puissant Navy . . .

In assessing the ordnance we have to make a most important distinction between the weight of the gun itself and the weight of the shot it fired. Cannons fired the heaviest shot but were not necessarily the heaviest guns; long guns like the demi-cannon could weigh more than a cannon firing a heavier shot. Range and muzzle velocity must also have been important factors. A smallish shot travelling exceedingly fast is likely to do quite as much damage as a heavy shot moving slowly, besides being more accurate. The difference between the rifle and the pistol is a modern example.

That said, the *Mary Rose* guns include examples of the cannon royal, a short-barrelled gun with a bore of around eight-and-a-half inches (compared to the *Valencera*'s seven-and-a-quarter inches for a similar type of gun). In both cases, overall length was about ten feet. One of the *Mary Rose* demi-cannons was twelve feet long, and two of her culverins about the same. But again, the gunfounders, Italian and English, had not yet discovered Henry Ford. There is an attempt at standardization but it does not amount to much in our terms. However, Elizabeth's fleet seems to have favoured the culverin and the demi-cannon, giving range and, initially, a comparatively flat trajectory which helps aiming considerably; and gives, one would think, better penetration at short ranges.

As no Armada wreck found so far is at all comparable to the *Mary Rose* in completeness of hull and contents, the old documents must still be used, illuminated now by the new discoveries, not only from the Armada but from Henry VIII's vice-flagship. For me at any rate, the English inventory of the captured *San Salvador*, of the Guipuzcoan squadron, blown up by her German gunner, means more than it did in 1963. The Spaniards listed her as of 958 tons, 396 men and twenty-five guns, while the English put her down as a Biscayan-built carrack of 600 tons; that is, a ship of the same type as the 700-ton *Mary Rose* but slightly smaller. What that means can now be gauged exactly by visiting the *Mary Rose* herself, next to HMS *Victory* in Portsmouth Naval Base. Most of her guns are on exhibition nearby.

In 1588 the English removed from the *San Salvador* fourteen bronze guns together with shot for cannons, demi-cannons and culverins – the same basic types as the *Mary Rose*. But there is a great difference in the weights. For instance, one of the *Mary Rose* cannon royals weighed over forty-two hundredweight and one of her culverins more than forty-three hundredweight. The *San Salvador* had two really big cannon of fifty-two and fifty-three hundredweight, but the four cannon pedros were only twenty to twenty-five hundredweight and the two culverins twenty-eight hundredweight. So, two big siege guns and the rest lighter versions of an English armament of forty-three years earlier.

This does not take into account the fact that the *Mary Rose* is listed as carrying twenty-four iron guns of some size, as against six iron guns found in the *San Salvador*, which the English noted down as 'iron pieces, minions, old pieces, a bad sling, 2 old fowlers'. The minion had a three-and-a-quarter-inch bore and was probably a cast-iron muzzle loader. My own interpretation of the others is that they are built-up breech-loading guns. The first gun I raised from the *Mary Rose* was a long, thin gun with a bore of three-and-three-quarter inches loaded with a three-and-a-half-inch iron shot; the next was a short, stubby gun with a bore of eight inches loaded with a six-and-a-half-inch stone shot; while the third was a shortish gun with a bore of four-and-a-half inches loaded with a stone shot. The first gun was welded, the other two were made of staves and hoops, like a beer barrel. I judged them to be a sling, a port piece and a fowler respectively, on the basis of a very contemporary document, Cecil's Memorandum Book of about 1555 (Lansdown MS f.118) which lists the iron ordnance of the time as:

Bombards	12″ to 21″	(shoots stone only)
Port Pieces	5½″ to 12″	(shoots stone only)
Slings	2″ to 4½″	....
Fowlers	3″ to 5½″	(shoots stone only)
Basses	½″ to 2″	(shoots lead)

Probably such guns were obsolete in the English fleet by 1588, whereas not only did the *Gran Grifon*, flagship of the hulk squadron, mount them, but so did the *San Salvador*, a warship of a fighting squadron.

Because her guns had been put ashore or given to the English fleet before she sank off Studland on her way to Portsmouth with a prize crew aboard, the *San Salvador* is not as vital a piece of evidence as she might be. Nevertheless, she was not pounded to death on rocks or in the breakers off some far-off beach, but went down in deep water between two big ports on the south coast of England – Portland and Portsmouth. The type of seabed where she sank is critical: if soft to a considerable depth, this carrack and the rest of her contents could be well preserved (not the treasure, of course, because the Spaniards were careful to remove that before they abandoned her and her dreadful cargo of burnt men). In 1978 I took part in a side-scan sonar survey of the track we thought she would have taken, organized by the Bournemouth Branch of the British Sub-Aqua Club. A number of anomalies showed up, but nothing definite. Probably a sub-mud sonar is required, a type which can penetrate below the sea floor.

Off Irish beaches there are still many wrecks to be found. Little of the hulls may remain but enough of the guns and ammunition may be discovered to help complete the picture. The *Rata Encoronada* seems to have been burnt in the shallows of Ballycroy with all her most formidable armament. The *Duquesa Santa Ana* was also stranded, somewhere off Rosberg. There were two wrecks at Killbegs, one aground and the other 'cast away' outside the harbour, which might be better preserved. There is the *San Marcos* on Mutton Island and the *Anunciada* at Scattery. Some may already have been found and discreetly looted. There are rumours of recoveries from a wreck at Cloughglass. Most recently, a team of divers exploring the long sweep of Streedagh Strand in Donegal, where Captain Cuellar survived from a triple shipwreck and the English executioners, met with success.

Steven Birch first became interested in the Armada through reading the books written by Robert Sténuit and Colin Martin about the discoveries they had made underwater. In 1985 he went to Ireland to visit some of the places off which there were supposed to be wrecks, and found the locals most helpful: they could show him artefacts found on local beaches – iron and stone shot, pewter plates, musket stocks, ships' timbers – and they could retell the folklore associated with the sites. It took him four months to prepare a three-week expedition, then at the end of April, 1985, the twelve-strong Streedagh Armada Group set off for Ireland.

The search was precisely and logically planned. Knowing that these were stranded wrecks and assuming that the three ships drew around fifteen feet of water, then the least depth must be around twelve feet. The team used three small boats, each equipped with a proton magnetometer (which detects large magnetic anomalies at a distance), an echo-sounder (to check the depth being searched), a Decca Navigator (to record where any anomalies were found), and an underwater metal detector (to locate precisely on the seabed the positions of completely buried and invisible objects). The three boats were worked side by side, so that the search pattern covered a wide path along Streedagh Strand. It was like a swimline search, but carried out in air on instruments at a higher speed. The only diving was to check contacts with a metal detector.

Within the first five days, we had located three major areas of scattered concretion, representing the vessels which Cuellar describes being wrecked simultaneously, in his vivid account. Looking from the Strand out to sea, we numbered the sites 1, 2 and 3, from left to right. Sites 1 and 2 are 320 metres apart, and 2 and 3 a distance of 410 metres apart, approximately. The wrecks lie in 4–5 metres (about 15 feet) of water and are completely covered in 0.5 to 2.5 metres of sand. The only evidence of visual wreckage was on site 3, in the form of siege-train wheels (as discovered on the site of the *Trinidad Valencera*), sections of connected and disconnected timbers (the wood being generally of sound condition), areas of concretion containing cannon balls of varying size, three bronze cannon partially showing through the sand, and overlying the site, three anchors, the largest measuring a total length of 4.6 metres.

Sites 1 and 2 had no artefacts or concretion showing at all, just large plains of flat, gently rippled sand.

The team carried out a pre-disturbance survey and then dug a short trial trench through site 3, using a sand dredge. This revealed more areas of concretion, containing pottery sherds, musket balls, lead sheathing and one intact pewter plate. Many disconnected timbers were uncovered. Just before they had to leave, Colin Martin visited them, but suggested that as the guns were vulnerable to looting by other divers, they should be raised.

The two short guns were bronze *pedreros* (the 'cannon pedros' of the English inventory of the *San Salvador*). They were two metres (just over six feet) long with a bore of 145 mm (approximately six inches). One of them had a marking resembling a flame round the touch hole. The third bronze gun was longer but with a smaller bore – three metres (about ten feet) and 90 mm (about four inches) respectively. In Spanish, it was called a *sacre* and was similar to what the English called a saker. On the breech was an effigy, the name 'St Severo', a date – 1570 – and the weight of the piece in Venetian pounds.

The team were able to come back again late in July to tidy up the sites in advance of the winter storms. They dived first on site 3, which they believed to be that of the *Juliana*, and were surprised to find that the bay had scoured during the summer.

Much of the sand was missing, larger areas of concretion were showing, five siege-train wheels and, most interesting of all, a completely intact rudder, 12 metres long, complete with pintles. Under one end of the rudder was another large bronze gun, partly buried. After excavating some sand, two lifting dolphins could be seen, also the effigy of another saint: running the length of the gun were ornate flames and scrolls.

Now the question was: had the sand been scoured away on the other two sites?

Site 1 consisted of the usual level sand with nothing showing at all, but site 2 had areas of black concretion sticking out. The muzzle of a much smaller gun could be seen protruding. After much frantic fanning of our hands, a breech-loading cannon emerged before our eyes. It measured 2 metres (just over 6 feet) in length and had a bore of 50 mm (2 inches).

The bore is the same as that of the largest type of English base, an anti-personnel swivel gun.

Colin Martin told Steven Birch that he had new evidence from the Spanish archives to name the three vessels wrecked at Streedagh as the *Juliana*, 860 tons, 32 guns, 395 men; the *Lavia*, 728 tons, 25 guns, 274 men; and the *Santa Maria de Vision*, 666 tons, 18 guns, 307 men. All three were from the Levant squadron, the *Lavia* being the vice-flagship.

The group have not been able to follow up their neatly planned discovery because of what they see as political red tape. But there may be other factors, such as the logistics of excavating such remote sites and preserving the multitude of possible finds in a campaign which could easily last for ten years. On the other hand, if authority simply does nothing, only the inevitable pirates will profit.

More than twenty years ago (in 1964), I suggested a marriage between the facts as suggested by the eye-witness narratives and the technical details to be had from discovery of Armada ships. This approach, I wrote,

can be tested, both for strengths and weaknesses, by reference to modern weapons where the technicalities are known. For instance, one could build up a good general picture of how the Tiger tank compared to the Sherman and Churchill, merely by reading contemporary battle stories. One would be able to deduce that it must have been formidably armed and armoured, although perhaps mechanically weak, even if the witnesses had failed to give a single technical specification.

But suppose they had. Would an historian, 400 years later, be able to assess with accuracy the really crucial differences between the Tiger's 88-mm gun and the Sherman's 75-mm? And how easy it would be to misinterpret facts which were in themselves indisputable! For example, photographs would show Shermans carrying spare tracks on their hulls; therefore they were carried as spares, he would assume. And he would be wrong. They were lashed on as extra protection, to offset the superior thickness of German armour and the superior accuracy and hitting power of their guns. Further, in some Canadian units, all tank commanders were given individual discretion to modify their own tanks as they saw fit – and this in the standardized twentieth century! If only photographs survived, what odd assumptions historians would make.

Therefore, although we must not ask too much of eye-witness narratives, we must be positively cautious when it comes to detailed technical specifications. We must check, if we can, only from a specimen of the actual weapon.

After more than twenty years of underwater exploration, this is now possible. I put the whole question to Dr Colin Martin, of the Scottish Institute of Maritime Studies, a diver-scholar who has seen more Armada wrecks than most people.

The wrecks themselves have of course given us a good deal. *El Gran Grifon* has yielded a good sampling of her armament, and shown that her heaviest guns (Spanish-cast demi-culverins) were badly made and, at best, grossly under-used. We recovered 50 per cent of the ammunition allocated to them, so they failed to fire off half plus whatever percentage of shot we failed to find – unquantified but probably considerable. That this ship was heavily and closely involved in the fighting is confirmed both by documentary sources and by the discovery of expended English bullets on the wreck site – confirmation indeed of engagements 'at half musket shot'.

The *Trinidad Valencera* gave us a clue as to the reasons for the supposed Spanish predominance in heavy cannon-types. In fact, they were siege guns, intended for use ashore: though apparently attempts to use them at sea were made, they were clearly ineffective. Most of the other guns were actually quite small – in weight of armament the English were in fact much the stronger side (there is of course a simple equation to explain this – ships carrying troops, invasion stores, and provisions for an extended campaign clearly have less capacity for performance and/or strength of armament than those operating close to home base and without a requirement to carry deadweight). The *Trinidad Valencera* gunnery instruments gave us an insight into the confusion unstandardized guns and shot, and the wide range of measuring standards involved, must have caused.

The limited ship structure we were able to examine (on the *Santa Maria* and *Trinidad Valencera*) showed that these two converted merchantmen were ill constructed to withstand gunfire, or indeed the stresses of their own artillery. I am sure I am right about Spanish artillery tactics – i.e. one salvo prior to boarding, though obviously a good deal of improvisation will have gone on when the English intention to 'play dirty' and avoid clapping sides became clear. I am sure you are equally right about the difficulty of damaging a wooden ship by gunfire, especially in the modest quantities and lack of skill which I think characterized the efforts of both sides in 1588.

In 1956 I wrote the Trafalgar Day programme for the BBC, basing it on the narratives of people in Portsmouth at that time, and I was struck by the description of the arrival home of some of the worst-damaged ships: 'The *Temeraire, Tonnant* and *Colossus* arrived here this day, under jury masts, from Gibraltar. They are much mauled in their sides.'

This was the result of a general engagement between fleets of ships equipped with many more guns, with a much higher rate of fire, many fighting lashed together, side-by-side, gun port to gun port almost, at ranges of about six to ten feet. The officers afterwards, discussing it together, debated why it was that, with so much artillery blazing away point-blank, the casualties were so remarkably low compared to that of an equivalent land action. When I was discussing the matter recently, during lunch on the gundeck of HMS *Victory*, my companion was surely right when he said that the reason ships like this had to have so many guns (more than a hundred) was because the guns were so ineffective.

As it happens, we do have battle-damage reports from both fleets during the Armada campaign. The most revealing evidence of the effect of Spanish gunfire is surely Howard's statement: 'My own pinnace hath been well beaten and hath had 18 great shot, which hath torn her hull and sails.'

A pinnace is the opposite of a battleship; it is a fast, lightly built vessel probably of less than 100 tons. One would expect that being hit by 18 *great* shot (my italics) would have knocked it to splinters; but nothing of the sort.

The English gunnery was certainly more effective, but let us consider exactly what it achieved at the height of the action off Dunkirk, against the prime target, the Duke of Medina Sidonia's flagship, the 1000-ton *San Martin*. According to Calderon:

At seven o'clock in the morning the enemy opened a heavy artillery fire on the Duke's flagship, which continued for nine hours. So tremendous was the fire that over 200 balls struck the sails and hull on the starboard side, killing and wounding many men, disabling and dismounting three guns, and destroying much rigging. The holes made in the hull between wind and water caused so great a leakage that two divers had as much as they could do to stop them up with tow and lead plates, working all day. The crew were much exhausted by nightfall, with their heavy labours at the guns, without food.

Medina Sidonia endorses Calderon: 'The enemy's flagship, with the greater part of their fleet, assaulted my flagship, with great shooting of ordnance, approaching within musket shot, or even harquebus shot.'

Fray Gongora, who was with Medina Sidonia in the embattled *San Martin*, paints an apocalyptic picture: 'It was the greatest war and confusion that there has been in the world, in respect of the great amount of fire and smoke and of there being ships on the shores of Flanders.'

Quite so. I have been guilty of writing pieces like that (and believing them, what's more) during the first year or so of the Second World War. But there is a similarity. Gun battles between fighting fleets were not exactly new – there had been one in Henry VIII's time, in 1512, off Brest – in which the *Mary Rose* crippled the French flagship and two ships locked together caught fire, and became a funeral pyre for both crews. It was not, however, a common experience, and for many people taking part in the Armada campaign on both sides, history was being made. Just so, in 1940, the air battles spearheading a possible invasion were unprecedented. No one knew then what the bomber could do. This, unfolding before our eyes, was the experiment.

What notable damage was done to the *San Martin*? Three guns dismounted . . . What ordeal did her crew have to endure? Two hundred shot hits over a period of nine hours . . .

I could put that in perspective even from my own unremarkable experiences. Often, the main effect of bombardment weapons is that, hopefully, they will frighten far more than they kill. This is true nowadays and it was true then, for the various Fighting Instructions issued for fleets during the sixteenth century do stress the value of an initial salvo to confuse and intimidate the enemy.

How much Spanish gunnery was affected by the nerve-shattering noise and shock of the English bombardment has not been recorded; but was probably not negligible. The exact noise level cannot be known but certainly, like that of a modern bombardment, must have been well above the level which can be transmitted by television (and is therefore beyond the understanding of most modern audiences under forty years of age). Most of the Spaniards would have been forced to stand it as mere targets, unable to reply, which is not a pleasant experience.

Perhaps the most important fact to emerge from the examination of actual Armada ships is that the Spaniards were not, as we had been led to believe, entirely out of ammunition; although it seems that the English were, when the Armada abandoned its invasion mission and fled with the wind to the north – and, for many of them, a terrible end on savage gale-beaten coasts.

But what would have happened if, instead, they had anchored in the Thames Estuary and attempted a landing? That is a different and intriguing scenario for debate.

The Witnesses

The story is told in extracts from the orders, reports, letters, diaries, pleas, narratives, interrogations, and reported speech of the following:

IN THE ENGLISH AND DUTCH FLEETS
Lord Charles Howard, Lord Admiral of England: *Ark Royal*
Sir Francis Drake, Vice-Admiral of England: *Revenge*
Sir John Hawkyns, Admiral under Howard: *Victory*
Sir Martin Frobisher, Admiral under Howard: *Triumph*
Lord Henry Seymour, Admiral in the Narrow Seas: *Rainbow*
Sir William Wynter, Admiral under Seymour: *Vanguard*
Thomas Fenner, Captain: *Nonpareil*
Henry Whyte, Captain of fireship: *Bark Talbot*
　　　　　Transferred as Volunteer: *Mary Rose*
William Monson, Lieutenant of pinnace: *Charles*
Richard Thomson, Lieutenant of London ship:
　　　　　　　　　　　Margaret and John
Thomas Cely (late of *Estrella* galley), Captain of pinnace:
　　　　　　　　　　　Elizabeth Drake
Mathew Starke, Officer: *Revenge*
Nic Oseley, Merchant, Spy, Intelligence Officer: *Revenge*
Edward Wynter, Officer
Sir Horatio Palavicino, Genoese Banker, Volunteer with the English Fleet
Sir Arthur Gorgas (or Gorges), Volunteer in the Fleet
William Borlas, Liaison Officer, with Fleet of Sir P. van der Does
Giles Napper, Mariner; escaped slave from Turkish and Spanish galleys

Patrick Catnihavil (?), Catholic Irish Student; served unwillingly and by accident: *Ark Royal*

Simons of Exeter; Master of a Bark of Mousehole; Fisherman of a Bark of 'Hampton, etc., etc.

IN ENGLAND

The Council:	London
Sir Francis Walsyngham, Principal Secretary of State:	London
Lord Burghley, Lord High Treasurer of England:	London
Sir Thomas Heneage, Vice-Chamberlain of the Household:	London
Earl of Leicester, Army Commander:	near London
Marmaduke Darell, Victualling Agent for the Navy	
Sir Francis Godolphin, MP for:	Cornwall
John Popham, Attorney-General and Spymaster:	Wellington
Sir Walter Raleigh, Governor:	Plymouth
William Hawkyns, Mayor of:	Plymouth
Richard Pitt, Mayor of:	Weymouth
John Jones, Mayor of:	Lyme Regis

John Gilberte } Deputy Lieutenants *Rosario*, Torbay and Dartmouth

George Cary } of Devon: *San Pedro el Mayor*, near Salcombe

Sir Anthony Ashley, Official, Devon: *San Pedro el Mayor*, near Salcombe

George Trenchard } Justices of the Peace for Dorset: *San Salvador*, Weymouth
Francis Hawley }

John Thoms, Dockyard Clerk:	*San Salvador*, Portsmouth
Earl of Sussex, Garrison Commander:	Portsmouth
Sir George Carey, Garrison Commander:	Isle of Wight
Rychard Barrey, Governor:	Dover Castle
Petruccio Ubaldino, Florentine Historian	
Dorothy Cely, Wife of Captain Thomas Cely	

IN IRELAND

Sir Wylliam Fytzwylliam, Lord Deputy of Ireland:	Dublin
Sir Richard Bingham, Governor of Connaught:	Athlone
Sir John Popham, English Official	
Mr Secretary Fenton, English Official	
Lady Denny, Wife of Governor of:	Tralee
James Trant, Official:	Dingle
Auncyent Dallawaye, Official:	Ulster

Sir Henry Bagnall, Soldier: Ulster
Eustace Harte, Merchant: France and Ireland
David Gywnn, Interpreter: Drogheda
Sir George Carew, Master of the Ordnance, Dingle
and Salvage Operator: and Dunluce

MISCELLANEOUS

The States of Zealand: Report on *San Felipe, San Mateo, San Antonio de Padua*

Prince Maurice of Nassau: Report on the interrogation of prisoners from above

IN THE ARMADA

Don Alvaro de Bazan, Marquis of Santa Cruz
Don Alonso Perez de Guzman, Duke of Medina Sidonia:
San Martin
Don Jorge Manrique, Inspector-General of the Armada:
San Martin
Captain Marolin de Juan, Navigator-General of the Armada:
San Martin and galleass *Zuniga*
Prince of Ascoli, natural son of King Philip II:
San Martin and a pinnace
Don Luis de Miranda, Staff Officer: *San Martin*
Captain Vanegas, Staff Officer: *San Martin*
Juan Martinez de Recalde, Vice-Admiral of the Armada:
San Juan of Oporto
Emanuel Fremoso, Portuguese Mariner (POW):
San Juan of Oporto
Emanuel Francisco, Portuguese Mariner (POW):
San Juan of Oporto
John de Licornio, Biscay Mariner (POW): *San Juan* of Oporto
Piero Carr (?), Flemish Mariner (POW): *San Juan* of Oporto
Miguel de Oquendo, Admiral of the Guipuzcoa Squadron:
Santa Ana
Don Pedro de Valdes, Admiral of the Andalusia Squadron:
N.S. del Rosario and POW in *Revenge*
Vicente Alvarez (POW), Captain of: *N.S. del Rosario*
Gregorio de Sotomayor (POW), Portuguese Gentleman:
N.S. del Rosario

Fray Bernado de Gongora, a Friar: *N.S. del Rosario*
transferred *San Martin*
Pedro Coco Calderon, Auditor-General of the Armada:
vice-flag hulk *San Salvador*
Log of: vice-flag hulk *San Salvador*
Marcos de Aramburu, Purser of the Castile Squadron:
San Juan Bautista
Pedro Igueldo, Purser of the Biscay Squadron: *Santa Ana*
Francisco Cuellar, Captain of: galleon *San Pedro*
and placed under open arrest in Levanter *Lavia*
Don Alonso de Luzon, Camp Master, *tercio* of Naples (POW):
La Trinidad Valencera
Master of: *La Trinidad Valencera*
Juan de Nova, Servant to Don Juan de Idiaquez:
La Trinidad Valencera
Francisco de Borja: *La Trinidad Valencera*
Don Diego de Pimental, Camp Master, *tercio* of Sicily (POW):
San Mateo
Six prisoners from: *San Mateo*
Pedro Estrade, Reinforcement Officer: *San Marcos*
A Gentleman of Salamanca (POW): flag galleass *San Lorenzo*
Witness of Capture (crew member?) flag galleass *San Lorenzo*
Juan de Saavedra, Captain, *tercio* of Naples: galleass *Zuniga*
Summarized Diaries of the Crew of: galleass *Zuniga*
Italian Mariner: galleass *Girona*
David Gywnn, Welsh galley slave: galley *Diana*
James Machary of the Cross, Pressed Man: *Duquesa Santa Ana*
Antonio Maneses (or Monana), Son of the Pilot of:
S.M. de la Rosa
Ensign Esquival, commanding: pinnace
Master of: Seville ship
Don Juan de Monsalve, Captain of: hulk *San Pedro el Menor*
Gonzalo Gonzales (POW): hospital hulk *San Pedro el Mayor*
Statement of the captured Crew of:
hospital hulk *San Pedro el Mayor*
Log of: hulk *Paloma Blanca*
Don Balthasar de Zuniga
Padre Geronimo de la Torre
Antonio de Taso Aquereis, Infantry Officer

Hassan, the Marquis of Santa Cruz's freed slave
Two Dutch Mariners (deserters); 14 Dutch Mariners (deserters); etc., etc.

IN EUROPE

Philip II, King of Spain

Alexander Farnese, Duke of Parma:	Bruges
Don Bernadino de Mendoza, Spanish Ambassador:	Paris
Don Diego Guzman de Silva, Spanish Ambassador:	London
Count de Olivares, Spanish Ambassador:	Rome
Giovanni Gritti, Venetian Ambassador:	Rome
Father Robert Parsons, emigré leader:	Rome

Captain Luis Cabreta, Naval Adviser
Garcia de Villego, Naval Official

Marco Antonio Messia, Genoese, Spanish Agent:	London
Antonio de Vega, Spanish Agent:	London
Miscellaneous Spies and Couriers in and from:	England

Miscellaneous Agents: Bruges, Dunkirk, Antwerp, Rouen, etc.

Sources

The bulk of the English documents are contained in: *State Papers relating to the Defeat of the Spanish Armada*, Vols. I and II, edited by Professor John Knox Laughton (Navy Records Society, 1900, and republished, 1981, for the Society by Kenneth Mason, Emsworth).

The bulk of the Spanish documents (in English translation) are contained in: *Calendar of Letters and State Papers relating to English Affairs preserved in, or originally belonging to, the Archives of Simancas*, Vol. IV, Elizabeth, 1587–1603, edited by Major Martin S. Hume (HMSO, 1899).

But both these works contain documents from the other side: English reports sent to Spain by Spanish agents, and Spanish documents taken from captured ships by the English; the interrogations of Spanish prisoners and deserters are, naturally, in the English records, as well as letters written by some of them when in England.

The bulk of the Spanish documents (in Spanish) are contained in: *La Armada Invencible*, edited by Captain de Navio C. Fernandez Duro, and *La Armada Invencible: Documentos Procedentes del Archive General de Simancas, 1587–1589*, edited by Enrique Herrera Oria (Valladolid, 1929).

Some additional Spanish documents, printed by Oria, are available in English translation in: *The Spanish Armada*, edited by G. P. B. Naish (Navy Records Society), which also contains Ubaldino's *Commentary*, published 15 April, 1589.

Captain Cuellar's original narrative is No 7, Folio 58, in the Salazar collection, Academy of History, Madrid. There are two English translations: *Captain Cuellar's Adventures in Connacht and Ulster*, edited by Hugh Allingham (Elliot Stock, London, 1897), and *A Letter written by Captain Cuellar to His Majesty*

King Philip II, translated by Henry Dwight Sedgwick, Jn. (Elkin Mathews, London, and George H. Richmond & Co., New York, 1896).

Pedro Estrade's narrative, in English translation, is from the Calthorpe MSS, edited by M. Oppenheim (Navy Records Society XXIII); the narrative of Fray Bernado de Gongora, in Spanish, is Appendix C to J.P. Lyell's *A Commentary* (Bodleian Library, Oxford and Harvard).

The *Naval Tracts of Sir William Monson*, edited by M. Oppenheim (Navy Records Society, 1902) give much useful background by an officer who fought the Armada.

Gorgas' Seafight, contributed by Tom Glasgow Jr. to *The Mariners' Mirror*, the journal of the Society for Nautical Research (and here quoted by permission of the Author and the Society) is another piece written by a volunteer in the English fleet.

Fighting Instructions 1530–1816, edited by Sir Julian Corbett (London, 1905, and Conway Maritime Press, 1971) quotes from various sixteenth-century Spanish and English authorities.

Diving operations on the Irish wrecks are reported in *Calendar of State Papers, Carew*, 1589–1600 (HMSO). The wrecks generally are usefully documented in two articles: 'The Wrecks of the Spanish Armada on the Coast of Ireland', by W. Spotswood Green, Chief Inspector of Irish Fisheries, in *The Geographical Journal*, May, 1906; and 'Armada Losses on the Irish Coast', by Caoimhín ó Danachair, in *The Irish Sword*, Journal of the Military History Society of Ireland, Vol. II, No 9, 1956. A translation of Marcos de Aramburu's narrative (from Duro), together with an account of Recalde and the Blasket sinkings, are contained in an article, 'Armada Ships on the Kerry Coast', by W. S. Green, in *Proceedings of the Royal Irish Academy*, Vol. XXVII, 1909. A useful recent work is *The Armada in Ireland* by Niall Fallon (Stanford Maritime, 1978).

It now seems almost certain that the 'Tobermory Galleon' is indeed the *San Juan Bautista* of Ragusa, as stated by Captain Marolin de Juan, but that this is the same ship as the *San Juan de Sicilia* (so-called because she was in Sicily when requisitioned for the Armada).

Recent Armada wreck discoveries are described by the divers

concerned in five books: *The Treasures of the Armada* by Robert Sténuit (David & Charles, 1972), *Full Fathom Five* by Colin Martin (Chatto & Windus, 1975), *In Search of Spanish Treasure* by Sydney Wignall (David & Charles, 1982), *Trésors de l'Armada* (Crédit Communal, Brussels, 1985), *The Tobermory Treasure* by Alison McLeay (Conway Maritime Press, 1986). For the specialist there are technical reports in various issues of *The International Journal of Nautical Archaeology and Underwater Exploration* (Academic Press). I must also acknowledge the most useful discussions and/or correspondence over the years with John Grattan, Colin Martin, Sydney Wignall and latterly, Steven Birch.

The story of the *Vasa* and her recovery has been described in *Vasa, the King's Ship*, by Bengt Ohrelius (Cassell, 1962) and *The Raising of the Vasa* by Roy Saunders (Oldbourne, 1962), and of course by her discoverer Anders Franzén in *The Warship Vasa* (Norstedts, 1966); and I must acknowledge also most helpful discussions and correspondence with Anders Franzén and others professionally concerned with this actual post-Armada galleon.

I must express my gratitude to the Central Library, Portsmouth, for research facilities afforded in their extensive Naval Collection; to Mr L. Sargeant, of Hayling Island, for some translations from the Spanish; and to Maurice Young for both the map on pp. 6 and 7 and the Fighting Ships diagram: The Vikings to the Victory, on p. 57.

Index